The design and printing of EPHEMERA in Britain and America 1720–1920

1. Benjamin Franklin in John Watts's printing house, London, in 1725. Note the simple construction of the wooden printing press. The operations of inking type, laying paper, and winding the forme under the platen were identical with the operation of the later Columbian press (26). The wooden press, however, did not have the mechanical advantage of levers; the impression bar acted directly on a screw working within the 'head' – the wooden cross-piece seen here. Franklin, a teetotaller, was dubbed the 'water American' by his hard-drinking companions. Wood-engraving *c.*1890 (xx%) *St Bride Library.*

The device on the title-page is an Art Ornament from the American Type Founders' *American Specimen Book of Type Styles*, 1912. (76%)

THE DESIGN & PRINTING of *Ephemera* in BRITAIN & AMERICA 1720–1920

No. 84008 40c

GRAHAM HUDSON

THE BRITISH LIBRARY

OAK KNOLL PRESS

2008

First published 2008 by
The British Library
96 Euston Road
London NW1 2DB
and
Oak Knoll Press
310 Delaware Street
New Castle
DE 19720

British Library Cataloguing in Publication Data
A catalogue record for this title is available from The British Library

ISBN 978 0 7123 4904 8 British Library
ISBN 978 1 58456 224 5 Oak Knoll Press

Design by Graham Hudson
Typeset in Garamond by
Norman Tilley Graphics Ltd, Northampton
and printed in Hong Kong by
Paramount Printing Company

Contents

Acknowledgements

NO HISTORICAL STUDY can be essayed without drawing on what has been written before, much of which may be found only in specialist libraries or through recourse to inter-library loan or the internet. So thank you to Nigel Roche and his staff at the St Bride Library, London; and to Kathleen Godfrey and her staff on the Canterbury campus of the Kent Institute of Art & Design (now the University College for the Creative Arts) through whose good offices several long out-of-print works were tracked down.

Thanks also to Michael Twyman of the Centre for Ephemera Studies, Reading University, and to my copy-editor John Trevitt for their invaluable appraisals of the work in its various stages. Here too my appreciation of David Way of the British Library, and Kathy Houghton who located several of the pictures.

Special thanks are due to Iain Bain for permission to reproduce the previously unpublished designs and extracts from letters received by Thomas Bewick from his customers; to Dr Kathy Haslam and Emma Hardy of the Geffrye Museum, London, for facilitating the photography of the napkin rings shown in illustration 141; to Wendy Shadwell of the New-York Historical Society and my friend the late Peter Jackson for providing background information on the 1775 Anthony Lamb trade card; to Mic Relf of GeorgeBaxter.com for advice on dating and other aspects of Baxter prints; to Eleanor McD. Thompson of the Winterthur Library, Delaware, and Emily Thompson of the Boston Public Library, for assistance in locating the 1854 Boston *Lady's Almanac*; Harry Searles and Susan and Michael Mangus of the Ohio Historical Society for biographical information on W. D. Howells; Heather Walker for her loan of the menagerie bill shown in illustration 104; Anthony Wells-Cole of Leeds Museums & Galleries, and Melanie Baldwin of the Castle Museum, York, for their help in locating the Charles Greaves trade card.

Valuable information and assistance was provided by Martin Andrews of the Department of Typography and Graphic Communication, Reading University, Robert Bell of the Wisbech & Fenland Museum, Hugh Dixon of the National Trust, Giles Guthrie of the Maidstone Museum and Bentlif Art Gallery, Kate Hebert of the American Museum in Britain, Andrew Gold, Michael Heseltine, Bernth Lindfors, Diana Mackarill, Barry McKay, Dr Arthur Percival of the Faversham Society, Charlene Peacock of the Library Co. of Philadelphia, Ann Smith of the Reading Central Library, Jeremy Smith of the Guildhall Library, Kim Streets of the City Museum & Mappin Art Gallery, Sheffield, Paul Wakeman and Lawrence Wallis.

For their friendly advice, help and continuing interest, thank you also to Lord Briggs, President of the Ephemera Society, to Sally de Beaumont its current chairman, and Amoret Tanner who, with the author and six others, was a co-founder of the Ephemera Society.

Graham Hudson
Dunkirk
Kent
July 2007

2. Old-style ornament from the Edinburgh type-founders Miller & Richard's *Specimens of Book, Newspaper, Jobbing and Ornamental Types*, 1895. (100%)

Introduction

THIS BOOK CONSIDERS the changing appearance of British and American printed ephemera over a period of two hundred years and discusses the part played by *design* in the thinking of those who created it.

Produced to meet the needs of the passing day, in content and form ephemera are wholly part of the culture within which they are created. This has nowhere been better expressed than in Arnold Bennett's *Clayhanger*, where the author evokes a picture of old Clayhanger's printing shop, its dusty ephemera of old jobs hanging from the rafters and proof sheets of current work scattered here and there below:

> These printed things showed to what extent Darius Clayhanger's establishment was a channel through which the life of the town had somehow to pass. Auctions, meetings, concerts, sermons … bill-heads, hand-bills, addresses, visiting-cards, society rules, bargain-sales, lost and found notices: traces of all these matters, and more, were to be found in that office: it was impregnated with the human interest; it was dusty with the human interest; its hot smell seemed to you to come off life itself.[1]

Though separated from Bennett's Five Towns by close on six thousand miles of land and ocean, the Ohio print shop that novelist T. B. Howells remembered from childhood turned out much the same range of work; but it was the craftsmen who did the printing that formed Howells's earliest recollections: 'the compositors rhythmically swaying before their cases of type; the pressman flinging himself back on the bar that made the impression … the apprentice rolling the forms, and the foreman bending over the imposing stone'.[2]

These were letterpress printers, but though the ephemera that one studies and collects today are as likely to have been printed from an engraved plate or a lithographic stone as from type and blocks, the ambience of the workshop will have been much the same.

The *Encyclopedia of Ephemera* contains well over five hundred separate articles, covering subjects as diverse as: ballad sheets, 'at home' cards, billheads, dance programmes, funeralia, inn tallies, posters, sheet-music covers – everything from 'ABC primer' to 'Zöetrope strip/disc'.

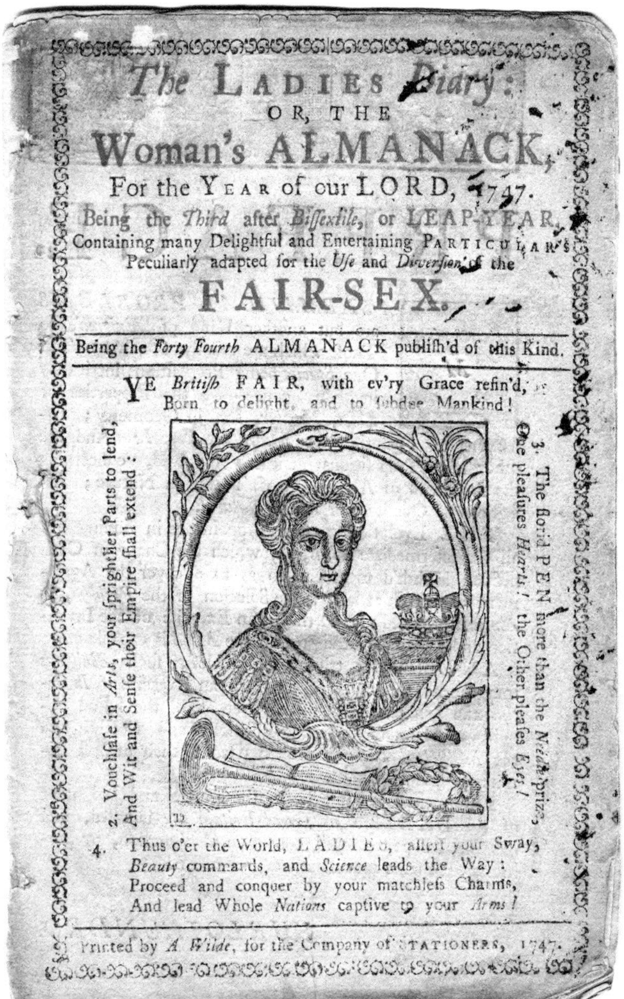

3. Letterpress printing, almanac of 1747 printed in black and red by A. Wilde, decorated with a wood-engraving of Queen Anne in whose reign the almanac was first published. The overall horizontal and vertical stress of the layout is characteristic of the letterpress process. (82%)

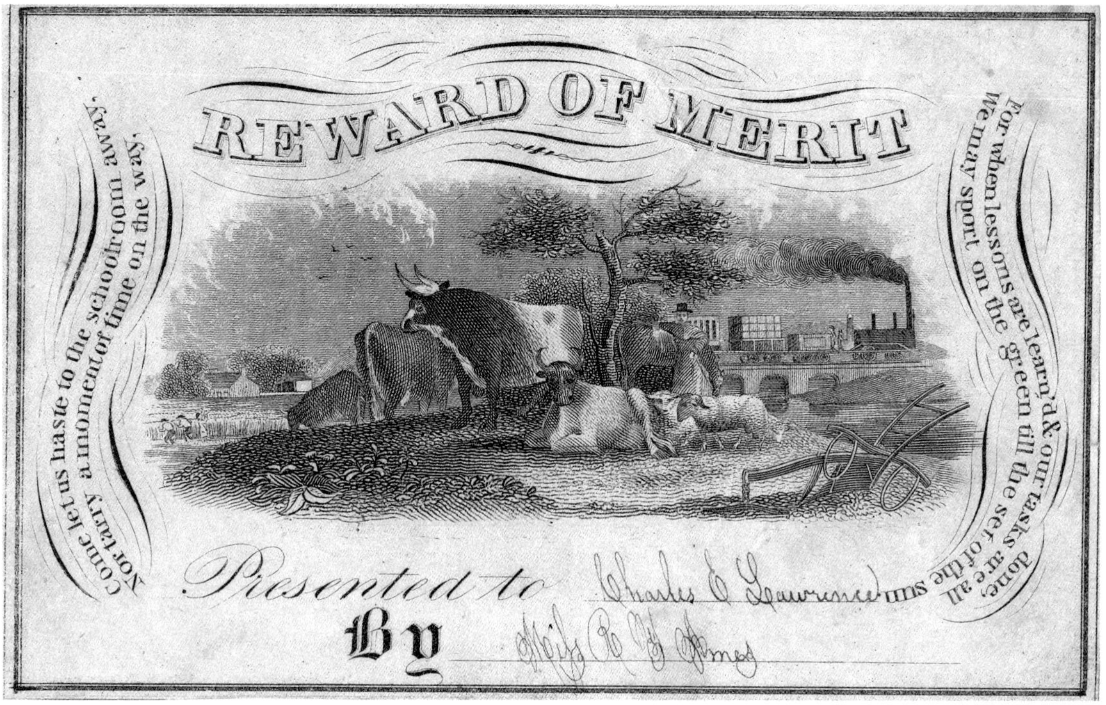

4. Engraving. Reward of merit awarded to Charles Lawrence by his teacher Miss Ames, *c.*1840, enlarged to show the fine detail. The integration of the vignette and the curving lines of lettering into one unified composition are typical of the process. The greater part of this design has been left at the etched stage, with firmer lines here and there showing where the graver has been used. Rewards of merit were a far more common form of ephemera in America than in Britain. (150%)

To consider the design of each of these individually is scarcely feasible, and would indeed be repetitive, for the factors that have affected the design of each of them are those that have affected all. It is therefore these factors, and the part they have played in the changing appearance of printed ephemera, that are the subject of this book. The factors are three: function, process and period.

Function is self-explanatory, for it concerns the purpose for which an item of ephemera was produced. Illustrated writing paper intended for private correspondence was naturally presented differently from commercial stationery; and a circular was graphically different from a poster, the one small for leisurely perusal, the other larger, and more boldly displayed to attract attention in the busy street.

Process relates to the means by which ephemera were printed. In the period under discussion these would chiefly be letterpress, engraving or lithography, and their related media and methods, e.g. wood-engraving, engine-turning, printing in gold, lace-paper decoration, etc. Each of these had its individual qualities and thus, either clearly or with subtlety, each had its effect on the look of what was printed. The letterpress printer could set several hundred words for a leaflet or programme in a fraction the time it would have taken an engraver to etch them in copper, and this would be equally so with ephemera utilising more limited copy, such as a trade card or a ball invitation. Yet letterpress also imparted a characteristic horizontal and vertical stress on printed matter that was not easily disguised, while the engraver suffered no such limitation, leaving him free to create designs as complex and elegant as he could wish or his customer would pay for.

Period concerns the historical period in which an item of ephemera played its brief part in the historical record. Here the effects on design are expressions of both commerce and culture. Improving communications in the eighteenth century brought the large typefaces needed for the printing of easily seen mail- and stagecoach bills, while tradesmen's cards were tricked out with the Rococo detail that elsewhere found expression in contemporary domestic furniture; and on ephemera also, the purveyors of hardware, patent medicines and other goods once household names presented their wares, and vaudeville and music-hall stars now long forgotten enjoyed their floreat days.

The design histories of ephemeral printing in Britain and America are inextricably woven. Colonial printers and engravers imported British type and equipment, took instruction from the same manuals, drew inspiration from the same exemplars. In 1798 the establishment of the first successful American type-foundry gave American printers a source of type nearer home, but those types were cast with strikes from British founders' punches; and though American punchcutters were to be at work early in the following century, the forms of their bold new display

5. Lithography. Allegorical vignette from the billhead of Italian lithographer Scipione Lapi, shown in the London-based *Printers' International Specimen Exchange* 10, 1889, illustrating stages in the lithographic process. The boy represents the artist/designer, here making a drawing of a factory in his sketchbook. On the right, a child artist draws on litho stone watched by another carrying an ink roller. The goddess Minerva with her attendant owl displays an album of Signor Lapi's work. On the left a putto plays with a pair of ink dabbers, as used by both lithographers and letterpress printers prior to the introduction of rollers in the 1820s. As is clearly indicated here, the nature of the lithographic process gave the printer a freedom in design equal to that of the engraver. (90%)

letters would be closely modelled on those of Britain.

It was in the years of stability and enterprise following the Civil War that American graphic design established its own identity. In Britain printing in colours was achieved by a variety of means but in America colour printing meant essentially chromolithography, and the focused development of this process in the latter part of the nineteenth century resulted in an efflorescence of colour-rich trade cards, cigar-box labels, rewards of merit, calendars and other ephemera that was essentially American. In Britain from the 1860s, typeface design stagnated, but from America a wealth of inventive new types now crossed the Atlantic en route to printing offices in London, Edinburgh, Dublin and elsewhere. Yet *ideas* travelled in both directions, for the development of expertise in designing with these new typefaces (and other innovations of the period) depended on jobbing printers learning from each other, and the scheme of specimen exchange that achieved this was set up in and administered from London.

The art of the printer relates as much to artifice – the making of things – as it does to Art, but while most printers of ephemera would not have claimed to be fine artists (though some in the later nineteenth century would do so) it is self-evident that many did exercise aesthetic considerations when laying out their work. The difficulty is – whether concerning visual qualities or adherence to particular conventions – printers rarely put pen to paper regarding why they did what they did: their work was too much an everyday activity to warrant record. A case in point is the long, narrow Victorian playbill, discussed on pages 37-41: the reasons for the development of this format must have been common knowledge in the trade, but in the absence of written record we can now only surmise. One has to glean what one can from the early manuals and – fortunately in rather more detail – the occasional articles in the trade journals. As to why a particular printer chose this type or letter-form rather than that or one arrangement rather than another, we cannot know; though we may realistically surmise.

It was in the 1720s that the young Benjamin Franklin worked for a period as a printer in London, before returning home and starting his own business in Philadelphia. All then was grist to the printer's mill – books, newspapers and general jobbing. A century or so later those three aspects of the one trade would become separate fields, with jobbing printers large and small undertaking the endless miscellany of trade cards, playbills, music covers, posters and other classes of ephemera now so avidly studied and collected.

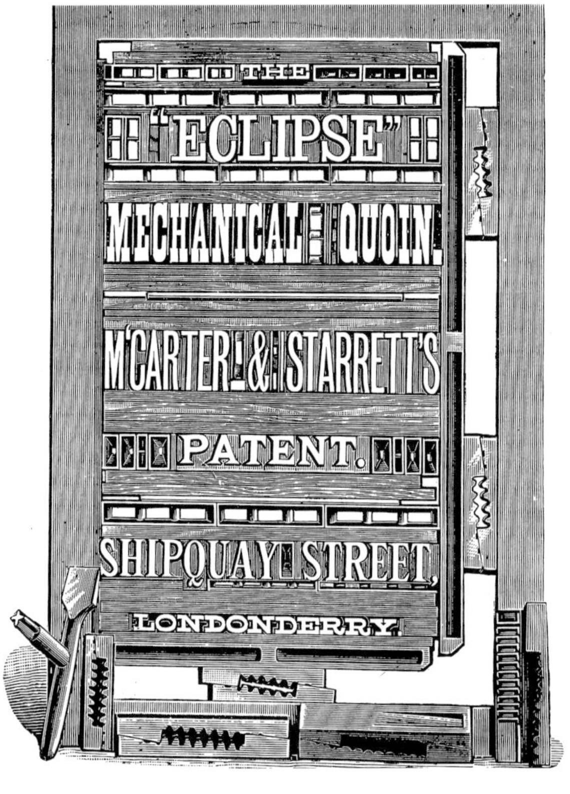

6. *(Above)* Compositor setting type. Capitals were stored in the upper of the two cases and small letters in the one below, from which derives 'lower-case', the term still used for the small letters today. *(Left)* Forme ready for printing, showing how the shape of the type and the rectangular chase that enclosed it imposed a characteristic horizontal-vertical stress on letterpress setting. Type and spacing material are here locked in place with *mechanical quoins.* These were a nineteenth-century invention, earlier quoins being simple beech-wood wedges. Reproduced from: Howells, 'The Country Printer', p. 543; and *Printing World*, n.s. 4 (1893), p. 176.

1

The wooden press

WHEN BENJAMIN FRANKLIN was working in London in 1725 there were, in both England and America, but two methods of printing: letterpress and copper-plate.

At its simplest the principle of letterpress is akin to that of the fingerprint: the image is in relief, higher than its background, and the impression is achieved by inking the image and bringing it in contact with paper. Today the same principle is employed in the pictorial linocut – though when illustrations were needed in the eighteenth century they were cut in wood, as will be discussed. The chief business of the printer however was not pictures but words: words in books and newspapers, words on ballad sheets, on playbills, on reward notices and other ephemera; and for all of these *type* was required.

Type consists of small square-section columns of lead alloy of standard height, each with a letter or other character cast in reverse on its upper surface. Type was available to the printer in a range of sizes to suit everything from a footnote to a broadside.

Franklin learnt typesetting as a twelve-year old apprenticed to his half-brother James in Boston. When setting type he would have before him two shallow cases positioned one above the other, containing all the characters and spaces that English-language setting called for (6). In his left hand he would hold a *composing stick* into which, following hand-written copy, he would transfer the type letter by letter. When sufficient copy had been set, the lines of type would be locked into an iron *chase*, the whole then constituting the *forme* (6), which Franklin would pass on to the pressmen.

The printing press was still much as it had been when invented close on three centuries earlier. It was built of wood and printing was effected by pulling on a bar acting directly on a screw (1). The size of the *platen* or pressure plate which the screw forced down averaged around 18 × 12 inches (456 × 304 mm), and as paper was made in sheets around twice this size and the power of the press was dependent on the strength of a man's arm, printing a large broadside or the leaves of a large-format book would require two pulls on the bar, the pressman raising the platen and advancing the forme between impressions. Printing was a two-man activity, one inking and the other laying and taking off paper and working the press. It was hard, physical work but, depending on the size of the sheet and the care required, a printing rate approaching 200–240 sheets per hour could be achieved.[1]

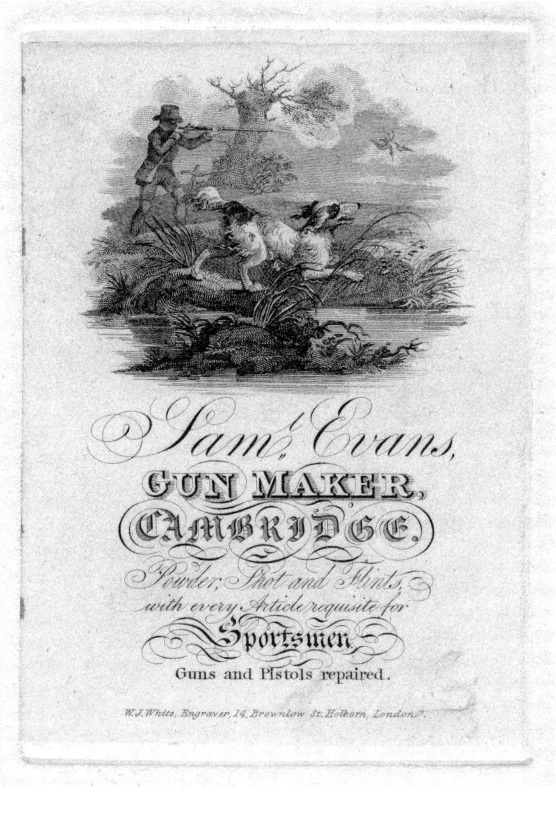

7. Proof of a trade card by W. J. White of London, *c.*1820. The proof has been taken on a slip of thin tissue laid over a coarser, more robust paper, thereby ensuring a sharp, finely detailed print. The image is surrounded by a prominent plate mark – the shape of the copper plate impressed in the paper surface – which would be trimmed on the cards printed for the customer. (100%)

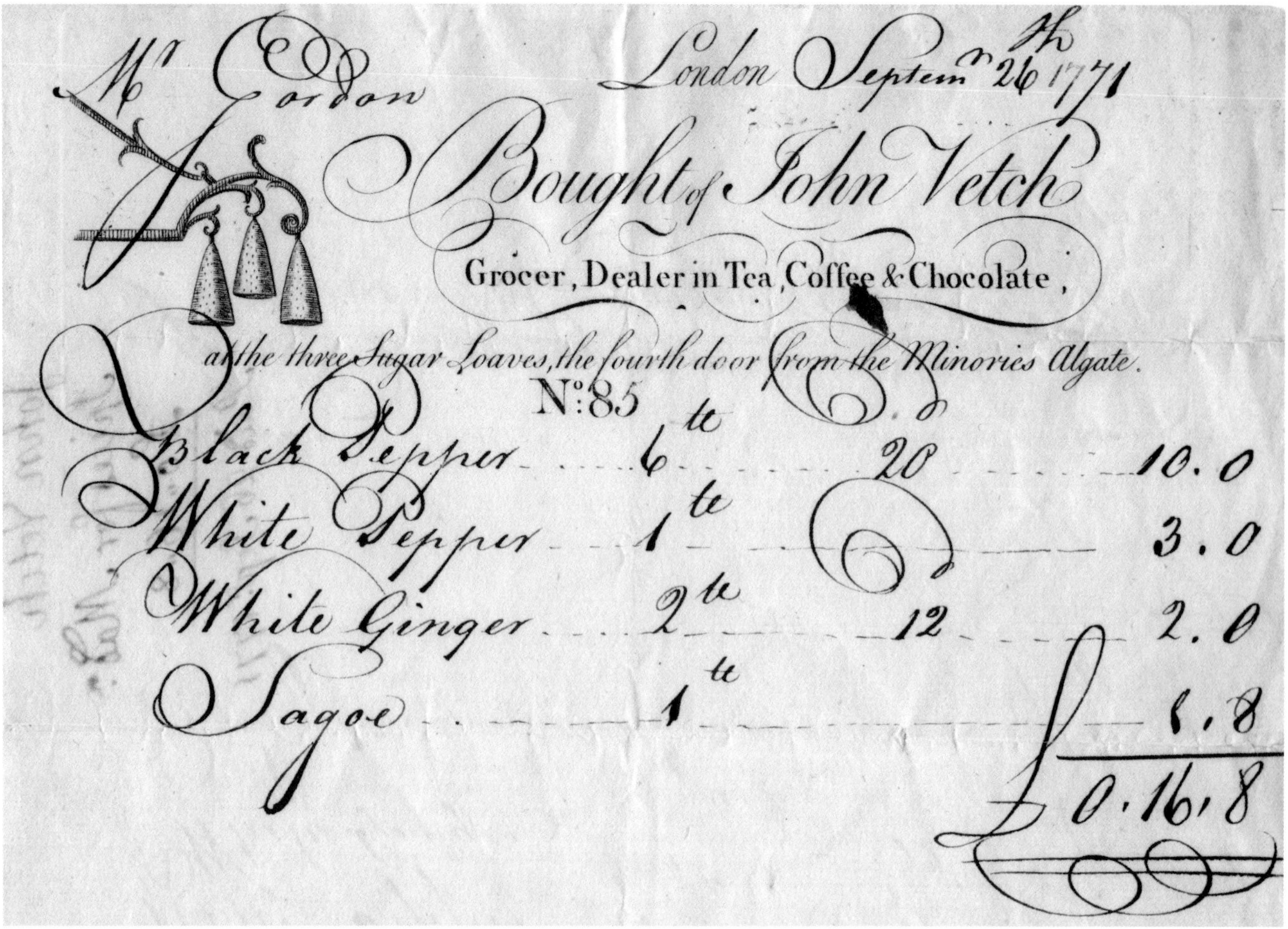

8. *(Above and below)* London tradesmen's signs on billheads. The street number on John Vetch's heading is clearly an addition, showing that the plate was originally engraved before the Act of 1766 prohibited trade signs extending over the street and house numbering was introduced. On Deacon & Wilkinson's heading the number is wholly integrated with the script, indicating that this is a later engraving. In both cases the script, whether engraved or hand-written, is English round hand, combined in the Deacon & Wilkinson design with elegantly decorated roman capitals. (87%, 91%)

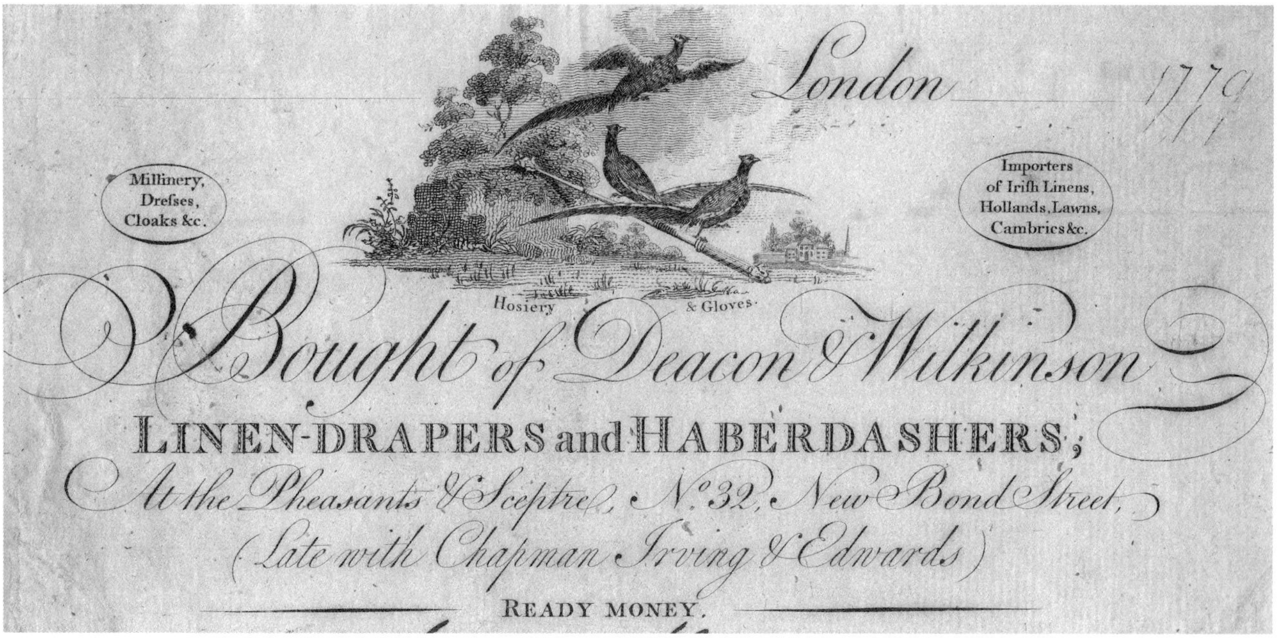

9. English song sheet, *c.*1750, the entire design etched in a single copper plate. The lighter tones were achieved by application of acid-resistant varnish to the copper after only a short period of etching, the darker tones resulting where the acid was then allowed to etch more deeply. The print has been closely trimmed and mounted on to an album leaf. (100%)

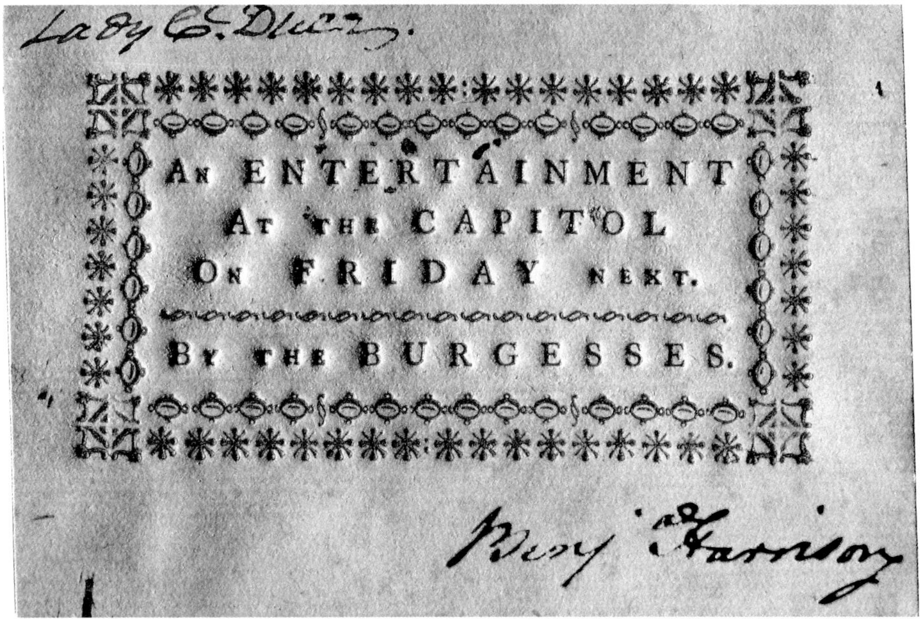

10. Letterpress ticket, Virginia, *c.*1770. Even so simple a job as this would have required the lifting and setting of upwards of 280 separate pieces of type and spacing material. Restricted by the nature of the process to horizontal lines and rectangular framing, the compositor has given elegance to his design by means of wide letter-spacing and a double frame of type flowers. Presswork is poor, however, excessive pressure having forced the type deep into the paper. *Special Collections. John D. Rockefeller Jr. Library, Colonial Williamsburg Foundation.* (67%)

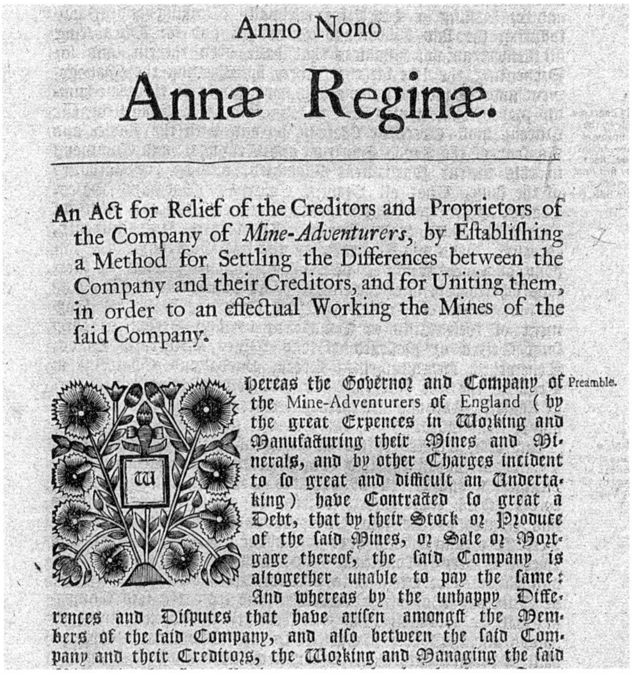

Anno Nono

Annæ Reginæ.

An Act for Relief of the Creditors and Proprietors of the Company of *Mine-Adventurers*, by Eſtabliſhing a Method for Settling the Differences between the Company and their Creditors, and for Uniting them, in order to an effectual Working the Mines of the ſaid Company.

Whereas the Governor and Company of the Mine-Adventurers of England (by the great Expences in Working and Manufacturing their Mines and Minerals, and by other Charges incident to ſo great and difficult an Undertaking) have Contracted ſo great a Debt, that by their Stock or Produce of the ſaid Mines, or Sale or Mortgage thereof, the ſaid Company is altogether unable to pay the ſame: And whereas by the unhappy Differences and Diſputes that have ariſen amongſt the Members of the ſaid Company, and alſo between the ſaid Company and their Creditors, the Working and Managing the ſaid Preamble.

11. Detail from the opening page of an Act of Parliament passed in 1711, ninth year of the reign of Queen Anne (1702–14), the text composed in black letter and the opening initial set within a wood-engraved factotum. The ill-cut roman type and bent printer's rule show the poor quality of English printing at this time. (55%)

The look of printing is always affected by the process employed. With letterpress, the physical shape of the square-cast types and the rectangular chase into which they were locked imposed a pronounced horizontal and vertical stress on design (3). For books and newspapers this was an advantage – an aid to sustained reading – but limiting for many sorts of ephemera. For this reason those desiring a freer treatment for their cards, bookplates, concert tickets and similar items would have them produced as copper engravings (61). Here, the entire design was first drawn on paper and a pencil tracing made. A copper sheet of corresponding size was given a smooth waxy coating or *ground*, and the image transferred to it by laying the tracing face down on the plate and passing all through a rolling press (15). The engraver than went over the image with an *etching needle*, delicately cutting through the wax to expose the copper, after which the plate was laid in a solution of nitric acid and the design thereby etched into the plate surface. After cleaning, the engraver then worked on the plate by hand with a sharp steel *graver*, deepening and developing the etched lines where necessary until the intaglio image was fully realised.

Printing was again a two-man activity. With the plate warmed over a charcoal stove the man responsible for inking worked vigorously over its surface with a leather *dabber*, forcing ink down into the etched and engraved lines. Then he cleaned off the surplus, starting with muslin and finishing with the edge of his hand dusted with whiting, a skilled procedure resulting in virtually a polished plate but with ink retained in every line. The plate was then laid on the bed of the press, dampened paper placed over it, a blanket over that, and the whole wound between the rollers, thus making the print.

Where engraving scored over letterpress was in the elegance with which the engraver could compose his design, with imagery and lettering freely integrated and taken to any degree of elaboration (16). But the printing rate was far slower, 300 impressions of a trade card taking perhaps a full working day.[2]

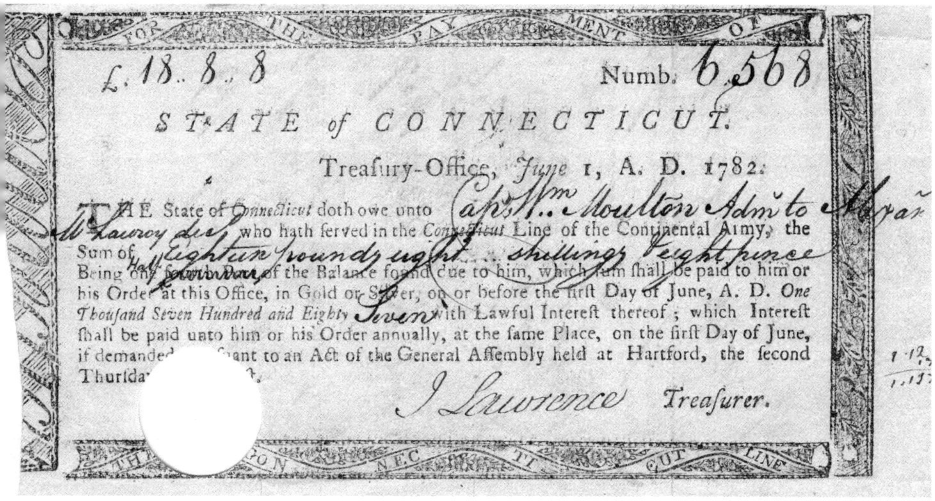

FOR THE PAYMENT OF

£. 18. 8. 8 Numb. 6568

STATE of CONNECTICUT.

Treasury-Office, June 1, A. D. 1782.

THE State of Connecticut doth owe unto Capt. Wm. Moulton Adm. to ... who hath served in the Connecticut Line of the Continental Army, the Sum of Eighteen pounds eight shillings & eight pence Being ... of the Balance found due to him, which Sum shall be paid to him or his Order at this Office, in Gold or Silver, on or before the first Day of June, A. D. *One Thousand Seven Hundred and Eighty* Seven with Lawful Interest thereof; which Interest shall be paid unto him or his Order annually, at the same Place, on the first Day of June, if demanded ... to an Act of the General Assembly held at Hartford, the second Thursday ...

J Lawrence Treasurer.

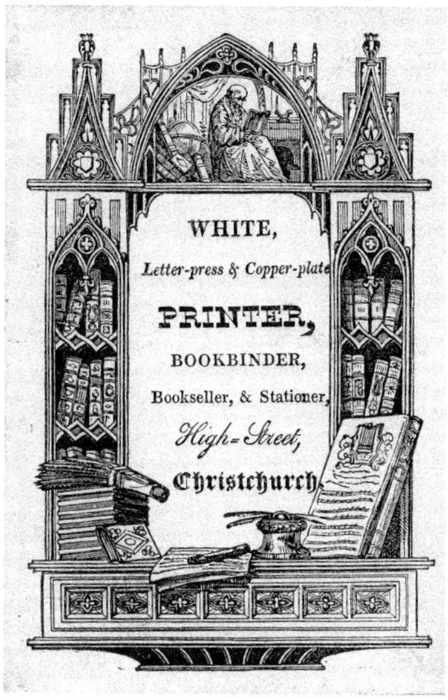

12. *(Left)* Treasury certificate, Connecticut, 1782, set throughout in Caslon type imported from London. The decorative border is an example of relief metal engraving, the small white circles at the corners showing where the metal was nailed to wooden spacing material enclosing the type. Cancelled with a circular punch, the certificate acknowledged money owing to Captain William Moulton for services during the War of Independence. (66%)

13. *(Right)* Printer's trade card, Christchurch, Hampshire, England, *c.*1850, the wood-engraved frame cut in the then fashionable Gothic Revival style. (66%)

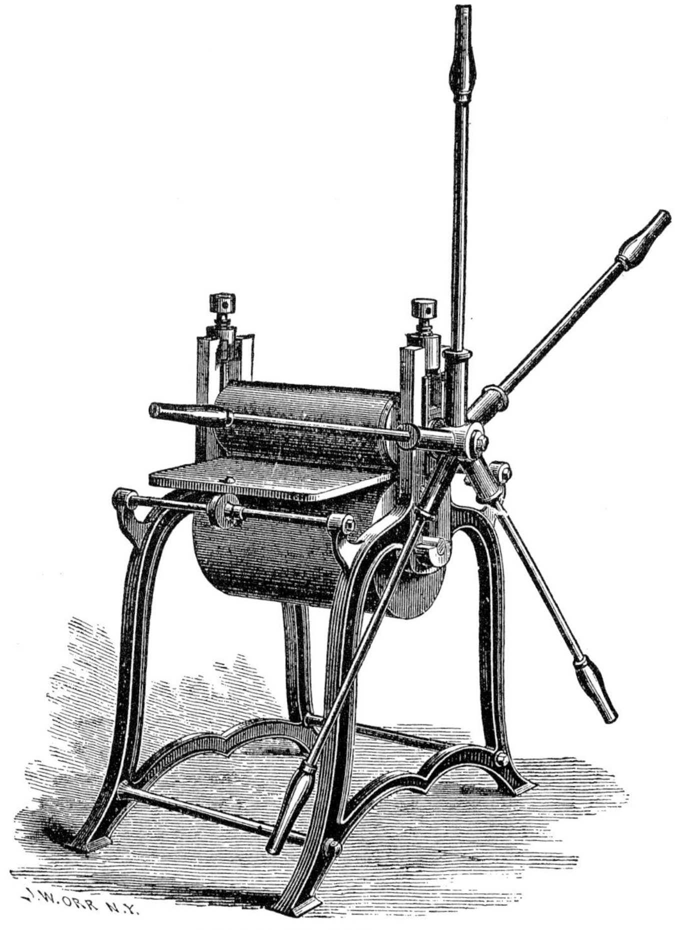

COPPERPLATE PRESS.

14. Engraver's proof of a rococo cartouche, possibly for a small trade card. Lettering would have been added to the plate following approval of this stage. (54%)

15. Nineteenth-century rolling press for printing copper- and steel-engraved plates. Wood- engraving by J. W. Orr, New York, from Ringwalt's *American Encyclopaedia of Printing*, 1871.

16. Trade card engraved by Henry Dawkins for Anthony Lamb, New York, *c.*1755, the elegance of its rococo frame somewhat at odds with the items of trade hung about it. Originally a Londoner, Lamb was transported to America as an accomplice of the notorious Jack Shepherd. Dawkins learnt his trade in London and emigrated to New York *c.*1753, where for a short time he worked for Lamb engraving scientific instruments; his penchant for the graver, however, led to his jailing for banknote forgery in 1776. *Courtesy of The New-York Historical Society, New York City.* (90%)

HONI SOIT QUI MAL Y PENSE
DIEU ET MON DROIT
HENRY HASTINGS,
NIGHTMAN
to His Majeſty's Offices & for the City & Suburbs,
At the KING'S Arms, Lombard Street, Mint,
SOUTHWARK.
WHERE Gentlemen, &c. may rely upon having their Bu-
ſineſs decently performed being always at the work Him-
ſelf: Also, empties Vaults, Seſpools; & unſtops Funnels,
at the loweſt Prices being in buſineſs upwards of 30 years.
I have the new invented Machine Carts for the quick Dis-
patch of Buſineſs. Gentlemen, &c. ſending a line ſhall be
waited on at the ſhorteſt Notice as above, or to the following
houſes, Viz. Lambeth, King's Head, High Street; the George
Vauxhall; City, Cooper's Arms, Botolph Lane; Horſe & Dorſet,
Bread Street; 1 Star, Old Change; Crown, Lad Lane; Marl
brough Head, Biſhopsgate Street; Holborn, Star, Lincoln's
Inn Fields, Southwark, City of Saliſbury, Horslydown &
the Crown Eating houſe, Prince's Street, oppoſite the
Manſion-Houſe; Hoop & Falcon, St. Martin's le Grand.

17. Trade card of Southwark nightman Henry Hastings, the hard lines of the overall image indicating that it was largely cut with a graver. Hastings claimed King George III to be among his clients and made the Kings Arms in the City of London his headquarters, hence his assumption of the royal arms as a trade sign. Performed at night, his occupation was emptying cesspools etc., as shown in the vignette. Written on the back of the card is a bill of October 1790 for emptying the workhouse privy in the parish of St George the Martyr, Southwark, signed with the mark of Hastings's widow Elizabeth. (77%)

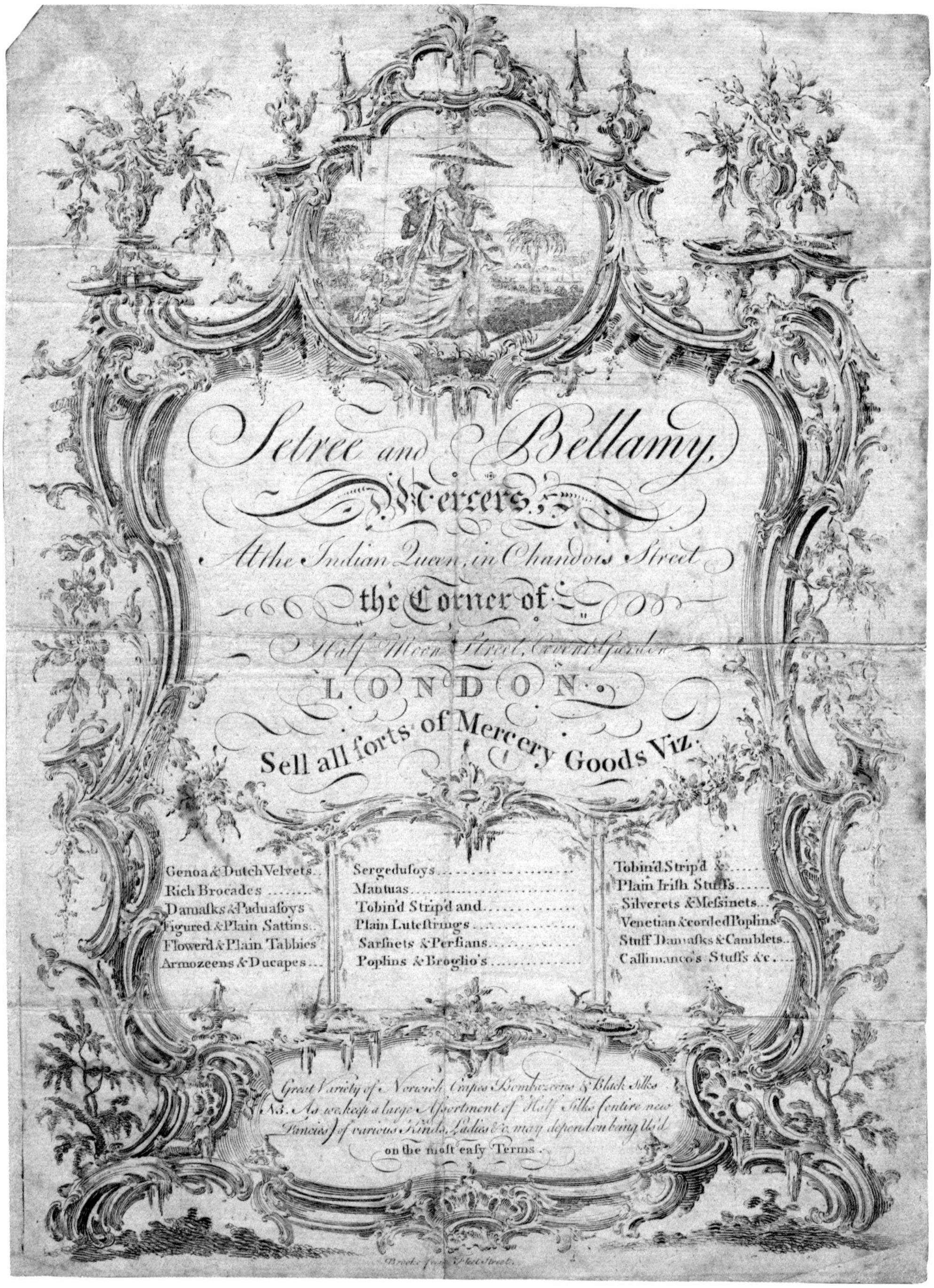

18. Trade card by Brooke of Fleet Street, London, for the mercers Setree & Bellamy. A faint pencil grid drawn over the trade sign at the top suggests that a copy was made from it in the engraver's workshop, though most likely by an apprentice for a practice piece as the grid is somewhat out of square. Rococo decoration as used here and on Anthony Lamb's card (16) was characteristic of domestic design generally in the period *c.*1740–*c.*1770. (63%)

In some cases a plate would be completed solely exploiting the qualities of etching, resulting in a design characterised by a somewhat freer line (4, 58). There was also from *c.*1770 the process of *aquatint* in which the ground was created with resin, either by dusting it over the plate and fusing with heat or floating on a solution of resin in alcohol and letting the alcohol evaporate. Such grounds being only partially acid-resistant, the acid textured the copper to produce soft tonal qualities in the print, longer etching producing deeper tones. With *mezzotint* the entire face of the plate was first laboriously worked over with a special tool to produce a textured surface which (had it then been printed) would have printed as an all-over black, the image being created by selectively scraping and burnishing the copper to develop lighter-printing areas. These variants on basic engraving, however, were more

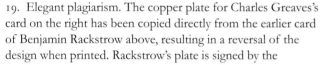

19. Elegant plagiarism. The copper plate for Charles Greaves's card on the right has been copied directly from the earlier card of Benjamin Rackstrow above, resulting in a reversal of the design when printed. Rackstrow's plate is signed by the London engraver H. Copeland and dated 1738. Greaves is recorded as working between 1763 and 1774. (Rackstrow card) *Trustees of the British Museum*; (Greaves card) *York Museums Trust, York Castle Museum*. (57%)

common in the fields of book and print publishing than in the ephemera of the tradesman. Collectively, engraving and its variants are known as intaglio processes.

The commercial handwriting of eighteenth-century Britain and her colonies was English round hand. This style was promulgated via the books of writing masters, its clear forms developed through a synergy between the shapes natural to the pointed quill and those intrinsic to the etching needle and graver (8), for it was via copper-plate printing that writing masters reached their public. Also shown in these manuals were roman and black-letter forms which, though of limited application in commerce, were further developed by engravers, particularly in the second half of the century, when letters might be cut in outline only or filled in with pattern rather than solid black (8). The skill employed was considerable, for the engraver needed to be as adept at cutting letters in reverse on a copper printing plate as he was in engraving them right way round on presentation silver.

The qualities necessary for the apprentice engraver were outlined in *A General Description of All Trades*, 1747, where the anonymous author describes the aspirant as needing 'somewhat of a Genius, strong Inclinations, some Study, and almost indefatigable Application in Practice', and concluding 'but [it] requires good Eyesight, and, if a Youth is taught Drawing before he goes to it, it will be a great Help to him'.[3]

One can readily see that the drafting of a run-of-the-mill billhead would be easily managed in the engraver's own workshop, but for a topographical print or elaborate trade card the services of a designer were needed. Writing in 1761, Joseph Collyer observed that prerequisite for the designer was his ability 'to draw with great accuracy and beauty' and that he be 'a perfect master of the doctrine of light and shades'. The latter the designer would render in washes of ink or watercolour for the engraver to translate into the linear tones and crosshatching achievable with the graver. The accomplished designer could earn from a half-guinea to a guinea and upwards per day, though few if any were able to make this their sole employment, and most frequently designing was, Collyer averred, a sideline for the history painter. Less often would an engraver be his own designer, and then only if he were 'well skilled in drawing'.[4] Engravings of landscapes, country houses and similar

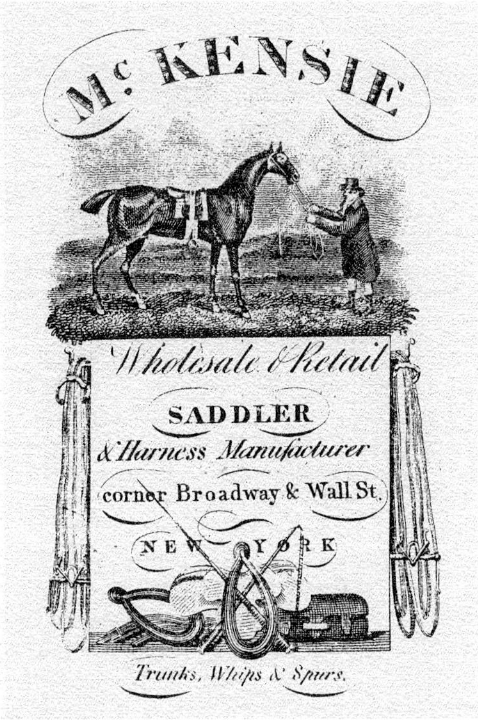

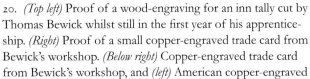

20. *(Top left)* Proof of a wood-engraving for an inn tally cut by Thomas Bewick whilst still in the first year of his apprenticeship. *(Right)* Proof of a small copper-engraved trade card from Bewick's workshop. *(Below right)* Copper-engraved trade card from Bewick's workshop, and *(left)* American copper-engraved card, *c.*1821, illustrating the continuing similarity in design in the graphic work of the two countries in the early nineteenth century. (Bewick items) *Trustees of the British Museum.* (American card) Jenny, *Early American Trade Cards from the Collection of Bella C. Landauer.* (100%)

subjects were based on the work of topographical artists.

Aptitude in drawing was certainly looked for by the north-of-England engraver Ralph Beilby when he took on the fifteen-year-old Thomas Bewick (1753–1828) as an apprentice in 1767. Bewick drew wherever he could – in the margins of books, on gravestones and the flags of his parents' hearth – until a family friend gave him pen, paper, brush and colours, following which he turned to painting pictures of the local wildlife. Beilby heard of the boy's talent through chance conversation and sought him out.

As with the majority of engravers, Bewick's master undertook a wide variety of work: clock faces, coffin plates, family crests on silverware, etc., as well as the copper plates for the cards, tickets, billheads and other ephemera of local commerce. Bewick expected drawing lessons, but in this he was disappointed, during his first days simply being given Copeland's *New Book of Ornaments* to copy from; but he progressed, and in due time was trusted to engrave mottoes on rings and armorial bearings on silver.[5] The latter would have been based on patterns

21. *(Top)* Wood-engraving for a horse dealer by Bewick and the trade card of Alexander Anderson, father of wood-engraving in America. *(Centre)* Wood-engraving for a stagecoach line by Anderson. *(Below)* 'The Spanish Pointer' from Bewick's *General History of Quadrupeds*: *(right)* by Bewick and *(left)* as copied by Anderson. (Bewick horse) Boyd, *Bewick Gleanings*; (stagecoach) Hornung, *Early Advertising Art*; (Anderson card and hound) Linton, *The History of Wood-Engraving in America*. (89%)

already drawn, and it is likely that much emanating from the average engraver's workshop was adapted from existing imagery (61). An engraver might also plagiarise another's design when an existing image provided a particularly apt model (19) thus saving on the designer's fee.

American and British ephemera differed but little in this period, for American letterpress printers worked with British type and equipment and colonial engravers learnt their craft from immigrant masters or were themselves immigrants (16). Colonial fashions in furniture design, silverware, pottery etc., were also influenced by the British, but here scarcity of labour and in some cases less sophisticated tools could result in less elaborate ornamentation;[6] but the copper plate imposed no similar restraint and colonial engravers were as free as the British when exploiting the graphic suggestions of their English pattern books, or adapting ideas from the scrapbooks of designs that had crossed the Atlantic with them.

The freedom intrinsic to engraving made it the medium of choice for the trade- or tradesman's card, 'card' here

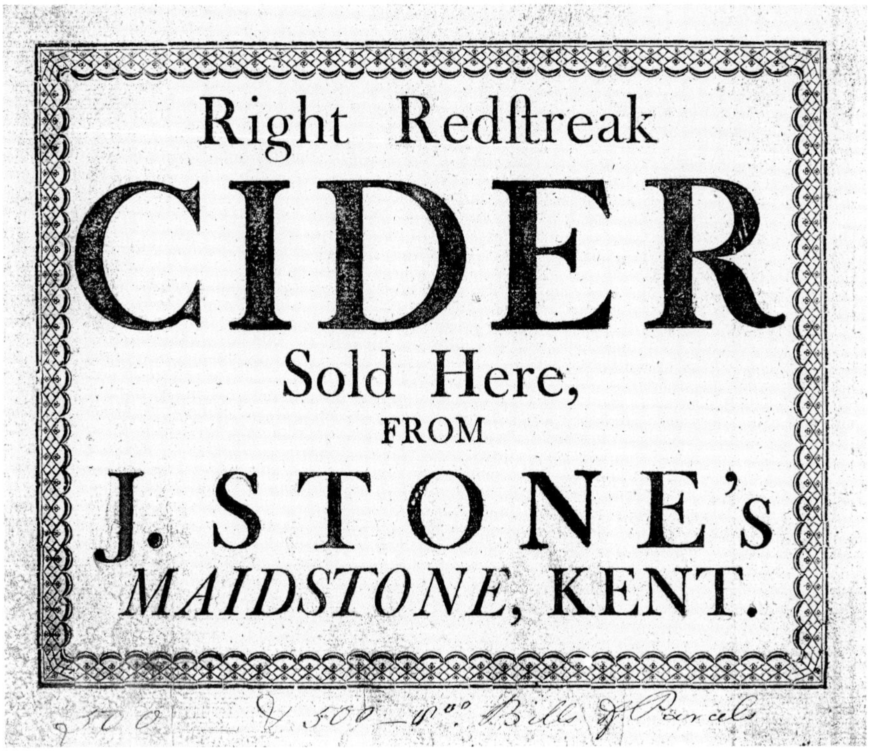

22. Window bill by John Blake of Maidstone, England, the main line set in Caslon's 19-line roman of 1780. The flowers used in the border are from the Fry & Steele foundry. Such advertisements were designed to fit within the upper small panes of a tradesman's window. (52%) *Maidstone Museum & Bentlif Art Gallery*

meaning a printed announcement rather than the small business card that modern usage might suggest. Eighteenth-century cards could be quite large, occasionally approaching modern A4 in size. Giving the tradesman's name and address and the nature of his trade, this versatile advertising medium served alike as compliments slip, handbill and small poster. The card was complemented by the billhead, on which the design was confined to the head of the sheet with the space below left clear for listing the goods or services purchased. This would usually require the engraving of a separate plate, though if the card itself were sufficiently small the one plate could be used for both purposes.[7] In some cases, tradesmen did without a billhead and simply wrote their account on the back of the card; and occasionally card and billhead were printed front and back on the same sheet.

The imagery employed in engraving changed as the century progressed, and these variations illustrate how functional, social and other factors could affect the appearance of eighteenth-century jobbing work. Shops in both countries were known by their trade signs, the Sugar Loaves (8) or Indian Queen (18) for example being associated with the trades of grocer and mercer respectively. As it was effectively his shop's address, the tradesman made the sign the chief feature of his stationery, so much so that a well-established sign might be retained even when the trade carried on in the building had changed. The earliest trade cards often bore no more than emblem and wording, but by the 1740s imagery was often enclosed in frames of increasing elaboration, their design reflecting current taste in the decorative arts – in turn baroque, rococo, Adamesque, etc. But aesthetics could be at odds with the needs of trade, the frame that had its counterpart in the elegant gilt surround of the assembly-room mirror being sometimes further embellished on the trade card with sextants, tea canisters, tin-ware or whatever else was the tradesman's line (16).

In England particularly, trade signs could be heavy three-dimensional structures extending over the highway, and it was not unknown for ill-maintained ones to collapse into the street below, with fatal consequences. From 1762 in Westminster and 1766 in the City of London, legislation forced their removal. House numbering was introduced, and though a tradesman might continue using his emblem it would now be on a relatively modest painted board. These changes were reflected not only in the addition of the new street numbers to existing copper plates (8) but, as fresh plates were engraved, the relegation of the emblem to a minor role on the card, the space thus freed being taken over by an extended list of goods and services. Occasionally vignettes showing the tradesman's premises or the trade being carried out (17) were included, but these were to become more common in the following century.

A further aspect of the engraver's workshop was the cutting of printing blocks for letterpress printers, occasionally in metal (12) but more often in wood. Here the procedure was the reverse of intaglio engraving, the background areas being cut away leaving the design in relief. For relatively coarse work the plank face of the wood was used and carved with small blades and chisels, but for finer work the wood was planed across the grain and the design cut with a graver, and here boxwood was the preferred medium. Ralph Beilby had no liking for wood-engraving and passed such work over to Bewick, who had an affinity for it. When still a first-year apprentice, Bewick engraved an emblem for the George & Dragon, Penrith (20), the little image proving of such quality that it greatly increased the workshop's business.[8] Thus began the wood-engraving career of Thomas Bewick, who in 1790 was to publish his *General History of Quadrupeds* and in 1797 and 1804 his two-volume *History of British Birds*, both illustrated throughout with wood-engravings.

The progenitor of wood-engraving in America was Alexander Anderson (1775-1870) (21), who even while studying medicine in his teens was engraving names on dog collars and cutting advertising emblems in type metal to sell to local newspapers. In 1793, from an imported copy of one of the many works by then illustrated by Bewick, Anderson saw how wood-engraving could afford a precision in cutting equal to that of copper. In 1795 he forsook medicine for engraving and from 1812 worked solely in wood, making cuts for trade cards, ballad sheets, playing-card wrappers and other ephemera; and book illustrations also, including those for a plagiarised American edition of Bewick's *Quadrupeds* (21).[9] Anderson was still engraving in the 1860s.

Although cut with the same tools as a copper-engraving, the fact that the printing surface was a relief image cut in wood rather than an intaglio incised in metal gave wood-engraving a characteristically different look (13). The advantage of the process in book production was that the blocks were included in the type forme rather than having to be printed separately like copper-engravings (25). In areas where a lighter tone was desirable the engraver would slightly lower the surface of the block to reduce printing pressure, and where darker tones were needed the pressman would insert slips of thin paper between the parchment and blanket of the tympan to increase it. But such subtleties would be unlikely in ephemeral work.

The utility of letterpress lay in the fact that type could be reset for different jobs. But there was a limit to the amount of type that any printer could stock. When the Philadelphia Quakers published a history of their movement in 1727 part of the work was undertaken by Benjamin Franklin, who at that time had sufficient type to compose no more than two pages at a time. This he had to set, print and distribute back into the cases each evening, ready for further setting on the morrow.[10] Franklin imported type

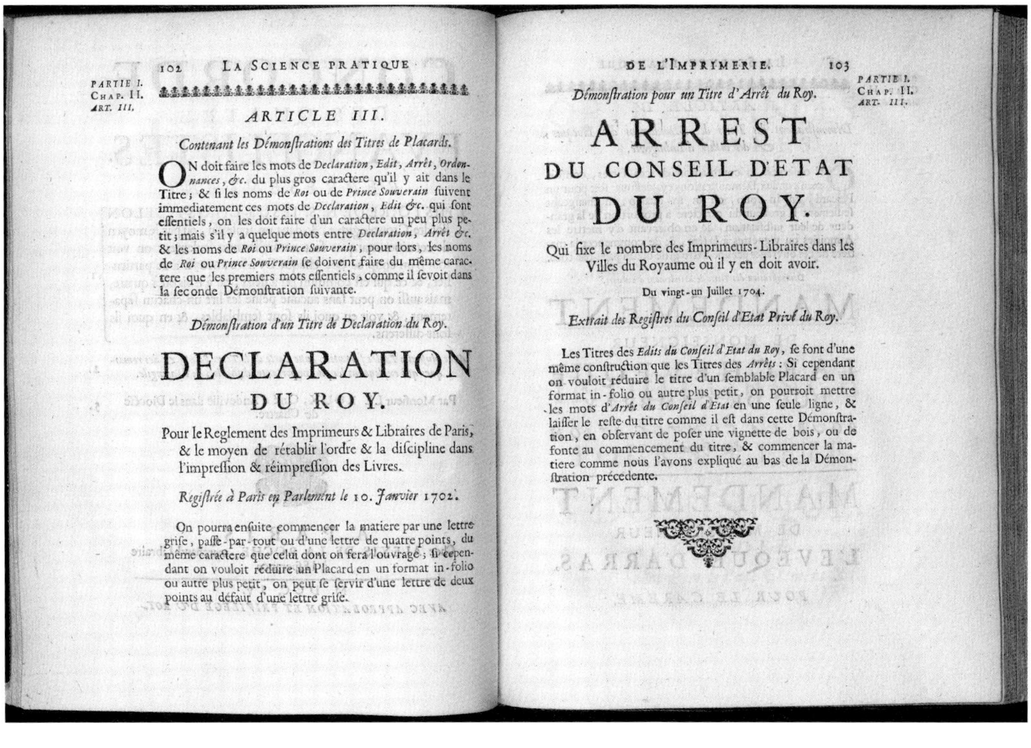

102 LA SCIENCE PRATIQUE

PARTIE I. CHAP. II. ART. III.

ARTICLE III.

Contenant les Démonſtrations des Titres de Placards.

ON doit faire les mots de *Declaration*, *Edit*, *Arrêt*, *Ordonnances*, *&c.* du plus gros caractere qu'il y ait dans le Titre ; & ſi les noms de *Roi* ou de *Prince Souverain* ſuivent immediatement ces mots de *Declaration*, *Edit &c.* qui ſont eſſentiels, on les doit faire d'un caractere un peu plus petit ; mais s'il y a quelque mots entre *Declaration*, *Arrêt &c.* & les noms de *Roi* ou *Prince Souverain*, pour lors, les noms de *Roi* ou *Prince Souverain* ſe doivent faire du même caractere que les premiers mots eſſentiels, comme il ſevoit dans la ſeconde Démonſtration ſuivante.

Démonſtration d'un Titre de Declaration du Roy.

DECLARATION

DU ROY.

Pour le Reglement des Imprimeurs & Libraires de Paris, & le moyen de rétablir l'ordre & la diſcipline dans l'impreſſion & réimpreſſion des Livres.

Regiſtrée à Paris en Parlement le 10. *Janvier* 1702.

On pourra enſuite commencer la matiere par une lettre griſe, paſſe-par-tout ou d'une lettre de quatre points, du même caractere que celui dont on fera l'ouvrage ; ſi cependant on vouloit réduire un Placard en un format in-folio ou autre plus petit, on peut ſe ſervir d'une lettre de deux points au défaut d'une lettre griſe.

DE L'IMPRIMERIE. 103

PARTIE I. CHAP. II. ART. III.

Démonſtration pour un Titre d'Arrêt du Roy.

ARREST

DU CONSEIL D'ETAT

DU ROY.

Qui fixe le nombre des Imprimeurs-Libraires dans les Villes du Royaume où il y en doit avoir.

Du vingt-un Juillet 1704.

Extrait des Regiſtres du Conſeil d'Etat Privé du Roy.

Les Titres des *Edits du Conſeil d'Etat du Roy*, ſe font d'une même conſtruction que les Titres des *Arrêts* : Si cependant on vouloit réduire le titre d'un ſemblable Placard en un format in-folio ou autre plus petit, on pourroit mettre les mots d'*Arrêt du Conſeil d'Etat* en une ſeule ligne, & laiſſer le reſte du titre comme il eſt dans cette Démonſtration, en obſervant de poſer une vignette de bois, ou de fonte au commencement du titre, & commencer la matiere comme nous l'avons expliqué au bas de la Démonſtration précedente.

23. Page opening from Dominique Fertel's manual *La Science pratique de l'impremerie*, 1723, showing scaled-down examples to demonstrate the setting of bills publishing royal proclamations and decrees. Fertel's instructions for the left-hand example are in translation: 'Make the words *Proclamation*, *Edict*, *Decree*, *Ordinances* etc. the biggest, and if the title of *King* or *Sovereign Prince* immediately follows as an essential part of the heading, then set it in slightly smaller type, but if there should be some words between *Proclamation* [etc] and *King* or *Sovereign Prince* set it in the same size type, as shown in the second example.' Then, concerning the text: 'Begin with a decorated letter, a factotum, or a four-line letter of the same face as the text. If however you wish to print the bill at folio [half-sheet] size or smaller, where a factotum would not be practical and you lack a decorated letter, then use a two-line letter.'
St Bride Library.

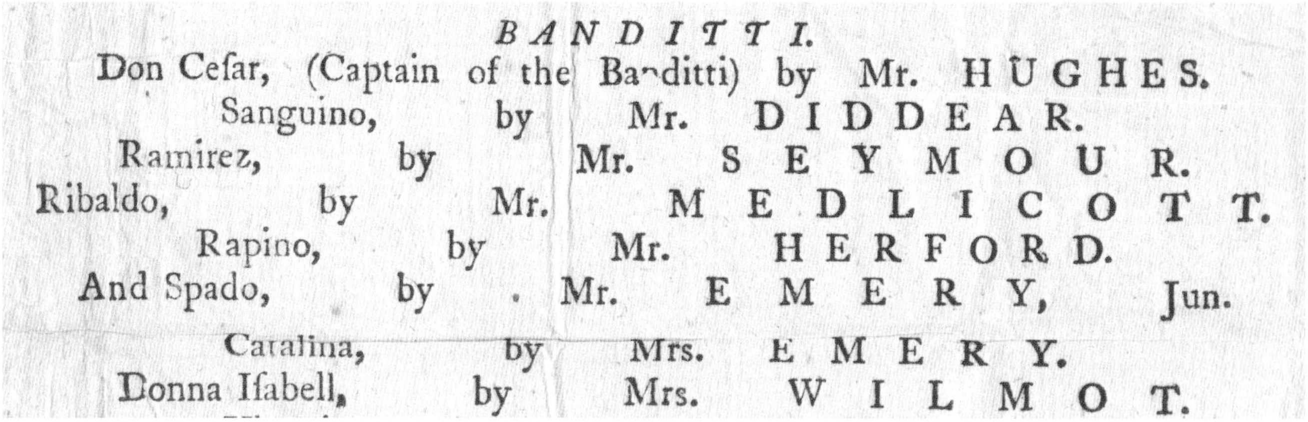

BANDITTI.
Don Cefar, (Captain of the Ba^ditti) by Mr. HUGHES.
Sanguino, by Mr. DIDDEAR.
Ramirez, by Mr. SEYMOUR.
Ribaldo, by Mr. MEDLICOTT.
Rapino, by Mr. HERFORD.
And Spado, by . Mr. EMERY, Jun.
Catalina, by Mrs. EMERY.
Donna Ifabell, by Mrs. WILMOT.

24. Letter spacing in excess: detail of a playbill by an anonymous Dover, England, printer, 1793. Here words and letters tend to link more readily with those above and below them than with those either side. The types are noticeably crudely cut, and may represent another founder's attempt to imitate Caslon. (98%)

from London, some at a later date from the foundry of William Caslon (1692–1766). Caslon was an engraver and adept at cutting the lettering tools used by bookbinders. The quality of his work was noticed by Franklin's old employer, John Watts, who with some others lent Caslon the money to start a foundry, Caslon's types (12, 27) subsequently initiating a renaissance in British type founding following publication of his first specimen in 1734. It was in Caslon's roman that in 1776 the printer John Dunlap would set the first printed copy of the Declaration of Independence.[11]

Sizes of type were identified not by measurement but by a sequence of names peculiar to the trade. *Pearl*, the smallest, was equivalent to 1/16 in. (1.6 mm), *pica* to 1/6 in. (4.3 mm), etc. The largest size commonly available up to the 1760s was no more than *five-line pica* – less than 7/8 in. (22 mm). Then in 1764 William Caslon's son issued a broadside specimen of a new 13-line roman – a set of capitals two inches (508 mm) tall – and in 1780 extended the range further to an imposing 19-line (three-inch/762 mm) (22). The *raison d'être* of these new, bold types becomes clear from the sample settings of the younger Caslon's 1785 specimen – 'Epsom, Windsor, Bristol, Southampton' – for these were big types for coaching bills, and any other large item of printing that might now be needed.[12] Thus did social change affect the look of printed ephemera.

In England the twenty-five years between 1750 and 1775 had seen considerable improvement in the state of the country's roads, with the provincial towns growing in prosperity as a consequence. Once there had been few printers outside London but by 1785 there were printing shops in market towns throughout England, Scotland and Wales. The situation was comparable in colonial America, where population and printing expanded with the frontier. By the time of the Revolution there were print shops in all principal American cities and an officially appointed 'Publick Printer' at work in each colony's capital. It was the towns' and settlements' increasing bustle that encouraged printing, for now there was need for coaching bills, inn tallies, auction and reward notices, and all manner of other ephemera. Local elections were busy times in Britain. Where there were two printers one might be favoured as the Whig shop and the other the Tory; yet this was not always the case, Stephen White of Norwich cheerfully printing the two parties' ballad sheets side by side in the same forme.

But inevitably there were slack times also, and thus it was not uncommon for country printers to ply more than the one trade. Stephen White kept himself busy as 'medicine vendor, painter, boat builder, and general artist',[13] while Ray of Barnsley, England, was both printer and hatter.[14] The Pennsylvania engraver J. D. Hechstetter made wooden legs and arms,[15] while the Philadelphia printer Robert Bailey kept a general store selling furniture, foodstuffs, hardware and liquor.[16]

The range of type styles available for English-language setting was initially limited to roman, italic and black-letter (11). About 1690 the Grover foundry cut the decorative Union Pearl (26A), a font of which Franklin imported and which also appeared on some early American currency notes;[17] but the type attracted little if any interest in England. Then in the second half of the century the printer's range was extended with a marked development of decorative types (26B–E), the founders' inspiration coming from both the fancy lettering of the engravers and the types of the Parisian founder Pierre-Simon Fournier, whose designs of 1764–6 were themselves inspired by engraved letterforms.

Although the letterpress printer could never achieve the freedom in design enjoyed by the engraver, these new typefaces enabled him to give added sparkle to ephemera. Already he could enhance his printing with *ornaments* – swags of fruit, allegorical figures and other motifs – cut in either wood or type metal, or decorate it with *flowers*, small motifs that could be composed into patterns and borders,

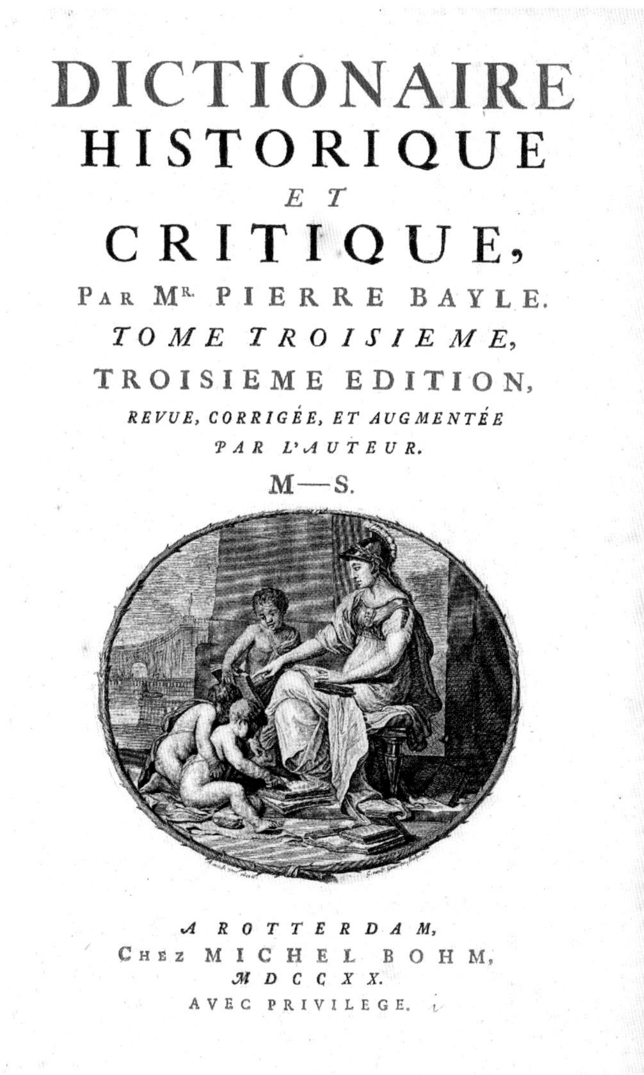

DICTIONAIRE
HISTORIQUE
ET
CRITIQUE,
PAR MR. PIERRE BAYLE.
TOME TROISIEME,
TROISIEME EDITION,
REVUE, CORRIGÉE, ET AUGMENTÉE
PAR L'AUTEUR.
M—S.

A ROTTERDAM,
CHEZ MICHEL BOHM,
M DCCXX.
AVEC PRIVILEGE.

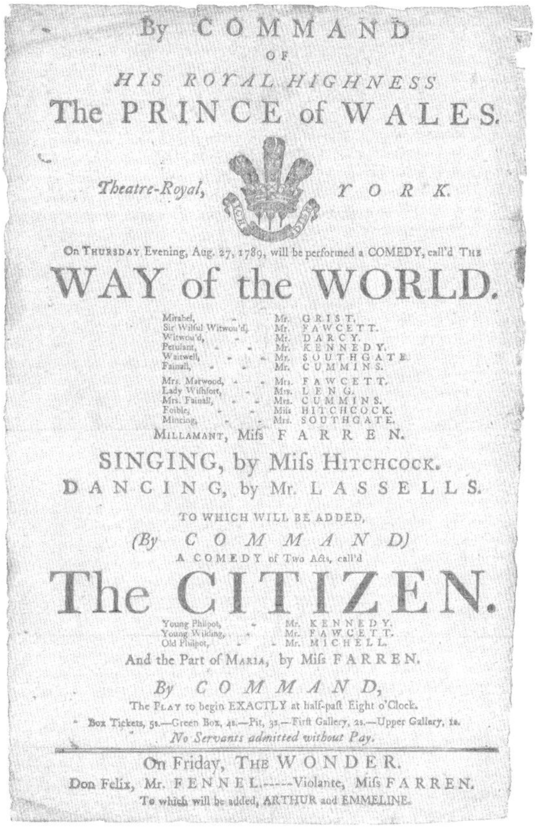

By COMMAND
OF
HIS ROYAL HIGHNESS
The PRINCE of WALES.

Theatre-Royal, YORK.

On THURSDAY Evening, Aug. 27, 1789, will be performed a COMEDY, call'd THE
WAY of the WORLD.

Mirabel,	Mr. GRIST.
Sir Wilful Witwou'd,	Mr. FAWCETT.
Witwou'd,	Mr. DARCY.
Petulant,	Mr. KENNEDY.
Waitwell,	Mr. SOUTHGATE.
Fainall,	Mr. CUMMINS.
Mrs. Marwood,	Mrs. FAWCETT.
Lady Wishfort,	Mrs. LENG.
Mrs. Fainall,	Mrs. CUMMINS.
Foible,	Miss HITCHCOCK.
Mincing,	Mrs. SOUTHGATE.

MILLAMANT, Miss FARREN.
SINGING, by Miss HITCHCOCK.
DANCING, by Mr. LASSELLS.
TO WHICH WILL BE ADDED,
(By COMMAND)
A COMEDY of Two Acts, call'd
The CITIZEN.

Young Philpot,	Mr. KENNEDY.
Young Wilding,	Mr. FAWCETT.
Old Philpot,	Mr. MICHELL.

And the Part of MARIA, by Miss FARREN.
By COMMAND,
The PLAY to begin EXACTLY at half-past Eight o'Clock.
Box Tickets, 5s.—Green Box, 4s.—Pit, 3s.—First Gallery, 2s.—Upper Gallery, 1s.
No Servants admitted without Pay.

On Friday, THE WONDER.
Don Felix, Mr. FENNEL.-----Violante, Miss FARREN.
To which will be added, ARTHUR and EMMELINE.

25. Folio title-page by Michael Bohm, Rotterdam, 1720, and an English playbill of 1789, showing how in the eighteenth century the printing of both books and ephemera was largely limited to the use of roman and italic types. It is in the presentations of their respective contents that differences arise, the page displaying the one title and ancillary information while the bill presents two titles and the fact of this being a royal command performance. The illustration on the title-page is a copper engraving by G. van der Gouwen, and as the page is printed in black and red it went to press three times: twice for the type and once through a rolling press for the engraving. (35%)

or enliven an opening paragraph with a *factotum,* a small ornament pierced with a square hole for the insertion of an initial letter (27). More fundamental than decoration, however, was the underlying structure of a design. It was rare for the eighteenth-century printer to do other than arrange his composition about a central axis, but still he had scope for the exercise of taste in his choice of type styles and sizes, and the spacing of the lines on the page.

The first manual of instruction for printers was Joseph Moxon's *Mechanick Exercises, or the Doctrine of Handy-Works applied to the Art of Printing.* Published in parts in 1683–4, this remained the printer's sole vade mecum until 1755; and it is from Moxon's advice as to the setting of title-pages that we get an insight into the printer's approach to display typography in this period.

Title-pages could at this time be very lengthy and Moxon advised that the compositor's first job was to carefully read through the author's copy to determine which word or words to present *as* 'the *Title* or *Name* of the *Book*'. That decision made, he was next to consider the words that would print above the title, judging whether to set them as one line or two, and which of those words might require their own emphasis. This copy he would then set, followed by the title word or phrase, the latter ideally making a single line equal in length to the width of a text page, which the compositor could achieve by careful choice between setting in capitals or capitals with lower case, in roman, italic or black letter. Following this, the compositor would continue with the matter to be set below the title. The arrangement had also to equal a text page in depth, and this

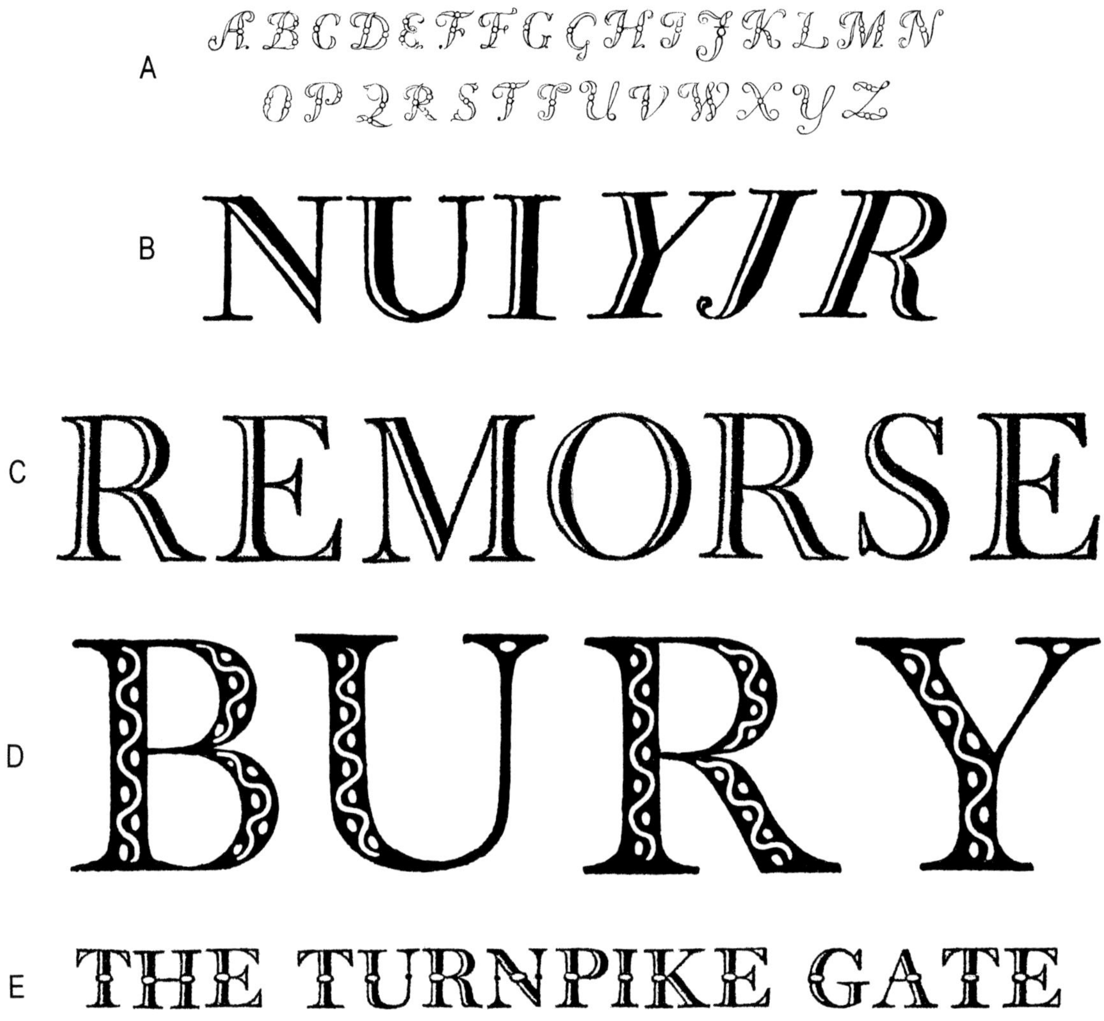

26. Various founders' ornamented typefaces. (A) Grover Foundry's Union Pearl, *c.*1690; (B) Fournier, 1766; (C) Fry, 1788; (D) Stephenson, 1796; (E) Figgins, 1801. (100%)

the compositor could achieve by inserting spacing material between the respective lines, grouping them in accordance with their sense. Mindful that the styles of title-page changed with time, Moxon ended with 'therefore a Lasting Rule cannot be given for the ordering them: only what has been said in general concerning Emphasis, and in particular to humour the Eye, the *Compositor* has a constant regard to'.[18]

Some seventy years later, John Smith declined to give similar detailed guidance in his *Printer's Grammar*, 1755, instead advising the compositor to study good examples: 'To furnish one's self therefore with proper conceptions for setting Titles, Dedications, Heads, and many other odd fragments, a *Florilegium Typographicum* would be of great help, especially to such as have made an early beginning to collect, and to secure in a Book, all such Scraps as will be of service and pleasure to refer to.'[19] Student graphic designers follow the same advice today, culling the flowers of contemporary ephemera as their exemplars.

Apart from Smith's 'many other odd fragments' neither authority makes reference to jobbing, though ephemera would constitute the everyday work of the majority of shops. However, from surviving printing of the period it is evident that the principles applicable in book production did carry over into the more ephemeral work. Indeed, the printer's intention in composing a title-page was not only for it to serve in the book per se but also to act as a *poster* to advertise it. Publishers would commonly paste up offprints of their title-pages in public places to give notice of publication – a contributory reason for the lengthy wording of many seventeenth- and eighteenth-century titles. In his account for printing Johnson's two-volume *Dictionary* of 1755 the printer William Strahan included charges 'For two Red Titles' meaning the title-pages in the volumes themselves, printed in red and black, and '250 Folio Titles to Stick up'[20] which, printed in black only, were the posters to advertise it.

The first printer's manual to address jobbing as well

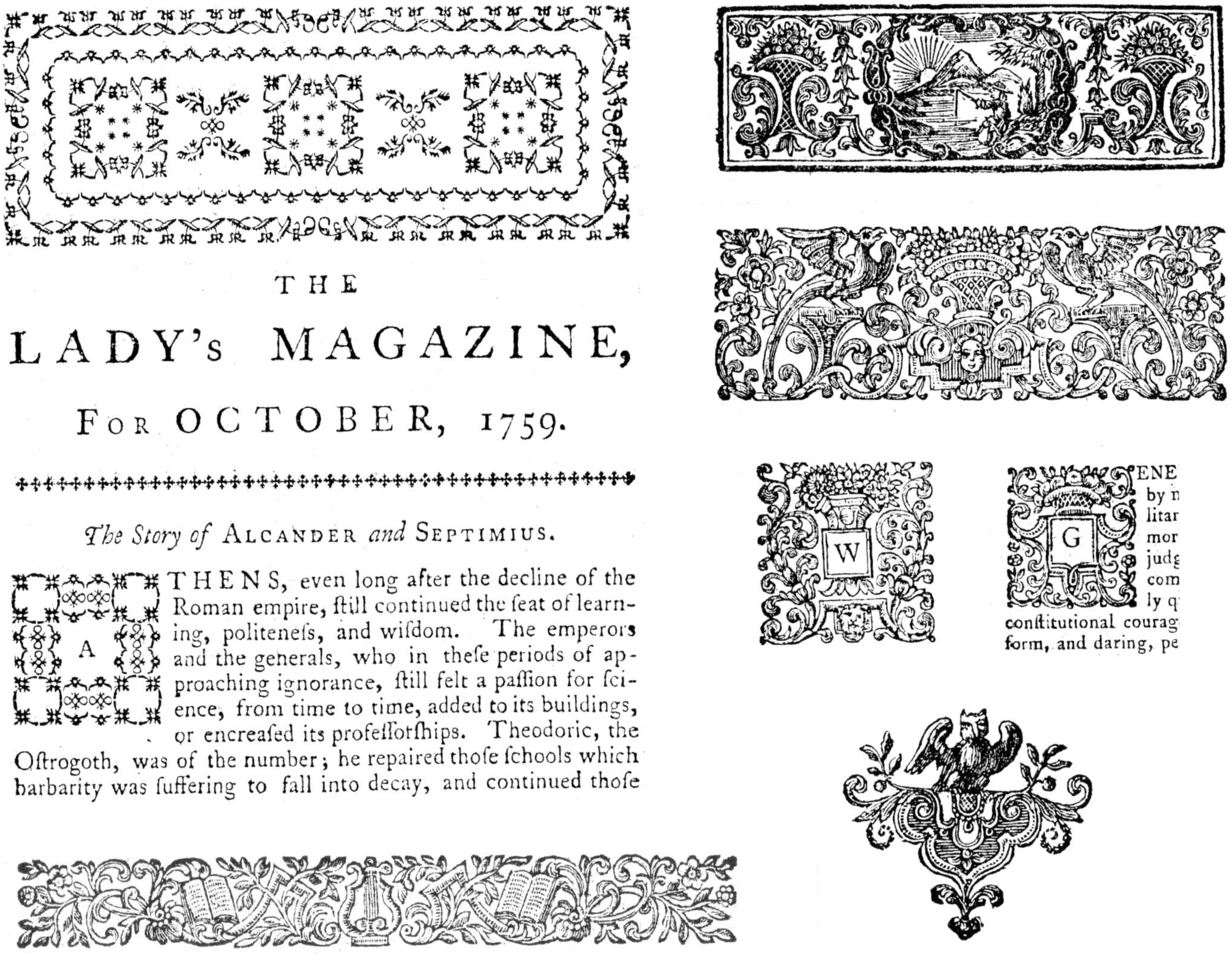
THE

LADY's MAGAZINE,

For OCTOBER, 1759.

The Story of ALCANDER *and* SEPTIMIUS.

A THENS, even long after the decline of the Roman empire, ſtill continued the ſeat of learning, politeneſs, and wiſdom. The emperors and the generals, who in theſe periods of approaching ignorance, ſtill felt a paſſion for ſcience, from time to time, added to its buildings, or encreaſed its profeſſorſhips. Theodoric, the Oſtrogoth, was of the number; he repaired thoſe ſchools which barbarity was ſuffering to fall into decay, and continued thoſe

27. *(Above left)* Detail of magazine opening page, 1759, set in Caslon type and with a decorative panel and factotum composed in printers' flowers. *(Right and below left)* Early-eighteenth-century printer's ornaments and factotums. (100%)

as bookwork was published in France in 1723: Martin Dominique Fertel's *La Science pratique de l'imprimerie.* What is particularly interesting about Fertel's manual is that he not only provided rules for guidance but demonstrated them in practice by skilfully resetting title-pages, posting bills and other large format jobs as facsimiles in small type (23).

Moxon advised that where a line was set in capitals, thin spaces should be inserted between the letters, but he cautioned against putting in too much letter-spacing. In the eighteenth century, however, noticeably wide spacing was often employed, this simple expedient momentarily slowing the speed of reading and imparting a feeling of dignity and elegance to the setting (10, 29). Taken to excess however, merely to stretch the lengths of a series of lines, the results could be visually confusing (24).

It is clear that the composition of much eighteenth-century ephemera was planned rather than set ad hoc, but it is unlikely that the compositor would first lay out his work on paper as the typographer of two centuries later would do. Rather, he would determine the relative importance of the various words in his copy and the types in which to present them by common sense and experience. A proof would be taken to check spelling, adjustments made perhaps to the inter-linear spacing, and the job put to press. Conceivably, a line might be reset in a different type if this was felt necessary, but it is unlikely this would occur often. Set by an experienced compositor the result would be a display in which the meaning of the whole was brought out as much through the sizes of type and the choices between capitals, lower case and italic as by the syntax. The reader viewing a play- or auction bill would read it not from top to bottom as he or she would a page in a book, but comprehend it according to the relative strengths of its display, the major lines being taken in at a glance and then, if the subject were found of interest, the subsidiary matter attended to more closely.

Little Chart Races.

On Wedneſday, the 2d of November, 1791,

Will be run for

A SADDLE and BRIDLE,

Of Two Guineas Value,

Free for any Horſe, Mare, or Gelding, that never ſtarted for any ſum whatever, to run the beſt three of two-mile heats: to enter at the SWAN, by twelve o'clock; to pay 2s. 6d. entrance or double at the poſt; to ſtart at THREE o'clock; no leſs than three to ſtart, to carry catch weight.

Alſo, on the ſame day will be run for,

A Whip, value Half-a-Guinea,

By HACKS, to run according to the above Articles.
To pay One Shilling entrance.

An ORDINARY at the SWAN, by ONE o'clock.

☞ Thomas Weſt will not run any thing for either of the Prizes.

28. Race bill, 1791, by John Blake of Maidstone. Space has been used effectively in the upper area of the bill, grouping the lines into separate blocks of information, but lower down the matter is crowded. The wood engraving is noticeably crude and should be compared with those of Thomas Bewick on page 21. In addition to printing, Blake was also publisher of the *Maidstone Journal* and operated a circulating library. He was elected mayor of the town in 1806. (83%) *Maidstone Museum & Bentlif Art Gallery.*

For the BENEFIT of

Mr. PILLOW.

AT THE

BULL-INN, MAIDSTONE,

On FRIDAY, the 18th of *April*, 1777.

WILL BE

A CONCERT,

OF

Vocal and Inſtrumental MUSIC:

CONSISTING OF

The following PIECES,

FIRST ACT.

Overture in the Occaſional Oritorio.

Song, Mr. PILLOW; HANDEL'S *Come ever ſmiling Liberty.*

Firſt Sinfonia, SCHWINDL.

Overture in ACIS and GALATEA, with the CHORUS *O! the Pleaſure of the Plains.*

SECOND ACT.

Overture, VANHALL.

Song, Mr. PILLOW; HANDEL'S *Happy Pair.*

ORGAN CONCERTO.

Second Overture, ABEL, and CHORUS, *Galatea dry thy Tears.*

To begin at Half paſt SIX o'Clock.

And to conclude with A BALL.

TICKETS 2s. 6d. each,

To be had of Mr. PILLOW, at Mr. PASSABLE'S, and at the BULL.

MAIDSTONE: PRINTED BY J. BLAKE.

29. Concert bill, 1777, by John Blake. Here the spacing has been well considered throughout, Blake skilfully employing different sizes of type set either in letter-spaced capitals or in lower-case to order the different levels of information. The sophistication of the design reflects the nature of the entertainment and suggests a more discerning customer willing to pay for quality work. (83%) *Maidstone Museum & Bentlif Art Gallery.*

2

The iron press

The year 1800 saw the introduction of the iron printing press. Invented by Charles, third earl of Stanhope, the innovation in Stanhope's press (32) was its system of horizontal levers. These magnified the pull of the pressman's arm, imparting greater force to the thrust of the screw. The platen could thus be made bigger, enabling large formes to be printed at a single pull. The press gained great popularity and two are known to have been exported to America, where some may also have been manufactured.

In Philadelphia in 1813 George Clymer introduced his Columbian iron press (30, 31), on which the levers acted vertically, transferring the pressman's pull to a beam bearing on a piston to push the platen down. The press was lavishly decorated: dolphins on the beam and counterbalance bar, rods of Hermes either side of the frame and a rattlesnake wreathed about the maker's plate. The most distinctive feature, however, was the Columbian's bald-eagle counterweight, which rose and fell clangorously with every impression.

But it is unlikely that Clymer sold more than thirty presses in America, and those mostly to New York newspapers.[1] Not easily discouraged, in 1817 Clymer sailed for England where his press was well received, and though it was but three years since Britain and America had been at war the eagle counterbalance was accepted with little comment. A laurel wreath replaced the rattlesnake, but more likely owing to the snake's wooden pattern being lost in transit than any concern for post-war sensibilities.

The Columbian's chief rival in Britain was Richard Cope's Albion press of 1820 (32) which utilised a powerful toggle action – two short levers set at an angle – to force down the platen, but few Albions appear to have been exported to America.[2] What was to prove the American iron hand press par excellence was Samuel Rust's Washington, the toggle action of which he patented in 1821. The virtue of the Washington was that its frame (the heaviest component on any iron press) could be dismantled into smaller parts for transportation – a major advantage in the years of westward expansion (39).

Typefaces too were to become radically different after 1800. In Europe in the eighteenth century an urge to rationalise type design led to the development of 'modern-face' types, with the first English version being cut by Robert Thorne in 1800. The letter-forms of Caslon and other earlier type founders were subtle in the contrasts of their thicks and thins but the chief characteristics of the moderns were abrupt contrast and reduction of the *serifs* – the minor strokes at the ends of letters – to hairlines. The novelty of the modern face encouraged founders to take contrast further and further, and eventually to such a degree that a classifiably *different* style of letter was created – the bulky 'fat face' (34B), the first of which was cut by Thorne *c.*1809.

This departure from centuries of tradition stimulated further innovation, 1815 bringing the first shaded or three-dimensional types (34E), followed in 1817 by the slab-serif Egyptians (in America known as antiques) – their name echoing the current interest in all things Egyptian (34F). But these new faces were far from universally welcomed, the London printer William Savage complaining of the Egyptian in 1822: 'The founders … have gone to a barbarous extreme … the rage is now which of them can produce a type in the shape of a letter, with the thickest

30. Advertising token of Sheffield printer John Blurton depicting a Columbian press, *c.*1850. The frisket is shown in the up position, with cut-outs appropriate to the printing of eight pages of a book. (59%)

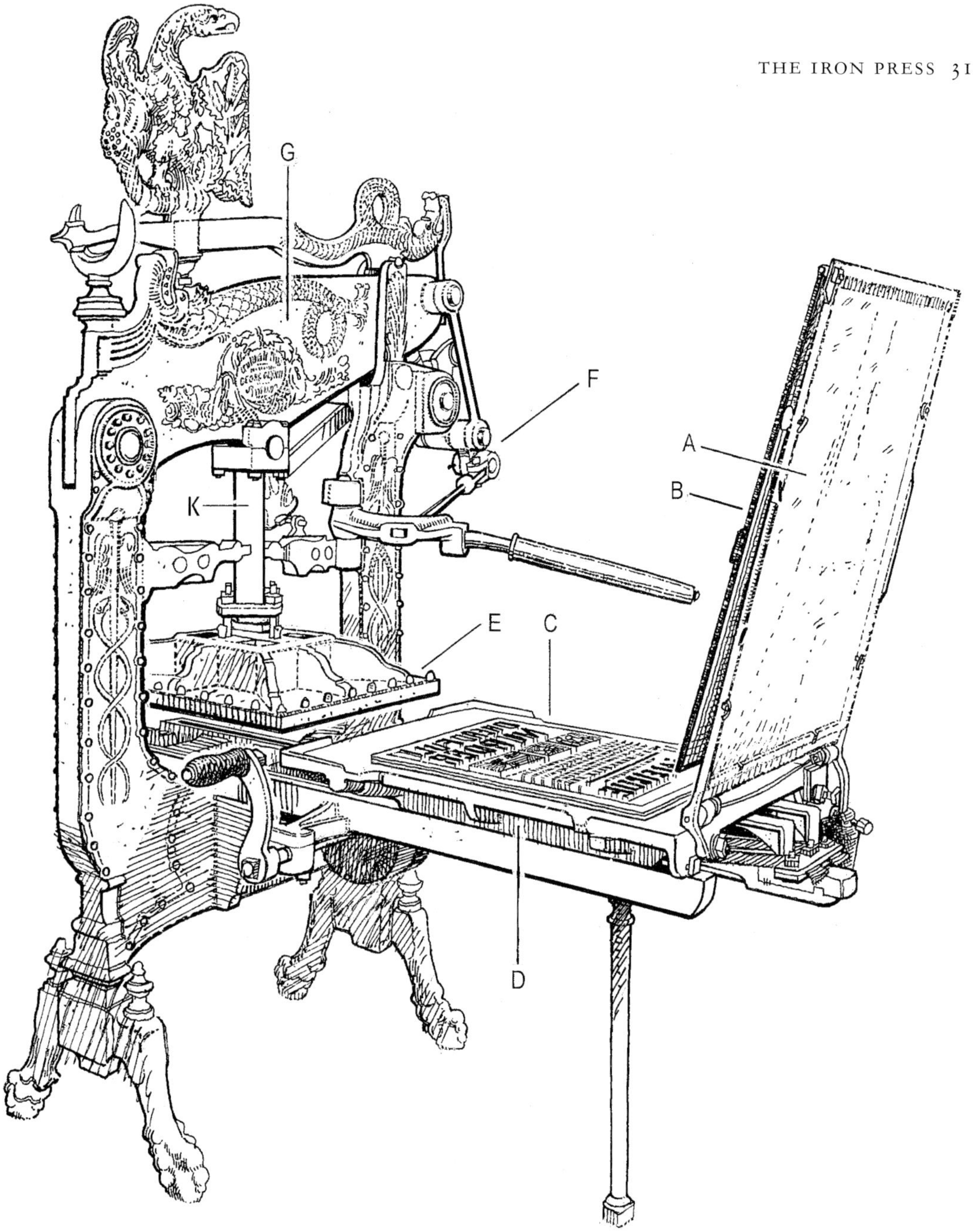

31. George Clymer's Columbian press, invented 1813. The sheet to be printed was placed on the front of the parchment-covered *tympan* (A), where it was held in position by steel *points* fixed to the tympan frame which pricked through the margins of the paper. Further support was afforded by the paper-covered *frisket* (B) which was hinged to swing down over the tympan, parts of the frisket paper being cut out so as not to cover the portions of the sheet to be printed. In printing, the type forme (C) was inked, the tympan-frisket assembly swung down over it, and the carriage (D) run under platen (E). Pulling on the bar then brought the platen down, making the impression, the force being magnified via levers (F) and beam (G). When the pressman relaxed his pull the eagle counterweight raised the platen, the carriage then being run back and the sheet removed ready for the next impression.

lines, and with the least white in the interior parts.' Savage's criticism arose from the use of these types on title-pages and other displayed elements in bookwork, but the founders responded that this was contrary to their intention, such types being designed 'solely for printing hand bills and posting bills, for the purpose of giving a bold effect to particular words intended to strike the attention of the reader and the passenger in the streets'.[3]

For those brought up in the classical tradition of the eighteenth century these bold new types were difficult to accept, James Ronaldson, co-founder of the first viable type-foundry in the United States, reflecting in 1816 that 'in some cases it became necessary for Binny & Ronaldson to imitate the Europeans, and, in some cases, contrary to

32. Stanhope *(top)* and Albion hand presses as stock cuts on printers' billheads. Both firms offered printing by copper plate as well as letterpress, and in Thomson's case by lithography also. Austen's heading effectively presents some of the fancy jobbing types at his disposal. (68%)

their own judgment'.[4] Writing nine years later, the London printer T. C. Hansard was particularly scathing over the Italian letter, introduced in 1821: 'a type in which the natural shape is reversed, by turning all the ceriphs and fine strokes into fats, and fats into leans' (34D).[5] But the quickening pace of commerce had need of these new display letters and the founders' innovations continued unabashed.

From the Egyptians/antiques there developed a host of related forms: Clarendons (35A), which first appeared in display sizes in the 1840s and were soon to be much used in text sizes as a means of emphasis; Grecians (35B), introduced in the 1840s; and the distinctly American antique Tuscans (35C), cut first as wood letter by Wells & Webb of New York in 1849. Also playing their part from the 1830s onwards were the new letters without serifs, usually known in America as gothics and in England as grotesques (34G), and a host of increasingly decorative types variously ornamented (34H). The introduction of new styles of type was continuous, and thus in promoting his stock to potential customers the printer might now describe it as 'new and *fashionable*' (author's italics).[6]

The spirit of the times was well expressed by the Boston printer and type founder Sam Dickinson (44) in 1846: 'Look at the public journals, and see the efforts there made by every class of businessmen to have their trade or calling favorably noticed, either by the editorial puff, or the flaring advertisement. Look at the corners of our streets, and there you will find almost every trade and business advertised in such bold and staring characters, that literally "he who *runs* may read".'[7] It was the iron printing-press that made possible these radical changes in the appearance of ephemera, both large and small, for the increased inking area created by an extensive setting of fat face or Egyptian demanded a printing pressure of which only an iron press was capable.

Much of this assertive new typography was printed from wood type. It was common practice for a handy printer to cut a word or a few necessary letters out of wood when a job called for them, but with his invention of the lateral router in 1827 Darius Wells of New York found the means of cutting complete founts – i.e. sets of characters – and at a lesser cost than their equivalent in metal. Foreseeing also that some printers might have ideas of their own regarding letter design, Wells advertised that they had 'only to draw one letter, and forward it on' to have a complete fount made in perfect agreement with the specimen sent.[8] Initially Wells's types were cut in sizes up to 28-line (4⅔ in./119 mm), but after the pantograph was added to the router in 1834 wood letter would eventually be cut in a range of sizes well beyond what was practical in metal, eventually up to 120-line (20 in./508 mm). Even bigger wood type was made, but cut or routed by hand. Wood letter also further extended the range of decorative styles at the jobbing printer's command, the material and its technology enabling letters to be embellished in ways impractical for the manufacturer of metal type.

Specialist poster houses with considerable capital invested in wood type were operating in New York by the early 1840s. Wells reflected in 1841 that when he had started his business in 1827 no posting bills above medium size (18 × 23 in./457 × 584 mm) had been printed, and those exhibiting but a limited typographic display; but now, in 1841, posters had increased both in scale and the power of their typographic display (43).[9] The size of the printed sheet was limited but separately-printed sheets could be

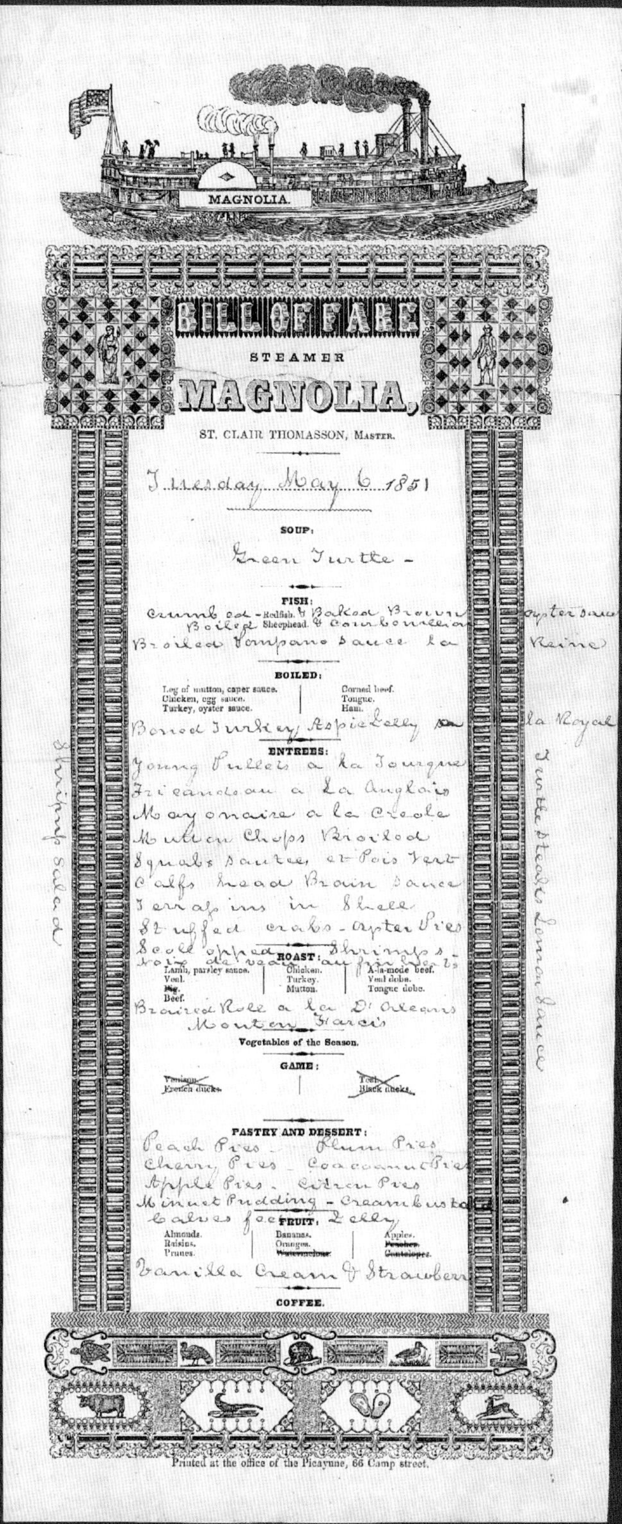

33. Decorative printing in letterpress and lithography. *(Left)* Steamboat bill of fare, 1851, printed letterpress in the jobbing office of the New Orleans *Picayune*. The design is enriched with a fine stock cut, though the fact that this is a mortised block with the vessel's name inset in type indicates that it is a generic image rather than a portrait of the Magnolia herself. The elaborate decoration has been built up piece by piece from no fewer than 563 separate units, including at the head images of Liberty and Washington cast on type bodies, and at the foot type motifs of turtle, turkey, oysters and other comestibles. 'Bill of Fare' is set in a type imported from Britain's Wilson foundry. *(Right)* Corset-box label, late 1880s, printed by lithography in cream, brown and black. The lithographic process afforded greater freedom in design than was possible for the letterpress printer, and by this date had forsaken the conventions of copper- and steel engraving that largely characterised lithographed ephemera until after the mid-century. (46%)

A WELL ACCUSTOMED INN,

B SOAPS,

C *Metamora*

D BRISTOL

E HANDEL

F JEFFERSON

G FREEMAN

H PUBLIC

34. Early-nineteenth-century typefaces. (A) Modern, *c.*1800 – marked contrast between thick strokes and thin; (B) fat face – contrast taken to extremes; (C) fat-face italic; (D) Italian – reversed contrast; (E) shaded; (F) antique/Egyptian – slab serifs; (G) grotesque/gothic – letters without serifs; (H) ornamented. Various foundries in both Britain and America produced versions of all these styles. (100%)

A NEW MUSIC BULLETIN

B MOUNTAINEERS

C FRESCH

35. British and American variants of the antique/Egyptian face. (A) Clarendon – bracketed serifs, the horizontals and verticals meeting with a curve; (B) Grecian – angled curves; (C) Antique Tuscan – concave forms. (100%)

---

pasted up together (40), two- and four-sheet posters becoming common.[10] The record before the second half of the century was almost certainly the 36-sheet poster mentioned by the soi-disant King of the Bill-Stickers in conversation with Charles Dickens in 1851.[11] Comprising four overlapping nine-sheet rows, its overall size would have approximated an immense 172 × 117 in. (4.37 × 2.97 m.)

The same period also brought advances in the technology of metal type. Medium- and small-size decorative types of some delicacy had been cast by hand for decades in Europe, but in America few workmen had the necessary skills. This changed with George Bruce's invention of the powered 'type caster', which enabled type to be cast with finer decorative detail. First used at the Boston Type & Stereotype Foundry *c.*1840, the type caster was introduced into Britain in 1849.

Means had also been found of modifying the pronounced horizontality so characteristic of letterpress printing. One method was to bend two *leads* – the lead strips normally used for interlinear spacing – into concentric curves and set the type between them. When placed in a chase with the rest of the typesetting, the unavoidable gaps were filled with whatever spacing material could be fitted in, then plaster of Paris was poured into the forme to make all secure (48). More sophisticated were *hollow quadrats*, which were virtually miniature chases rectangular on the outside and circular or oval inside (49).

Printers' flowers were now démodé in fine bookwork but in jobbing printing their use continued, with the addition now of bold motifs complementing the current styles of typeface (36). There were also the new 'mathematical combinations' imported from Jules Derriey of Paris, though of these the printer William Savage cautioned that 'unless the workman possess judgement with some taste, it is doubtful whether he will be able to produce a border, or any other subject, that will be gratifying to the eye'.[12] More extensive in their range than existing flowers, it was their very variety that made these new ornaments challenging to use (38).

The problems of design now facing the conscientious young printer, however, embraced more than flowers. With type now available in a variety of fancy styles and founders willing to sell it in small lots, the printer was tempted to buy as many different faces as he could afford. But the drawback was that he would be able to set only a limited number of words in a particular face before some letters ran out, and thus it was often necessary for succeeding display lines to be set in different types, with consequent effect on the unity of the whole. How best to use this wealth of new typographic material was the problem. Some help arrived in 1841, when Thomas Houghton published his *Printer's Practical Every-Day Book*. Houghton devoted his second chapter to job work, and this being

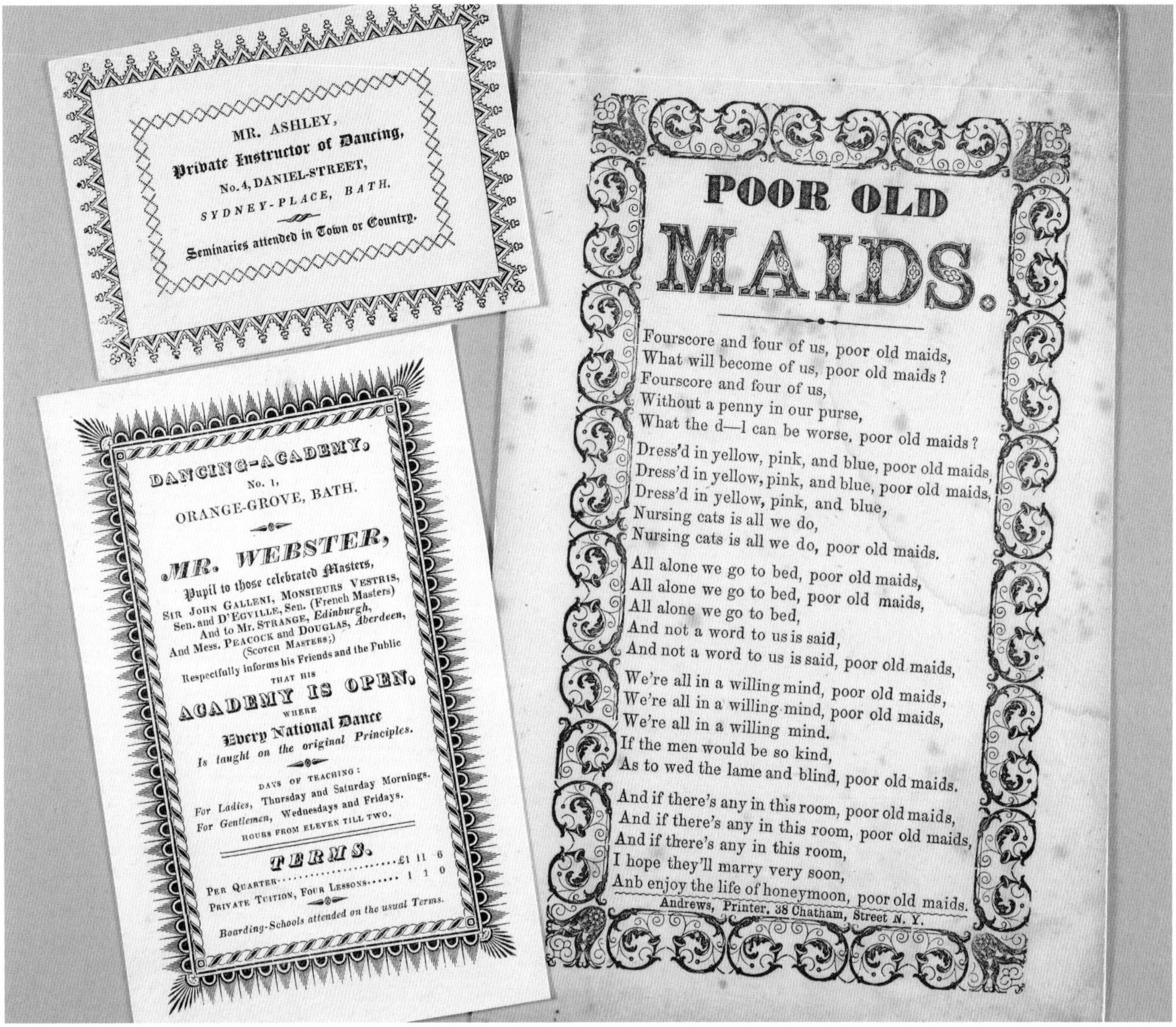

36. Printers' flowers. *(Left)* on Bath, England, dancing masters' cards *c.*1830s, new designs complementing the novel typefaces of the period. On Mr Webster's card the black-and-white contrasts of the decoration echo the contrasts seen in the 'open-face' treatment of the italic fat-face, while on Mr Ashley's, the gothic border unit harmonises with the black letter. *(Right)* Ballad sheet by Andrews of New York, *c.*1850, bordered with motifs from the foundry of Charles Derriey of Paris. The decorated type used here is from the Wilson foundry of London, Edinburgh and Dublin. (61%)

the first English-language printer's manual to deal with the subject, circulating in Britain, North and South America and the British colonies, Houghton's guidance is worth examining in some detail.

Houghton tells the young job compositor that it is only by observation that he will learn how different sizes and styles of type work in combination. By this means he will develop 'taste in display'– a grasp of the aesthetic qualities of type arrangement. But aesthetics were only part of the business: 'propriety' in display had also be cultivated, that is, the setting had not only to please the eye but also convey what it was meant to convey – 'the object for which the job is printed'. It is the ability to do this, Houghton observes, 'united with taste, that makes a good jobbing hand'.

In arranging a leaflet or circular the compositor should set it in 'the lightest form', no size of type above pica being used, with a pleasing arrangement achieved by suitably varying the lengths of the lines by letter-spacing and careful choice among the typefaces available. (Different types could vary significantly in 'set' or relative width; thus the compositor could make the same words run longer or shorter by choosing the appropriate type.)

On a human note, Houghton knew how the young compositor might suffer by having his work altered by

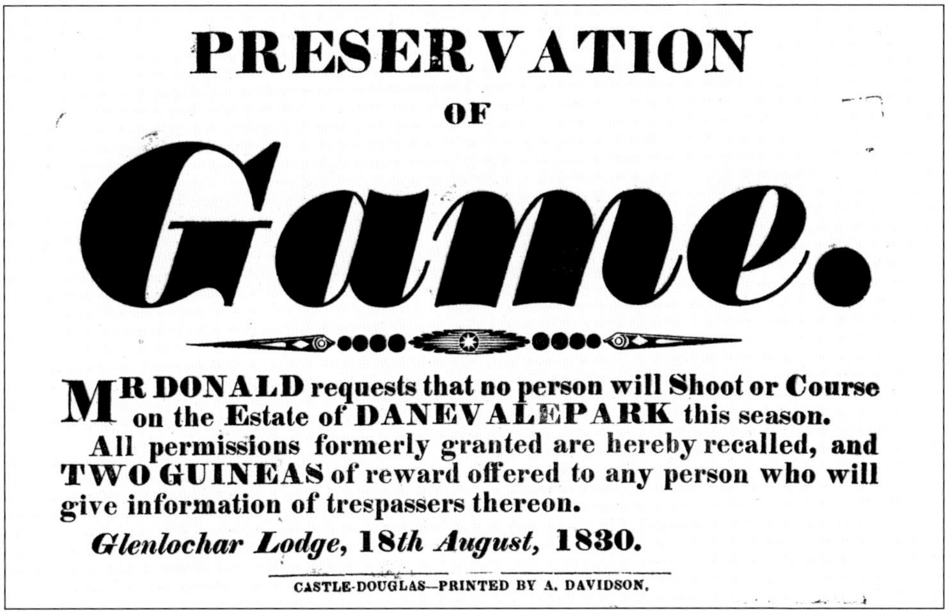

PRESERVATION
OF
Game.

MR DONALD requests that no person will Shoot or Course on the Estate of DANEVALEPARK this season.
All permissions formerly granted are hereby recalled, and TWO GUINEAS of reward offered to any person who will give information of trespassers thereon.
Glenlochar Lodge, 18th August, 1830.

CASTLE-DOUGLAS—PRINTED BY A. DAVIDSON.

37. Game notice, A. Davidson, Castle Douglas, Scotland, 1830. The printer gains the attention of those to whom the notice is solely directed – sportsmen and poachers – by focusing on just the one key word, and thereby produces an effective piece of graphic communication. The fat-face italic has great vigour, the G being a particularly strong design. (69%)

a meddling superior, through whom 'propriety is often sacrificed, and the taste and judgment of even the best practical workmen are thwarted'. But the compositor was not to be discouraged, for when the meddler had gone 'the workman, with taste, may so modify the alterations as to be but little detriment in appearance'.

In setting handbills and posters, however, clear communication was the sole aim and here aesthetics played no part. Houghton instructs that the key words be set in the boldest types 'that the substance may be read at a glance', and then, like Fertel in France a century and more earlier, he presents the reader with a miniature version of a poster and analyses it in some detail (42). Such work was to be set 'expeditiously' with no second thoughts over choice of type, for 'altering one line often requires an alteration of another, or two, which after all may make the bill no better than at first'.[13]

For ephemerists today, those bold Victorian handbills and posters have a real visual appeal, but it would be a mistake to credit too much of this to typographic subtlety on the part of the printer. Changes in visual texture from Egyptian to fat face within a phrase, or a contrasting of bold grotesque with condensed roman, have piquancy, but such juxtapositions are more likely to be due to the limited amount of any one size or style of type that the printer had to hand than to aesthetic choice. Houghton himself described handbills and posters as 'a rougher description of work, in which neatness yields to propriety and taste to effect' – it was more important that the typography catch the eye, and that 'the substance may be read at a glance', than that it be aesthetically pleasing. With the types themselves it is different, for many of those early-nineteenth-century display faces are minor masterpieces of design (37) and even the maligned Italian face has a graphic vigour we can respond to today (34D).[14]

LINES WRITTEN ON VIEWING THE
Wisbech Cemetery.

HAIL! sweet sequester'd silent spot,
Where human cares and toils forgot,
The body rests in peace.
'Twould almost cause a wish to die,
To have our dust and ashes lie
In such a place as this.

The vessel floats upon the tide,
And commerce travels by thy side,
But still ye heed it not:
No storms alarm—no tempests fright,
To thee alike both noon and night,
For all is now forgot.

Sleep on blest shades till that great morn
Of judgment and of justice dawn,
Rest—rest till *this* in peace:
Wait for the great appointed hour,
And trust his kind and gracious power,
To give thee sweet release.

Ye surely here can rest where bowers,
And shrubs, and evergreens, and flowers,
Invite, and shade, and bloom:
Where death seems plunder'd of his sting,
And art and nature join to fling
A fragrance round the "*tomb.*"

Saffron Walden. *J. S.*

38. Ornamented verses, *c.*1850, celebrating the newly opened cemetery at Wisbech, England. The greater part of the decoration – here appropriately arranged to represent a headstone – is composed with the 'mathematical combinations' designed by Jules Derriey of Paris. Both image and sentiments reflect the Victorian acknowledgement of death as part of life. (67%)

39. New Mexico, 1866: editor James A. Currant of the *Kingston Shaft* leans on the Washington hand press on which both his newspaper and the larger jobbing work were printed. The smaller ephemera of this frontier town were printed on the jobbing platen to the right. It was not unusual for a pioneer newspaper to be printed al fresco when a suitable building was not immediately available. *Photograph by J. C. Burge, courtesy Palace of the Governors (MNM/DCA). Neg. No: 14691.*

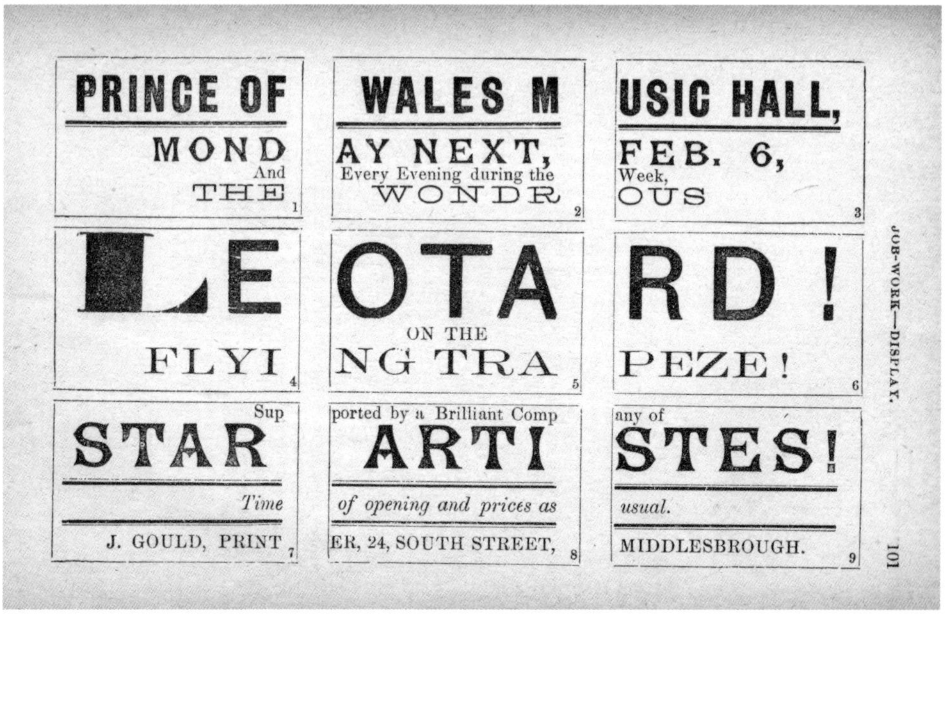

PRINCE OF MOND And THE 1	WALES M AY NEXT, Every Evening during the WONDR 2	USIC HALL, FEB. 6, Week, OUS 3
LE FLYI 4	OTA ON THE NG TRA 5	RD ! PEZE ! 6
Sup STAR Time J. GOULD, PRINT 7	ported by a Brilliant Comp ARTI of opening and prices as ER, 24, SOUTH STREET, 8	any of STES! usual. MIDDLESBROUGH. 9

JOB-WORK—DISPLAY.

101

40. Scaled-down setting demonstrating the make-up of a nine-sheet poster, from Joseph Gould's *The Letter-Press Printer*, fifth edition, 1893. (86%)

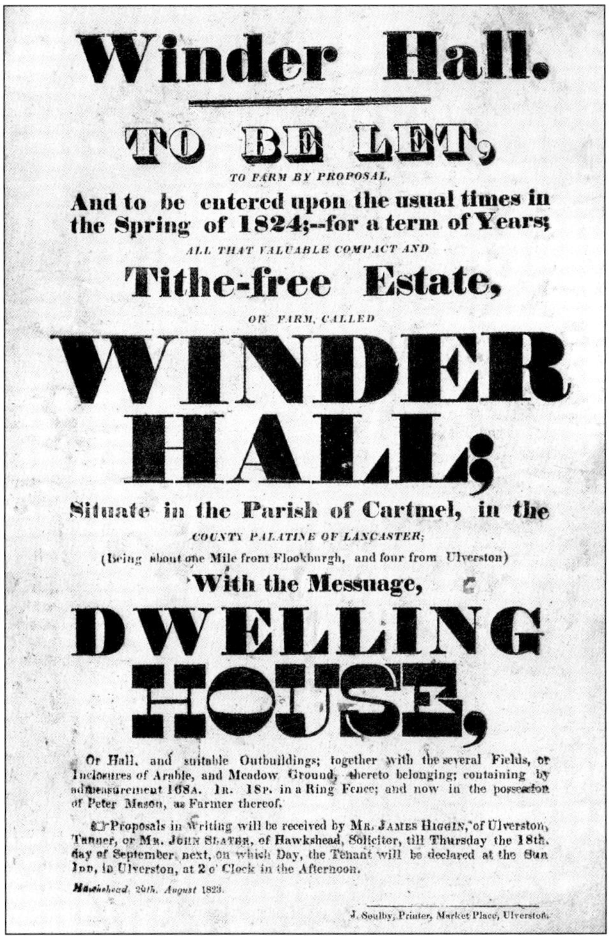

Winder Hall.

TO BE LET,

TO FARM BY PROPOSAL,

And to be entered upon the usual times in the Spring of 1824;--for a term of Years;

ALL THAT VALUABLE COMPACT AND

Tithe-free Estate,

OR FARM, CALLED

WINDER HALL;

Situate in the Parish of Cartmel, in the

COUNTY PALATINE OF LANCASTER;

(Being about one Mile from Flookburgh, and four from Ulverston)

With the Messuage,

DWELLING HOUSE,

Or Hall, and suitable Outbuildings; together with the several Fields, or Inclosures of Arable, and Meadow Ground, thereto belonging; containing by admeasurement 168A. 1R. 18P. in a Ring Fence; and now in the possession of Peter Mason, as Farmer thereof.

☞Proposals in Writing will be received by MR. JAMES HIGGIN, of Ulverston, Tanner, or MR. JOHN SLATER, of Hawkshead, Solicitor, till Thursday the 18th. day of September next, on which Day, the Tenant will be declared at the Sun Inn, in Ulverston, at 2 o' Clock in the Afternoon.

Hawkshead, 29th. August 1823.

J. Soulby, Printer, Market Place, Ulverston.

41. Property notice, John Soulby, Ulverston, England, 1824. By emphasising the phrases of greatest importance, Soulby has given structure to the information contained in some one hundred and seventy words, but the repetition of 'Winder Hall' seems purposeless and may be due to his having uncritically followed copy thus headed. (30%). *Museum of English Rural Life, University of Reading.*

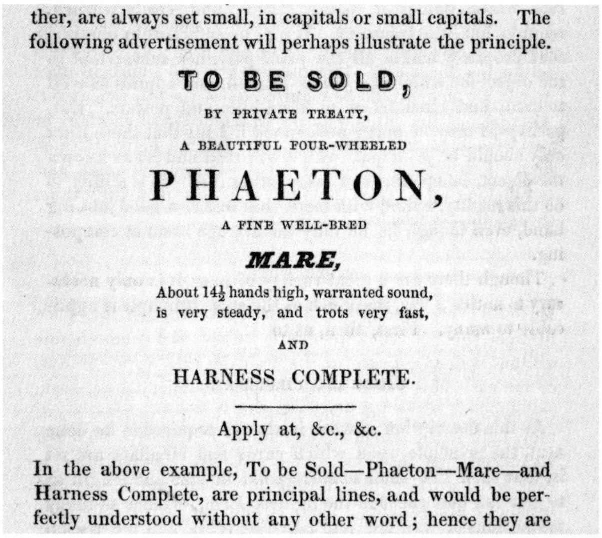

ther, are always set small, in capitals or small capitals. The following advertisement will perhaps illustrate the principle.

TO BE SOLD,

BY PRIVATE TREATY,

A BEAUTIFUL FOUR-WHEELED

PHAETON,

A FINE WELL-BRED

MARE,

About 14½ hands high, warranted sound, is very steady, and trots very fast,

AND

HARNESS COMPLETE.

Apply at, &c., &c.

In the above example, To be Sold—Phaeton—Mare—and Harness Complete, are principal lines, and would be perfectly understood without any other word; hence they are

42. Scaled-down setting demonstrating the composition of a posting bill, from Thomas Houghton's *Printer's Practical Every-day Book*, 1841. Houghton's observations here are: 'To be Sold—Phaeton—Mare—and Harness Complete, are principal lines, and would be perfectly understood without any other word; hence they are the largest, that they may be readily seen. By Private Treaty—About fourteen and a half hands high, &c.—are secondary-lines, or what would only be looked for if there were any desire to purchase. A beautiful four-wheeled—a fine well-bred—and—are catch-lines, because they are merely used to connect the lines and make them read smoothly. Apply, &c.—partakes more of the nature of a note, and hence the reason for being always cut off with a rule, and run on in smaller type. It is of little consequence what may be the size of the bill, whether for the hand or the wall, the *principle* which points out the leading and secondary lines is still the same.' *St Bride Library* (100%)

43. New York poster hoarding, *c.*1860, a medley of visually competing advertising. Such large-scale printing was a consequence of the development of wood type, which could be made in larger sizes than could be cast in metal. Stereo card by E. & H. T. Anthony, 'The brigade de "Shoe black", City Hall Park'. (xx%). *National Museum of Photography, Film and Television.*

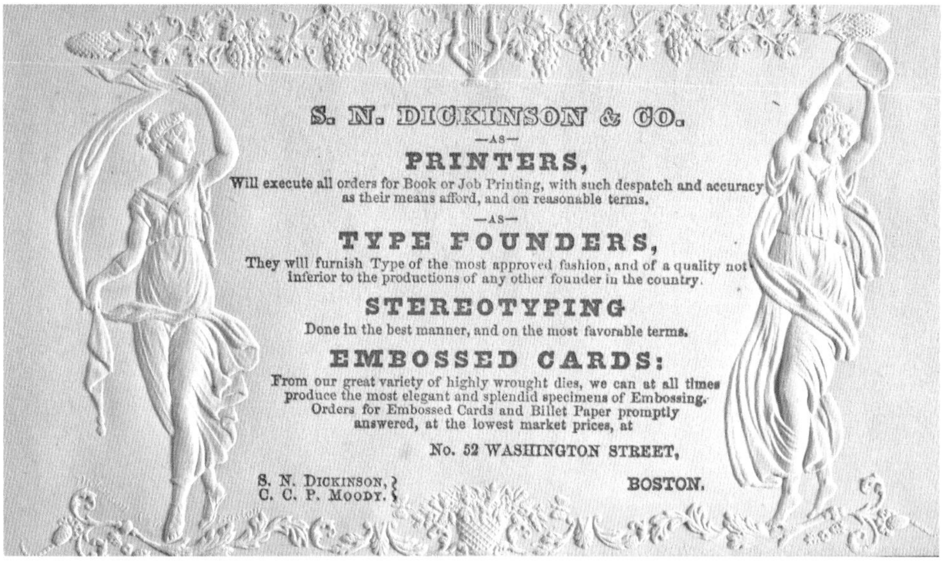

44. Embossing. *(Left)* Trade card of Samuel Dickinson & Co., Boston, MA, *c.*1840s; and *(below)* English Christmas card dated 1863. In both cases the modelling is of the highest quality. (97%, 93%)

45. *(Below)* Billheads as catalogues, 1860s and 1890s. The white-lettered cut on Henry Folsom's heading, engraved by W. Eaves of New York, lists a variety of the medicines that 'Doctor' Folsom could supply. On the Waterman design the images are almost certainly stock cuts, this heading also illustrating how ordinary rule-of-thumb jobbing continued at a time when a significant number of other printers in Britain and America were influenced by the Artistic-printing movement. (65%)

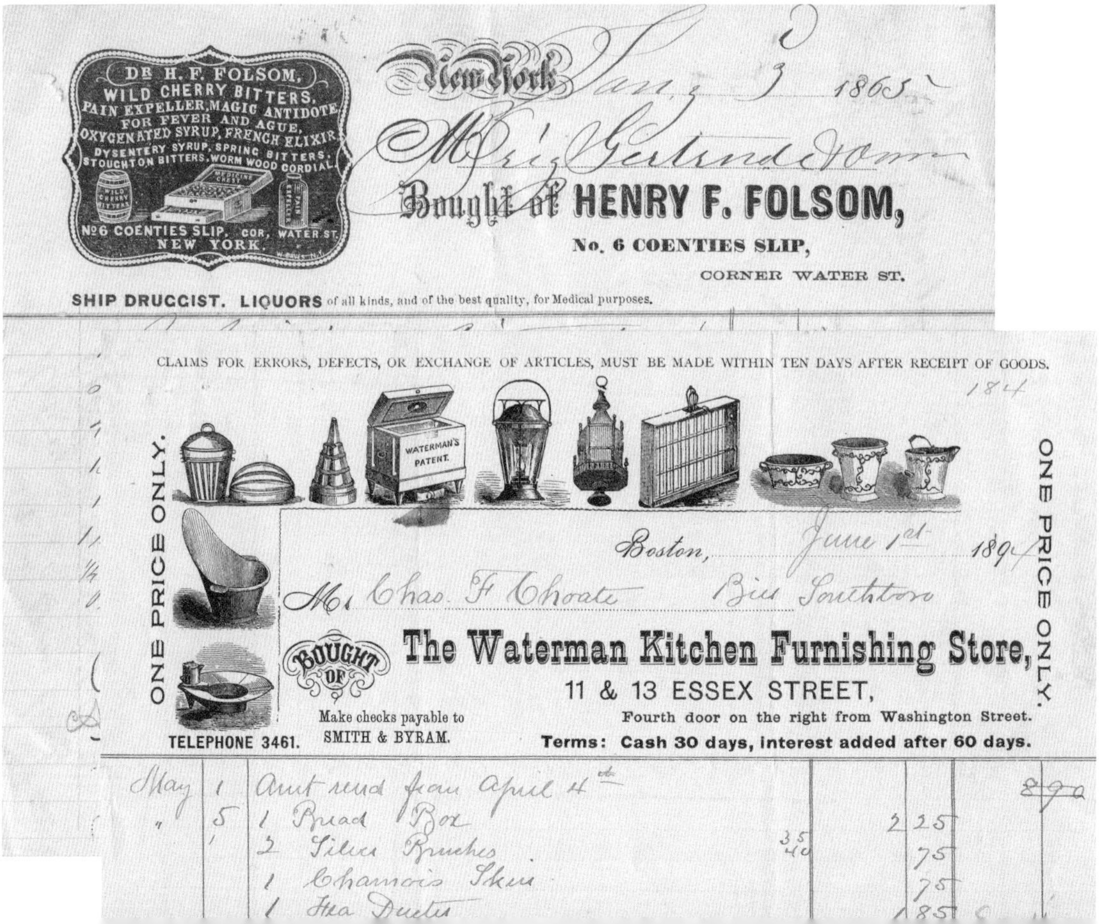

46. Uncut strip of small handbills, *c.*1890. By setting the job 'four-up' the printer would have reduced press time to a quarter, in the same way that a lithographer would employ multiple transferring. This job is additionally interesting for the changes in style from one setting to the next, a consequence of the limited amount of any one display type that the nineteenth-century printer would stock. (90%)

Occasionally a customer would give no more than spoken instructions, leaving it to the printer to determine the actual wording of leaflet, handbill or poster, and even with written copy the printer could modify the wording to make best use of what types were available or to achieve a more telling display. But there is evidence also that printers could at times follow copy uncritically (41), even to the point of absurdity. Examples are: 'Ten shillings reward. Any person found trespassing on these lands or damaging these fences on conviction will receive the above reward. Dogs poisoned', and 'Notice is hereby given, that the Marquis of Camden (on account of the backwardness of the harvest) will not shoot himself, nor any of his tenants, till the 14th of September'. The first was posted 'a few years back', at Osterley Park near Brentford, seat of the Earl of Jersey, and the second on the Marquis of Camden's Bayham Abbey estate in Kent in 1821. Both are quoted in Henry Sampson's *History of Advertising from Earliest Times* (1875) and are regarded as authentic.[15]

Where wood-engravings were needed, they would be commissioned either by the printer or by his customer. Letters sent to Thomas Bewick when in business on his own account give a flavour of the everyday exchanges between engraver and customer, and indicate the sorts of briefing an engraver would receive. In 1803 the North Shields printer Thomas Appleby ordered a cut 'with a handsome border' to be cut in brass for the Quaker tea importers Braithwaite & Atkinson. 'The Size and Inscription, they left for me & you to determine on as well as [style of] execution', he wrote, penning a rough sketch of a cut the firm had previously used (53A), and adding 'the Ornaments must be left intirely to you, only they want it very neat, and different to what they have had. – At the same Time, it may be necessary to remind you that they are *Friends*, and may not wish it too much ornamented.'[16]

Appleby also planned to publish an edition of William Falconer's *The Shipwreck* and enquired if Bewick had a cut of a storm at sea to illustrate the poem, but if not 'can you sketch me out something with your *Pencil* to send me by the Bearer for approbation?' Appleby specified that once the design was approved the cut be 'done in the best stile',[17] indicating that Bewick's charges varied according to the work he or his apprentices put into them.

An order of 1806 from James Jacobs of Skipton is headed with an impression taken from a crude old racing cut (53B), Jacobs writing:

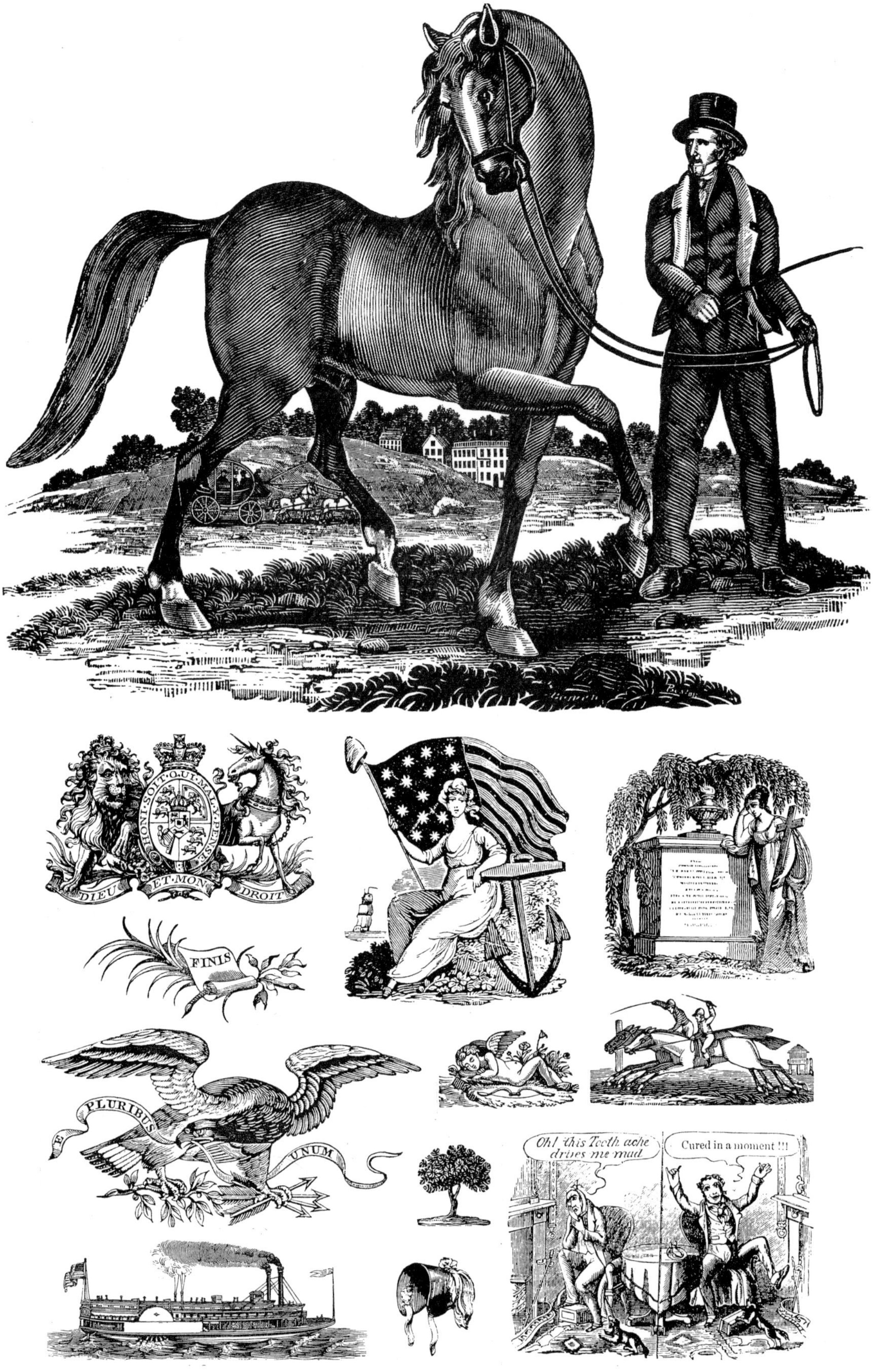

47. English and American stock cuts, the top example by Abel Bowen and the rest by uncredited engravers. Replicated from wood-engraved originals by the stereotype and electrotype processes, such cuts provided the letterpress printer with an inexpensive means of adding an extensive range of pictures to his work. (77%)

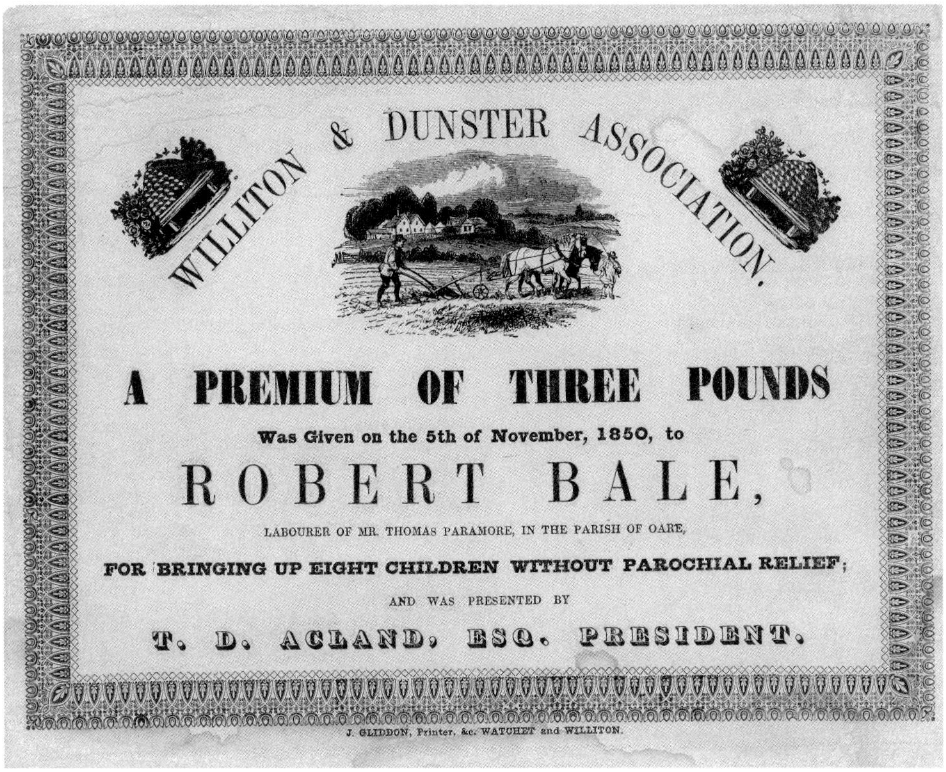

48. Agricultural association certificate by J. Gliddon of Somerset, 1850. To mitigate the horizontal/vertical stress characteristic of letterpress, Gliddon has somewhat crudely curved the upper line by manipulating the spacing material and then (very likely) securing the whole setting with plaster of Paris. Apart from its charm as an item of ephemera, the certificate gives an insight into social attitudes and a way of English rural life long gone. The beehive stock cuts are emblematic of industriousness. (69%)

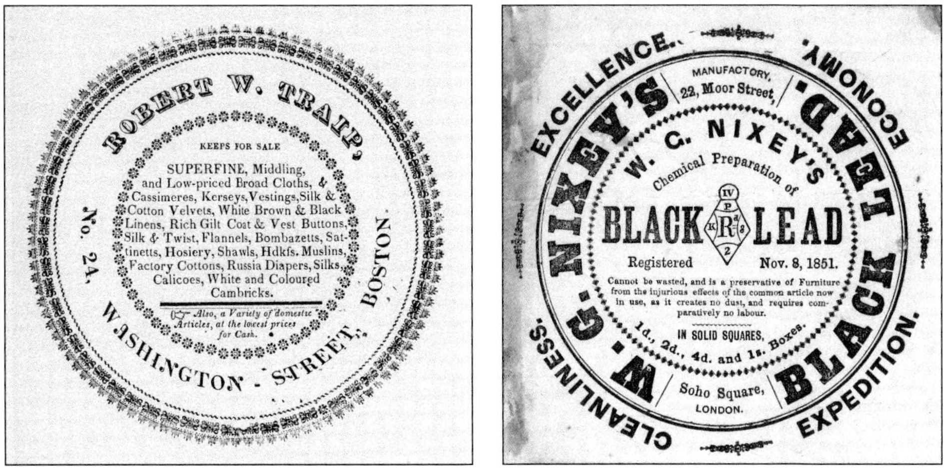

49. Setting in a circle. American trade card *c.*1826; and British black-lead label, 1851. Here the horizontal stress of letterpress is circumvented by setting the type within a nested series of lead strips curved into circles. 'Hollow quadrats', curved on the inside and square on the outside, were used for the outer formers. (American card) Jenny, *Early American Trade Cards from the Collection of Bella C. Landauer.* (51%)

Sir, The above is a sketch of the Engraving I should wish you to execute for me – tho' not done in the best stile, I trust your abilities will surpass it. The Length of the Engraving I should wish to be just four Inches, with any alteration you think proper; – you will also Engrave another, about Two Inches and a half in Length, for the Top of a Large Card. Shall thank you to execute the above order as soon as possible, as the Lists will not be printed till you send the above; you will also send your charges along with them, and your money will be return'd.[18]

An order received in 1808 from A. Soulby of Penrith reads: 'Mr Bewick will please cut me a Race Cut according to the Plan on the other side which I think you may make out by the Notes – it must be no larger than what I have marked. …' Soulby's plan was schematic in the extreme (53C), his instructions concluding 'The above Sketch is not taken from the Spot it is only to show the Plan upon which it is to be, so Mr Bewick may do it as he thinks it will look best; but do it as nearly to the above Plan as possible.' A man to leave no detail unspecified, Soulby could not resist adding 'Cut it upon Box wood' and 'Make it as beautiful as possible whatever the expense be'.[19]

Bewick became as revered in America as he was in Britain. In 1834, six years after Bewick's death, Boston's first wood-engraver, Abel Bowen (47), with six others including John Hall, one of Anderson's pupils, advertised in *Stimpson's Directory Advertiser* their readiness 'to take orders for engraving in wood, steel and copperplate

50. Razor strop and label, *c.*1820–30, the display line set in a vigorous open-face black letter. (76%)

51. American Nursery literature, 1830s, illustrated with wood engravings and enhanced with printers' flowers. The smaller engraving has been executed by the engraver removing the wood from between the lines of an ink drawing made on the block; on the larger, the engraver has mostly employed the earlier technique of translating the qualities of a tonal original into the textures natural to the graver. (57%)

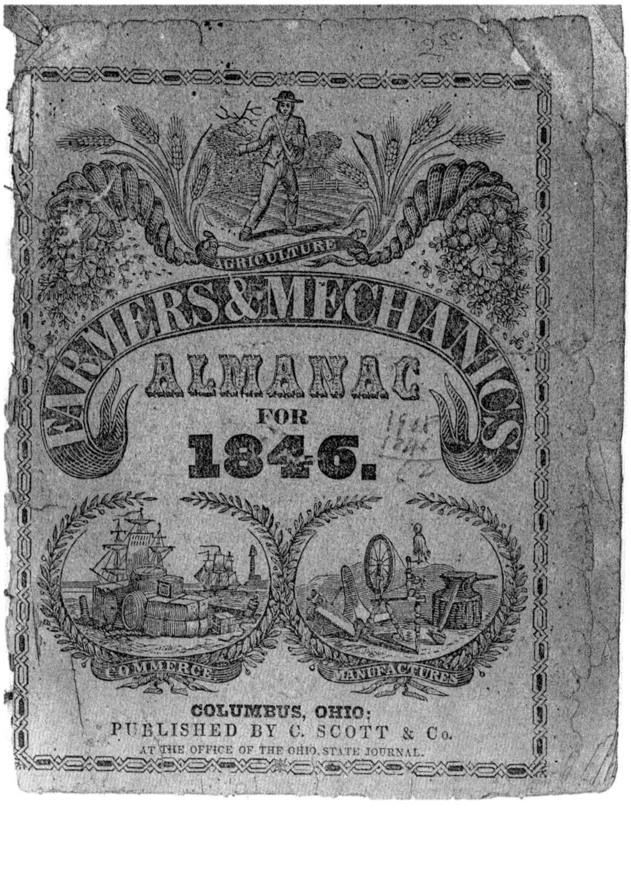

and for letterpress and copperplate [printing] in all its branches'. In honour of the 'restorer of the art of engraving on wood' the seven styled themselves the Boston Bewick Company.[20]

By this date it was usual to print not from the wood block itself but from a metal replica. In Britain from the late eighteenth century, type-founders had produced ornaments, decorative letters and other printers' imagery by 'taking a dab' – impressing the face of a wood-engraved original into metal sufficiently molten to take an impression, then casting from the mould thus formed. In the 1820s this was largely superseded by *stereotyping*, in which plaster of Paris was used for the mould, plaster in turn being superseded by papier mâché in the 1830s. By this means not only could wood-engravings be replicated but

52. Almanac cover, Columbus, Ohio, 1846. Imagery and title line are engraved in wood, with the block mortised to allow the insetting of 'Almanac', date, and the publisher's imprint in type. The date would change each year but the block would continue in perpetuity. In commissioning an engraving of this elaboration the publishers sought to achieve a freedom of design in their letterpress printing akin to that of engraving and lithography. (52%)

A

C

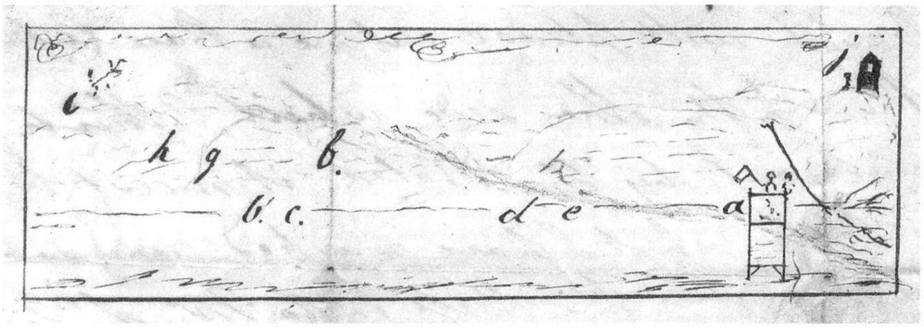

53. Rough designs sent by customers ordering cuts from Thomas Bewick. (A) 1803, representing a cut previously used, now to be superseded; (B) 1806, crude old woodcut, as a guide to size and arrangement only; (C) 1808, schematic accompanied by instructions: a. 'The Stoop with the Stewards in'; b,c,d,e. 'Four Race horses galloping with jockies on'; f. 'Huntsman on Horseback (make them coming in right)'; g. 'A *Wall* with Huntsman jumping over it on Horseback'; h. 'The Hounds'; i. 'The Stag turning up the hill'; j. Penrith Beacon, with a Man standing beside it viewing. Make the Hunters, Beacon, &c. appear as a little distant from the Racers, and small.' (79%) *Iain Bain MSS.*

so could entire type formes, thus freeing the type for other work. The finest replicas of wood-engravings, however, were those made by *electrotyping*, invented in 1839, in which a copper skin was deposited electrochemically on the inside of a wax mould and then backed up with type metal (141). Thus originated printer's *stock cuts*, general-purpose imagery of horses, trains, steam boats, bald eagles, royal arms and other motifs, with which the printer could enliven a customer's job at no extra charge (47). In America stock cuts from originals engraved by the Boston Bewick Company were syndicated to many foundries.

There is a marked difference in appearance between the images cut by Bewick, Anderson, Bowen and their contemporaries and those of the engravers of a later period. This is due to changes in the ways in which wood-engravings were designed and executed. Those earlier engravers would work from a watercolour or pencil drawing, *translating* its tones into the textures natural to the cut of the graver. There was an alternative technique, however, only occasionally used in Bewick's workshop, where the image would be drawn directly on to the block with pen and ink, the engraver then simply removing the wood from between the lines (51, 80);[21] and with the increasing demand for wood-engraving this procedure became the norm.

The greatest tour-de-force of early-nineteenth-century wood engraving, *The Assassination of L. S. Dentatus*, 1821, was executed by Bewick's former pupil William Harvey after the painting by Benjamin Haydon. The favoured process for fine-art reproductions was still copper-engraving and Harvey chose to cut *Dentatus* in close imitation of it. With dimensions of 15⅛ × 11⅛ in. (384 × 295 mm) the block was significantly large, taking Harvey three years of spare-time work to draw and cut. Problems arose when it came to printing. The press was a large Columbian. But even that, unmodified, proved insufficient to print so large a block effectively, and to increase the leverage the printer, John Johnson, had to have two inches cut off the connecting rod and an extra long bar made. Pulling the bar demanded the strength of two men working together. Johnson said that even Clymer was astonished.[22]

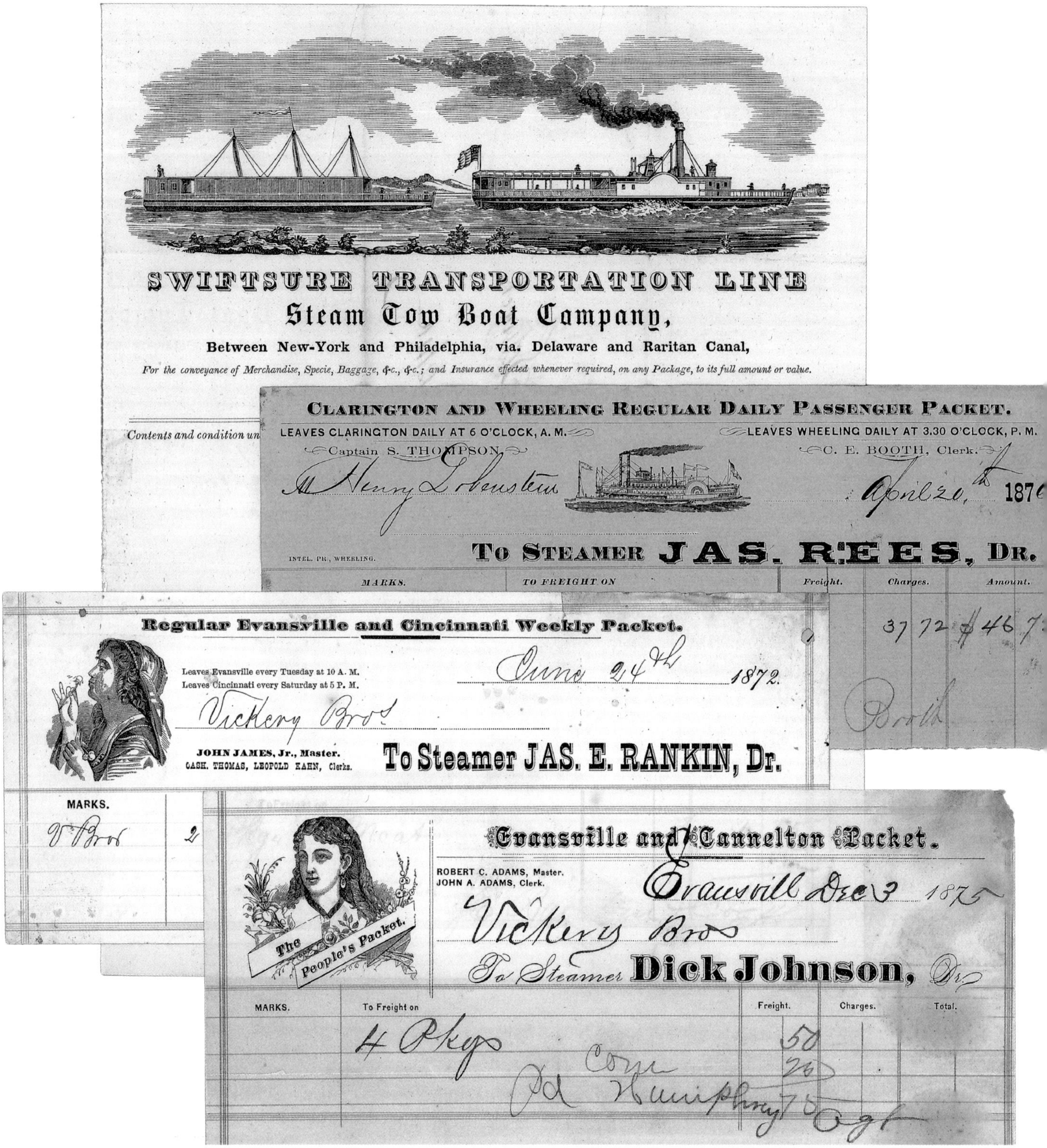

54. Imagery on American steamboat waybills, 1840s and 1870s. The wood-engraving on the Swiftsure bill is sufficiently specific in its details to suggest that it may have been specially commissioned by the line. The other images are stock cuts, that of the steamer *Dick Johnson* being a mortised cut, which has enabled 'The People's Packet' to be inset in type. This ephemera also displays an interesting variety of nineteenth-century types, that on the *James Rankin* item being a French Antique, a variant of Egyptian with the horizontals at top and bottom heavier than the verticals. The two on the *Dick Johnson* bill are 'outlined' forms, each letter surrounded by a fine line. On four of the other type faces a shadowed effect is achieved by restricting the fine line to the right and bottom edges. (70%)

55. Railroad imagery. *(From top)* Masthead of the British *Railway Times*, 1847, with locomotive, tender and carriages composed with seven separate four-line-pica (48-point) pictorial type units. *(Below)* Boston & Providence waybill, 1845, its little train comprising three paragon (20-point) units. *(Below)* North Pennsylvania waybill, 1864, with a somewhat crude stock cut. *(Bottom)* Late-nineteenth-century credit note, engraving on stone by the Union Bank Note Co. of Kansas City, Missouri: the image is drawn with skill but seen alongside the railroad cars the reduced scale of the incidental figures is slightly absurd. The display type used in the *Railway Times* heading is an 'open' face, what would otherwise be a sombre black letter being enlivened by an incised white line. (71%)

3

The rise of lithography

THE NINETEENTH CENTURY also brought iron into the world of the engraver, iron frames and steel rollers gradually replacing wood in the rolling press and the introduction of gearing making the press easier to operate. Yet it was not these that were to affect the appearance of ephemeral printing, so much as the use of steel for the printing plate.

Siderography was developed by the Philadelphian Jacob Perkins. Perkins's invention consisted of engraving on a softened steel plate, case-hardening it, then passing the plate back and forth beneath a softened-steel roller. This action copied the design in relief in the roller face, after which the roller was case-hardened and used to create duplicates of the original intaglio design, either in further plates or as multiple copies in a single plate. An advantage of the process was that portraits, emblematic figures, patterns, currency numerals and other imagery could be stored on rollers for use on future work, siderography finding its greatest application in postage stamps, banknotes, cheques and other security printing (57).

Although such specialist equipment was scarcely justified for the trade engraver, it became fashionable now to work in steel, the harder metal enabling the engraver to employ a delicacy of line that would quickly have shown wear had it been cut in copper. Steel engraving was employed in the drawing-room annuals fashionable in the 1820s and 1830s and on illustrated writing-paper (58), the latter becoming increasingly popular following the introduction of cheap postage rates in England in 1840 and in America in 1845. But steel did not supplant copper, for steel even when softened was the harder metal, making it difficult to achieve the depth of cut necessary for the swelling strokes of engraved script. Later, it also became possible to make a fine engraving in copper and protect it from wear by steel plating.

The range of engravers' lettering styles increased, the elegant round hand of the previous century now often interweaving with extravagantly decorated bold faces

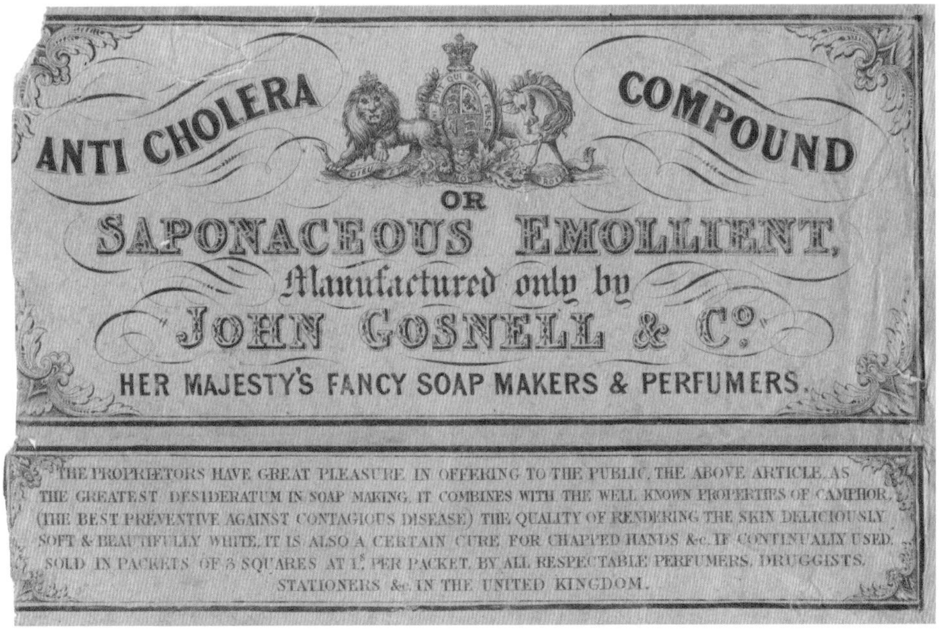

56. Copper-engraved wrapper for anti-cholera soap manufactured by John Gosnell & Co., soap makers and perfumers to Queen Victoria, *c.*1840. To those easily impressed, the manufacturer-devised 'saponaceous emollient' would hint at scientific validation, but in reality camphor was the only medicinal ingredient. (71%)

57. Front and back of railroad 'fare ticket' printed from a siderographic plate engraved by the American Bank Note Co., 1873. Background patterning to the numerals and other parts of the design have been engraved with a rose engine (also known as a geometric lathe). Used by railroad companies when making payments, such scrip gave a right to travel but otherwise had no monetary value to the recipient. (71%)

and fancy black letter (69A). In England in the 1820s and America around five years later (though there were some earlier examples), music publishers began to include illustrations on some of their covers, the imagery increasing in size until by 1850 it was often the chief feature in the design; though by this time such work was as likely to be printed by lithography (discussed below) as by engraving.

Engraving continued as the favoured medium for billheads and trade cards. With the latter, however, the new century saw a change in format, smaller pasteboard cards – ancestors of the modern business card – supplanting the leaflet-sized paper cards of the eighteenth century (possibly due to a scarcity of the linen rags needed for papermaking during the Napoleonic wars). Developments in paper technology led in the 1840s to porcelain cards, where white lead incorporated in the surface paper produced a hard sheen taking a finely detailed impression.

Both trade cards and billheads manifested a variety of imagery: sheaves of corn, sheep (an emblem particularly favoured by drapers), beehives symbolising industriousness (48, 119), Chinamen (representing the tea trade and thus by extension grocery in general (61)), native Americans and Scottish Highlanders for tobacconists. There were also female figures: Ceres with plough and cornucopia, Hope with her anchor (representing for the tradesman commercial reliability rather than hope against adversity) and general-purpose classically attired ladies included for the sense of good taste their presence imparted (60). Trade activities were also depicted: candle and needle making, women outworkers at their spinning wheels, the hosier at his stocking frame, the carpet weaver at his loom (59). There were the products of manufacture also: pumps and cisterns; bonnets, shoes and other fashionable attire; still-lives of kettles, saws and scythes; and in a period when shopping had become a pastime in its own right, often the shop front itself (59). That engravers could have resource to their pattern books when undertaking work of this kind is shown by the occurrence of similar imagery on jobs for different customers, and indeed the reworking of virtually entire designs (61, 62).

Recognising that not all who plied the engraver's trade would have drawing ability, in his *Engraver's Complete Guide* (1825) C. F. Partington described three methods of copying useful to the engraver: making the drawing paper transparent with oil (thus facilitating tracing); holding original and paper up to a window or against glass back-lit with a candle; and laying a sheet of square-gridded glass over the original and copying square by square on to a grid drawn on the paper. Partington also gave guidance as to the rendering of silk, satin, linen, smooth water, dark clouds and other textures; and the use of the ruling machine, with which fine, closely parallel lines both straight and curved could be drawn through the etching ground with a diamond point (66).[1]

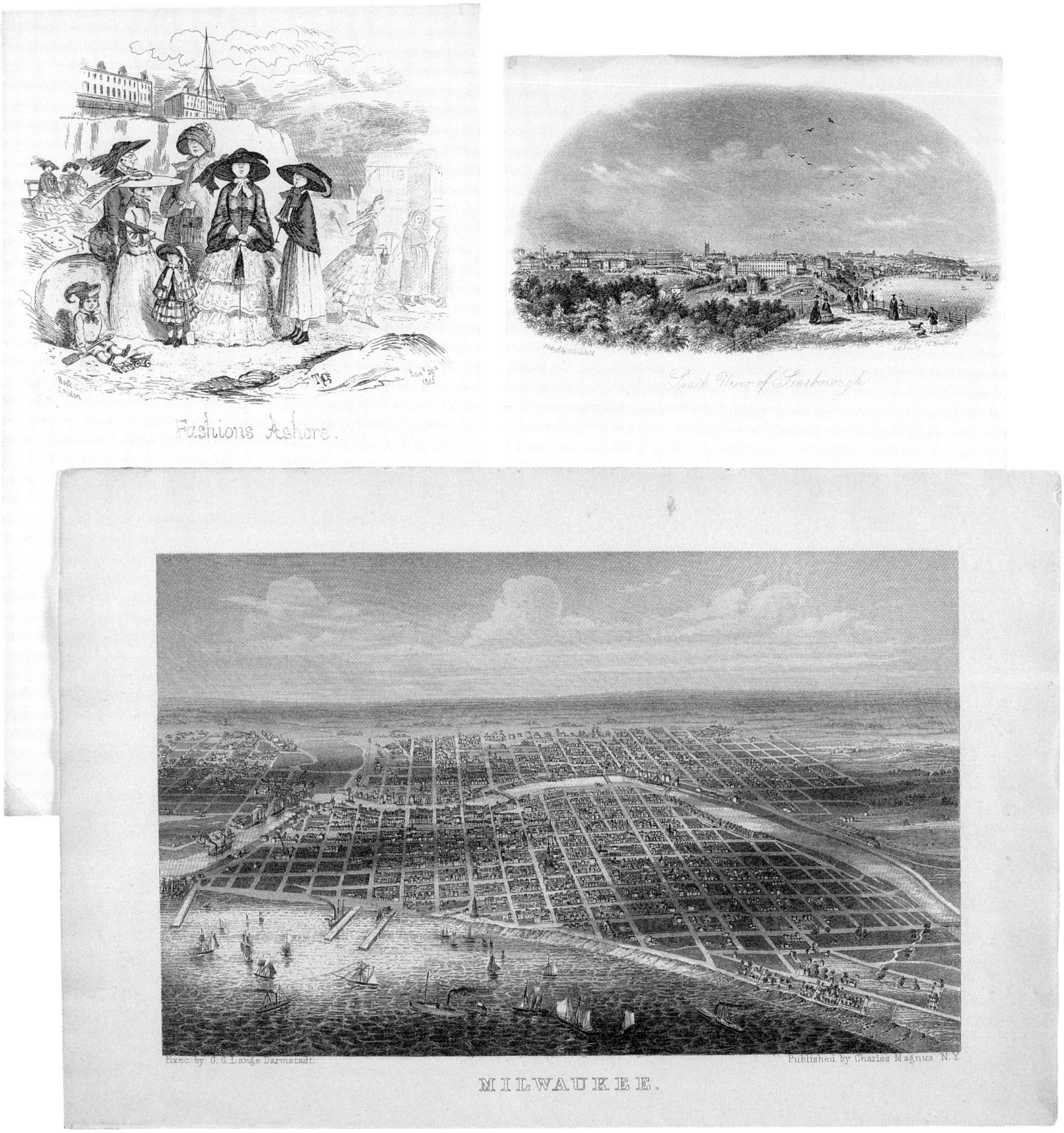

58. Illustrated writing paper, 1850s. *(Top left)* Etching by Thomas Onwyn published by Rock & Co. of London, 1855: the freedom in drawing is characteristic of the etching process. *(Right)* Panoramic view of Scarborough, 1850s, published by S. O. Bailey of Bradford: a stiffer style of etching, in this case based on a photograph by J. Goodchild. *(Below)* Steel engraving by G. G. Lange Darmstadt published by Charles Magnus of New York: based on city maps, such a bird's eye view would be largely conjectural. This form of pictorial stationery was to be largely supplanted by the picture postcard later in the century. (69%)

Occasionally an engraver might be required to alter a design, as for example when a business partnership changed and a different name had to be accommodated on the firm's billhead. The engraver would then work on the metal with hammer and punch to raise the appropriate area from the back, then tediously smooth away the old imagery with a steel burnisher preparatory to re-engraving.

Through repeated inking, cleaning-off and printing a copper plate would wear down. Fine lines were lost and the printed image became fainter. When this occurred, the plate might be refurbished by *re-entry*, the engraver deepening the worn lines of the image with his graver.

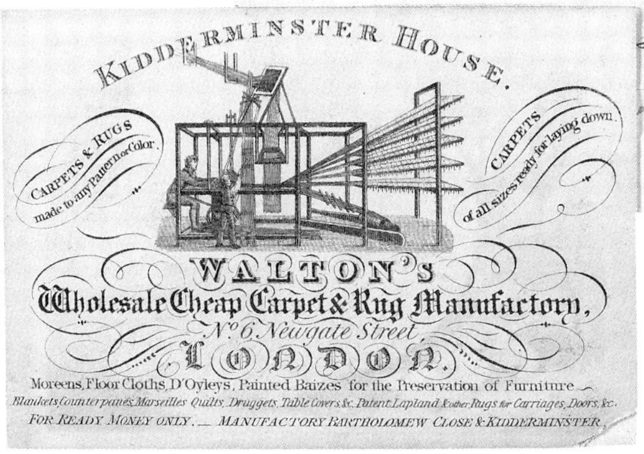

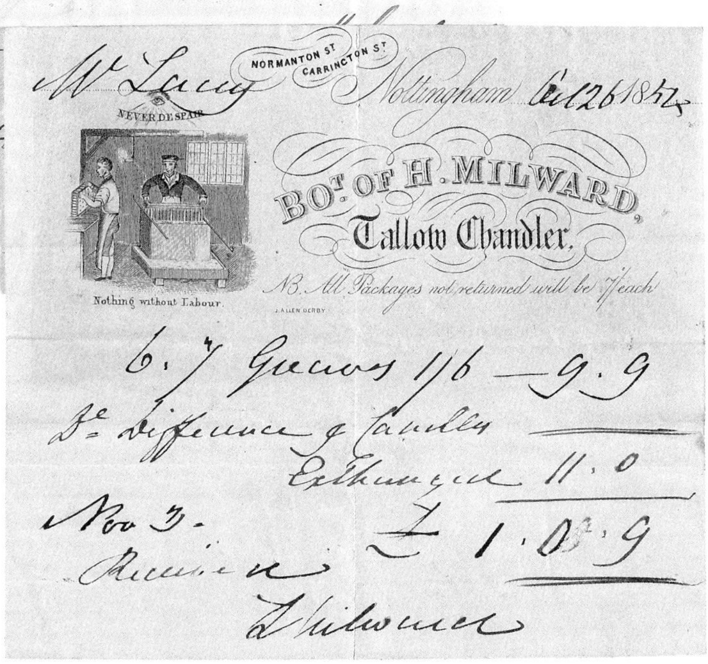

59. *(Top)* Billhead, copper engraving by Atkinson & Bayley of Manchester used in 1845, presenting a finely detailed shop front. *(Below, left)* Copper-engraved trade card *c.*1820–30 showing a carpet weaver at his loom. *(Right)* Tallow chandler dipping candles, detail from a billhead of 1854 engraved on stone by J. Allen of Derby, the two mottoes – 'Never despair' and 'Nothing without labour' echoing the self-help philosophy adopted by some among the working classes of the period. (70%)

60. Trade card, 1817–18, engraved by Francis Shallus of Philadelphia for the circulating library run by his wife Ann. Whether the girl represents Flora, the Roman goddess of flowers, or is simply a general-purpose classically attired figure is hard to determine. Jenny, *Early American Trade Cards from the Collection of Bella C. Landauer* (91%)

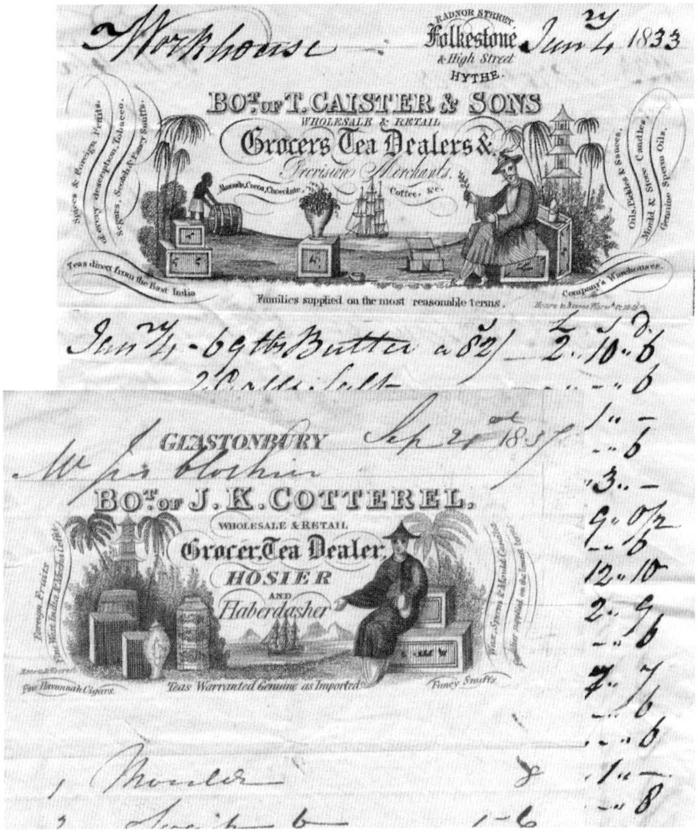

61. Copper plate for a grocer's trade card, *c.*1820–30, by Reeves & Hoare, London, and two billheads by the firm showing the same concept adapted for other customers. Drawn with an etching needle, the smallest lines of lettering are less than 1/16 in. (2mm) in height. Through his associations with the tea trade, the Chinaman became emblematic of grocery in general. (Caister heading) *Canterbury Cathedral Archives.* (62%)

Alternatively, a new plate might be ordered, the opportunity being taken perhaps to make changes to the layout. If it was necessary to repeat a vignette a skilled engraver could copy the existing image with remarkable fidelity, though with trade emblems he might simply copy directly from an existing print, with a consequent reversal of those images when printed.

Intaglio printing remained a slow process. It had been the practice since the eighteenth century to speed up production of small items such at hat-labels or watch-papers by engraving the same design several times on the one plate, each pass through the press producing several copies at one go. Whether the procedure was at that time also employed for items of larger format such as billheads is unclear, but it was certainly in use for this type of work in the nineteenth century. Evidence indicates that headings of the London tea importers Ridgway & Co. were being printed two-up in the 1840s (68) while those of the mineral-water manufacturers J. Schweppe & Co. were printed in fours – two images on each of two plates (67). In this time of growing commercial activity multiple engraving facilitated the printing of large orders, but it may also be an indication that by the 1840s trade engravers were beginning to feel the competitive pinch from the relatively new process of lithography.

Lithography, or 'printing from stone', was invented in Bavaria by Alois Senefelder (1771–1834). Initial experiments in creating a relief-printing surface by etching tablets of his local limestone met with only limited success, but through them *c.*1799 Senefelder developed true lithography, where the difference between printing and non-printing areas is determined not by relief but by chemical means. Senefelder obtained a British patent in 1801.

The design to be printed was drawn on the flat surface of the stone using ink with a high grease content. In printing, the stone was first sponged with water, which the background accepted but the grease in the design areas rejected, then rolled with ink, which the damp in the background rejected but the design accepted. Paper was then laid on and the stone passed through the press (64).

Initially lithography was largely seen in Britain as a medium for the art amateur, gentlemen hiring stones to draw on and then having their drawings 'multiplied' in the lithographer's printing shop; and the process only began to make headway after Charles Hullmandel and Rudolf Ackermann opened printing shops in London following visits to Munich, where lithography was already well established. By the early 1820s the process was finding favour with English topographical artists, many of whom had previously had their work largely reproduced in aquatint, leading to wider acceptance of lithography as a professional medium and a decline in intaglio reproduction. For jobbing printers lithography was to prove as versatile as engraving in the combining of images and words, and quicker both in preparation and printing.

The first lithograph printed in America was a drawing by the artist Bass Otis accompanying an article on the process published in the July 1819 issue of the *Analectic Magazine*, while the first successful American lithographic firms were those of Anthony Imbert, started in New York in 1825, and John and William Pendleton, who set up in Boston in the same year. The Pendletons were also suppliers of equipment, advertising that the firm 'being Agent for one of the German Quarries has always on hand, an extensive assortment of the first quality lithographic stones polished on both sides'.[2] The stones were

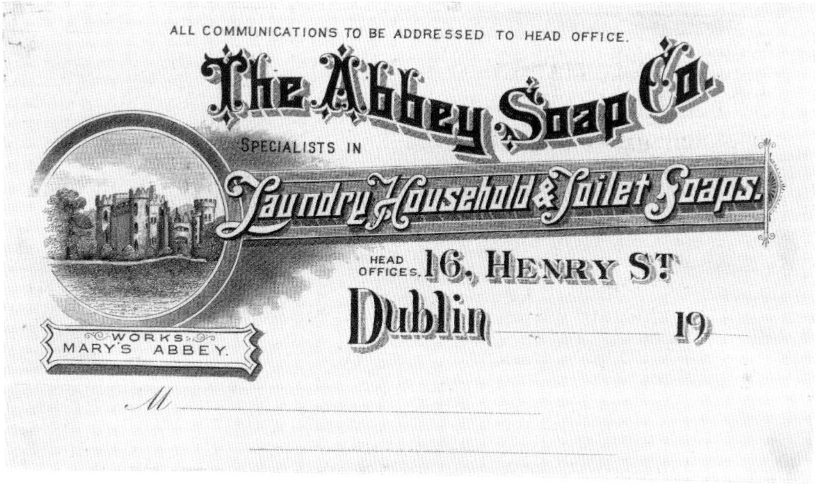

62. Proofs of engravings in either copper or steel by Waller & Co., Dublin, *c.*1900, designed for transfer to stone. The similarities in design suggest a standard style of layout and lettering adopted by the company. (63%)

imported via New York, the port's geographical location making it the natural depot for continental supplies and subsequently a leading centre for American lithographic printing. European immigration also furthered the development of American lithography, skilled printers and designers being among those fleeing the political unrest in their home countries.

What may have been the earliest lithographic press to have worked *between* Britain and America was operated by one Henry O'Neil, who crossed the Atlantic on board the *Great Eastern* when it was laying the first Atlantic cable in 1865. O'Neil edited, penned by hand, and printed the ship's one-voyage house journal the *Atlantic Telegraph* (63).[3] Bearing in mind O'Neil's situation, it is likely that he printed from zinc plates rather than lithographic stone, for suitably prepared zinc exhibited similar properties. 'Zincography' became common in England in the 1840s and is first recorded in America in 1849. Initially zinc was limited to simple line reproduction (making it ideal for O'Neil's purposes), with a shift towards more sophisticated imagery beginning in America in the 1870s. Overall, however, stone was to reign supreme for many years.[4]

A significant drawback to lithography was the weight of the stone. Even a 10 × 15 in. tablet would weigh nearly 30 lbs. The sheer bulk and weight of stone presented not only storage problems but positive dangers, as was to be tragically demonstrated in 1891 when the building partly occupied by Liebler & Maas of New York collapsed under the combined weight of machinery and stones, killing all but three of their staff.[5]

The best stone was quarried at Solnhofen near Munich, thus incurring heavy transportation costs. In Europe, experiments were made with the White Lias found near Bath, and some French quarries are known to have marketed stone on a reasonable scale. In America, home supplies were to be sought throughout the century. Bass Otis worked on stone quarried from Dirks River, Kentucky, while a ten-foot vein reported as 'very fine' was to be found in a cave in Indiana in 1892.[6] Yet for all round quality nothing ever equalled that of Senefelder's home district, and Solnhofen was to remain the chief source so long as lithographs continued to be printed from stone.

Lithography was a versatile medium, giving the artist choice of working with pen and/or brush on polished

63. Lithography on the high seas. The *Atlantic Telegraph*, house journal of the *Great Eastern*, written, drawn and printed by Henry O'Neil during the ship's cable-laying voyage from Britain to America in 1865. O'Neil's cover design shows captain, officers and VIPs – the exclusive readership among whom the magazine circulated. (62%) *British Library.*

stone, or with crayon (121) if the stone was prepared with a finely grained surface. There was also the technique of *engraving on stone* (65, 74), in which the stone was coated with a thin solution of coloured gum arabic, the artist then delicately engraving the design through the gummed surface with a fine steel or diamond point. When finished, the stone was rubbed over with ink, grease from which penetrated the stone via the engraved lines, thus creating the printing image. A small vignette or line of decorative lettering could take several days, but the quality achieved was akin to that of fine copper or steel engraving. Lithographic artists were also able to imitate etching and wood engraving (73), but these approaches were outmoded as the craft became better established.

An idea of the advantages of lithography to the jobbing printer can be gained from an advertisement of 1827. Robert Horniman ran a stationery, bookselling and letterpress-printing shop in Reading, England, and may

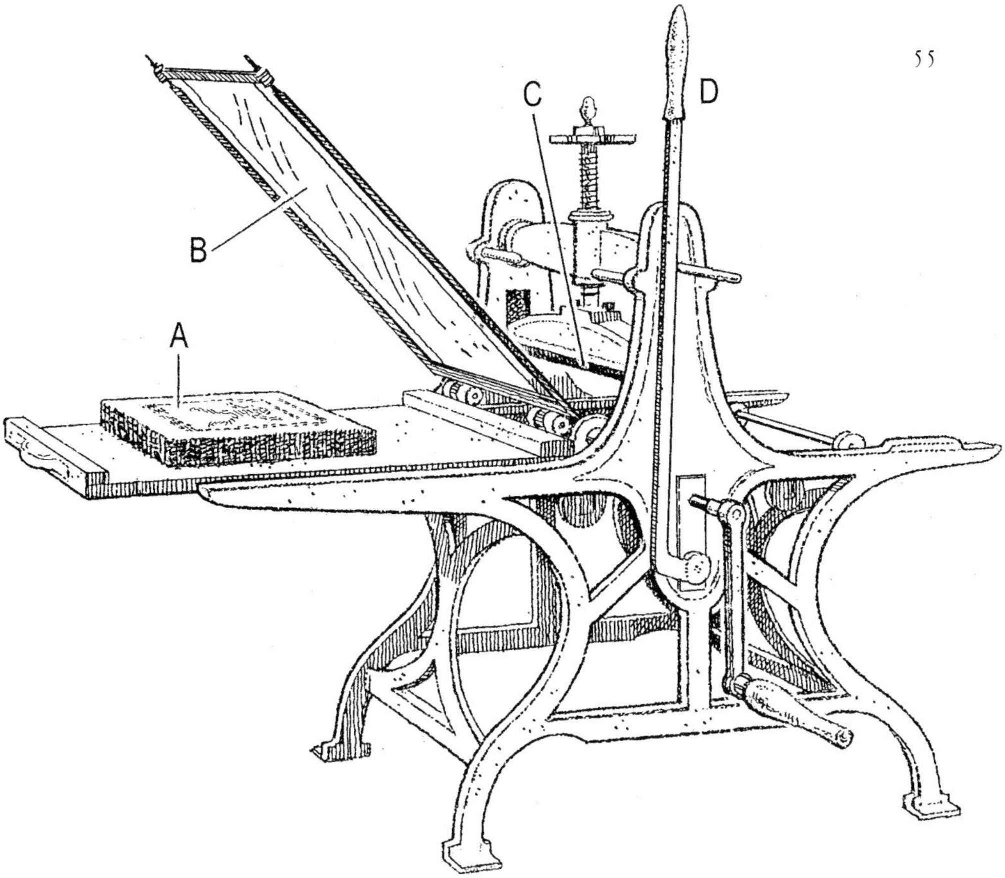

64. Lithographic hand press. The stone (A) was damped and inked, paper laid on and the *tympan* (B) lowered. The bed was then pushed forward beneath the *scraper* (C). Dropping lever (D) lifted the bed, bringing the tympan hard in contact with the scraper and the stone was then cranked through the press.

have added the process to his business only recently. 'Lithography', he declared, 'being nearly equal to Copper-plate, many avail themselves of it for Circular Letters, Maps and Plans of Estates, Chalk and Ink Drawings, ancient and modern Fac-similes, Manuscript, &c.'.[7]

Circulars and other ephemera involving the printing of scores of words had previously been the province of the letterpress printer, but this too was challenged by lithography, and with the advantage that a communication could be made to appear hand-written, giving each recipient the impression of its being a personal communication (70). Lithography equally lent itself to the printing of music (otherwise printed from copper plates or music types), as well as trade cards, billheads, illustrated writing-paper, show cards and other ephemera. The lithographic artist would also undertake the drawing of family trees, tables of statistics and other work, which demanded much ingenuity of a compositor but which an artist could draw with ease.

Horniman also operated a rolling press and took orders for both wood- and copper-engraving.[8] Like others in the provinces he may have continued to do so for many years, but in the industry as a whole lithography brought a gradual decline in engraving. Not only was it possible for the lithographer to achieve the integration of words and image so long unique to the older process, but *actual* engravings (both metal and wood) could be printed by lithography, prints being first taken on special transfer paper and thence transferred to stone. When in 1849 the Bristol, England, engravers and plate printers Harris & Mardon purchased two second-hand lithographic presses, it was because of their need to increase output and thereby attract customers with larger orders.[9] Printing could also be further speeded by multiple transferring.

Lithography began to find its way into the English provincial towns mostly after the mid-century.[10] The technology was by this time well established and it is likely that these new enterprises were started either by journeymen from the larger centres setting up on their own or by printers adding lithography to their existing businesses. Few, if any, of the latter are likely to have had the necessary

65. Twentieth-century lithographic artist engraving on stone, working with steel point and eyeglass. From Hackleman, *Commercial Engraving and Printing*.

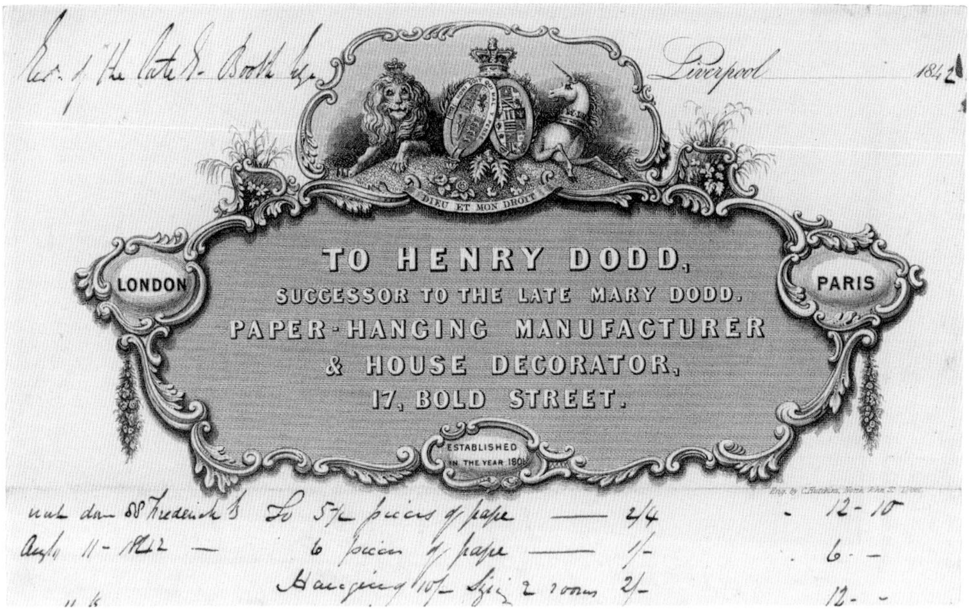

66. Letterhead engraved by C. Hutchins of Liverpool, *c.*1840. The antique/grotesque lettering shows the influence of contemporary letterpress styles and is set off against an etched tonal background achieved with a ruling machine. The design couples the royal arms of Queen Victoria with those of Albert the Prince Consort whom the queen married in 1840, though their presence on this heading would be a gesture of loyalty rather than an indication of royal patronage. (71%)

drawing or lettering skills, but here lithographic transfers provided the answer.

The London *Typographic Advertiser* was the trade paper of brothers J. & R. M. Wood's Austin Letter Foundry. In response to their country readers' demands, in February 1863 the Woods commenced a series of articles on lithography, and in the following issue announced the addition of mail-order transfers to their services, offering everything from simple circulars to elaborately lettered trade cards or bill headings. Customers had choice of scripts ranging from those 'usually adopted where customer gives no instructions' and 'facsimile "own hand" writing, gives impression that a circular is handwritten' to 'lady's hand, used by Ladies' Schools, Milliners, etc.' (70). Depending on the amount of work required, prices were from 1*s.* 6*d.* to 3*s.* 6*d.* (then equivalent to 53c–$1.24c) for octavo circulars and to 2*s.* 6*d.* to 5*s.* (89c–$1.77c) for quartos,[11] with additional charge if an ornamental heading was required. Foreseeing that readers might find these costs rather high, the Woods stated: 'We are aware that London Lithographers can get transfer writings done a little cheaper than these prices, but J. & R. M. Wood cannot undertake them for less, for the country customers, as, the transfer writers being few who work for the trade [i.e. on a freelance basis], there is frequently trouble in getting the work done, unless they are well hunted up.'

The firm also supplied transfers from custom-engraved copper plates, charges varying from 9*d.* (27c) a line for basic script or black letter for use on a trade card to 2*s.* 6*d.* (89c) a line for best-quality script and fancy lettering on the scale of a bill heading.[12] For safety in the post, all transfers were mailed in a tin case costing an extra sixpence.[13]

It is likely that many lithographic artists were recruited from the ranks of the engravers, bringing with them the older craft's established conventions of layout, lettering and illustration. So it can sometimes be difficult to determine whether an item of ephemera originated in copper or steel cut by an engraver or an engraving-on-stone executed by a lithographer. It would be some years before lithographic artists were to develop a style of design characteristically their own.

Transfers had very limited shelf life and it appears to have been rare for suppliers to provide the transfer equivalent of stock cuts. Borders and frames, trade emblems and similar imagery, however, were of such general application that having been originated for one job it was worth a firm's preserving them for use on future work. Images were therefore transferred to stones kept solely for this purpose. If subsequently a design needed modification, the redundant parts could be ground off with fine sand or carefully scraped back (depending on whether the surface was grained or smooth) then redrawn.

Surprisingly, in the latter part of the century it became possible to enlarge or reduce imagery without need for redrawing. The design was transferred on to a prepared sheet of thin rubber, which was then mechanically stretched all round to the desired scale and the enlarged image then transferred to the stone, reduction being managed by a reverse procedure. In 1889 a German version of the apparatus was said to cost around a thousand dollars, though Fred Buehring of New York could confidently advertise his own apparatus for a mere ten.[14] Eccentric though the procedure sounds, images were enlarged and reduced with remarkable fidelity, hence the extremely fine detail seen in many later-nineteenth-century vignettes (75, 150).

Working on lithographic stone had its problems. In his *The Grammar of Lithography* (1878), W. D. Richmond recommended that in cold weather the artist warm the stone by the office fire, lest his breath condense on it and prevent the ink or crayon 'taking'; and where warming was not possible the artist was to shield mouth and nostrils with an oval of cardboard held by a loop of twine gripped in the teeth.[15] Hair was another likely source of problems, the

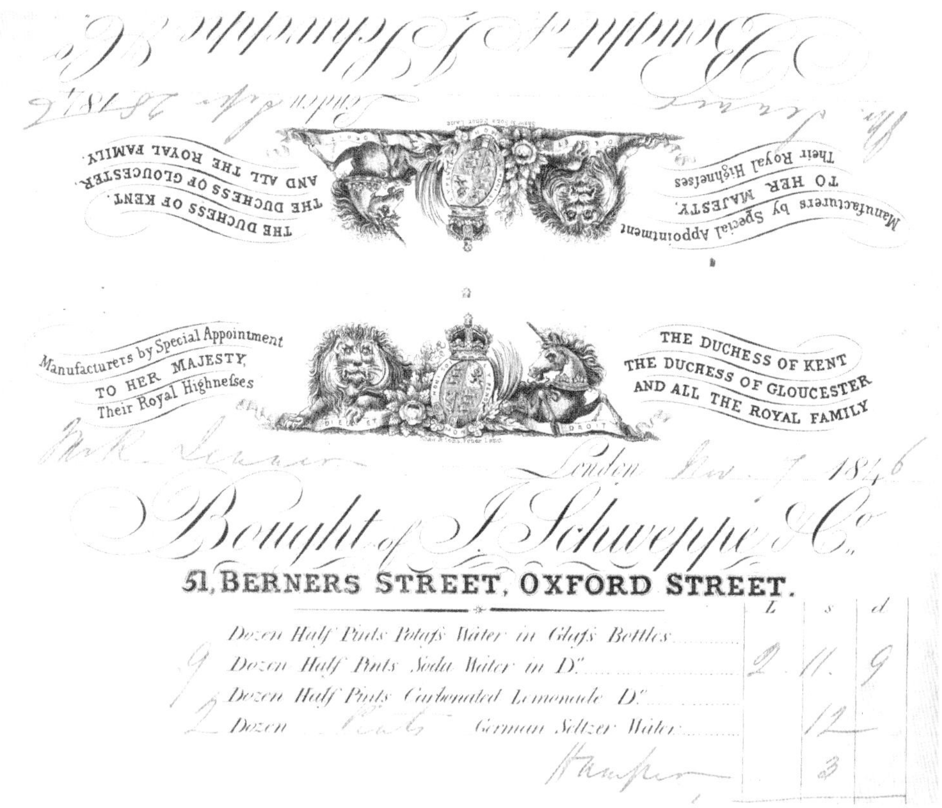

67. Two billheads of J. Schweppe & Co., by Shaw & Sons, London, in use mid-1840s, arranged to show how the two images were engraved head-to-head on a single plate. Note how in the lower example the tip of the crown from the second engraving is just visible in the top margin. (70%)

68. Copper-engraved billheads of Ridgway & Co., in use mid-1840s, showing variations on the same basic design. Two minutely differing examples of the upper design are known, suggesting that they were engraved as duplicate images on one plate. (91%)

69. Letterforms. A–A, copper engravings from music covers, *c.*1820. B–E, lithographic letterforms: B, Scroll from *Prang's Standard Alphabets*, 1878; C–E, Moderne Verzierte, Blumen and Amoretten from Weber & Co.'s *Collection of Ancient & Modern Alphabets*, *c.*1890. This selection clearly indicates the increasing inventiveness of the lithographic-lettering artist. (100%)

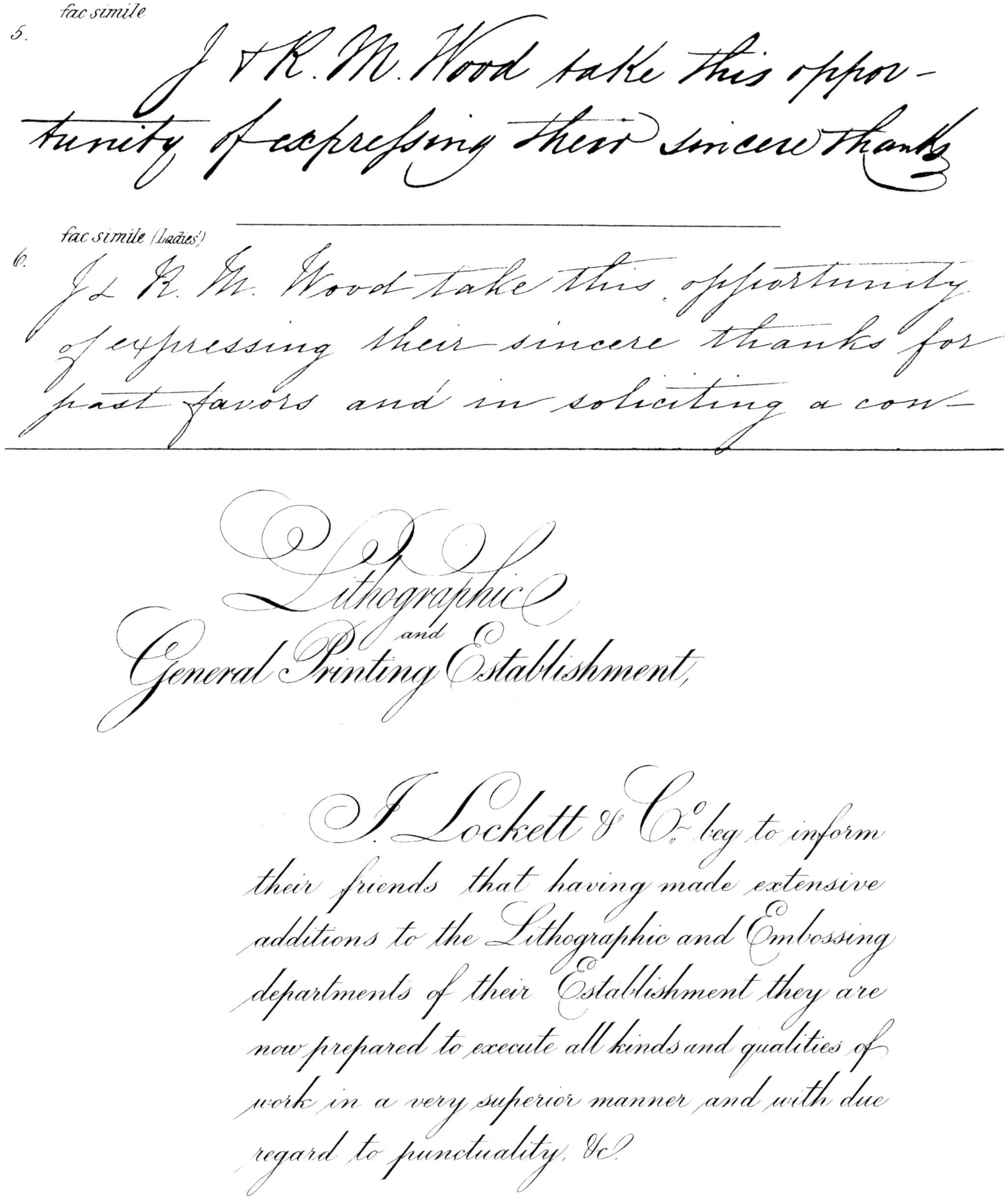
fac simile
5.
J & R. M. Wood take this opportunity of expressing their sincere thanks
fac simile (Ladies')
6.
J & R. M. Wood take this opportunity
of expressing their sincere thanks for
past favors and in soliciting a con-
Lithographic
and
General Printing Establishment,
J. Lockett & Co. beg to inform
their friends that having made extensive
additions to the Lithographic and Embossing
departments of their Establishment they are
now prepared to execute all kinds and qualities of
work in a very superior manner and with due
regard to punctuality, &c.

70. Lithographic writing. *(Top)* Samples of the facsimile 'own hand' and 'lady's hand' transfer-writing styles advertised by J. & R. M. Wood, 1865. *(Below)* Heading and sample of script from the entry by Frank Prescott, first-prize winner in a competition for transfer writing set by the *British Lithographer* in 1892. Woods' examples. *St Bride Library.* (100%)

advice here being that the artist wash head, face and beard to free them from dandruff, which might otherwise fall on the stone and 'by lying on it a short time, penetrate it, and roll up as black specks, very difficult of removal'.[16] Laughter too was a hazard, Richmond advising, 'the artist, of course, should cultivate a cheerful temper; but he must bear in mind that laughter is a fertile source of spittle-spots; so that if he wishes to indulge in that, or sneeze, he must jealously turn away from the stone'.[17]

As to drawing (a wholly separate field of study from the process itself), Richmond confined his instructions to hints on the crayon textures suitable for representing 'old walls, roads, shingly beach, and suchlike'. He also observed that the quality of some lithographers' drawing had led them to forsake the craft and become fine artists, while others 'somewhat deficient in artistic feeling' and thus still studio-bound, would 'engage some artist-friend to advise them as to effect, and to put the finishing touches to their work'.[18]

In addition to drawing skills, the lithographic artist needed the ability to design. As a stimulus to his own ideas, the wise artist would build up a scrapbook of imagery culled from various sources and keep a sketchbook to record any picturesque 'bits' he might see from day to day. For the benefit of its designer readers, in November 1886 the *American Lithographer & Printer* issued the first of a series of one-sheet art supplements of imagery and lettering. But the scheme did not long continue, possibly due to the logistical difficulties of both sourcing the imagery and having it printed elsewhere (the journal itself was printed by letterpress). In 1891 the newly founded *British Lithographer* commenced a series of artistic Plant Form studies, but these were not well received, probably because they were simply objective drawings of plants rather than designs based on them. Inviting readers to submit drawings of their own with half a guinea ($2.63)[19] promised for those accepted also 'turned out anything but a success' and the scheme was dropped.[20] Far more useful to its British and American subscribers were the journal's specimen alphabets, samples of ornament, design 'suggestions', and supplementary pages supplied by various firms promoting their own design and printing skills.

The lettering artist had the benefit of publications such as Freeman Delamotte's *Examples of Modern Alphabets, Plain & Ornamental* (London, 1859) and *Book of Ornamental Alphabets Ancient and Mediaeval* (London, 1863). In Boston in 1878 Louis Prang published *Prang's Standard Alphabets* (69B); and *c.*1890, though with examples dating back to 1883, Weber & Co. of Philadelphia brought out their *Collection of Ancient and Modern Alphabets and Ornamental Letters* (69C–E). Although published in the United States, the titling of the latter's plates – 'Fantasie Initialen, Moderne Americanische Schriften', etc – indicates this source book's German origins. Also circulating were collections of imagery and lettering published by Josef Heim of Vienna, and a sense of the usefulness of these to the office-bound artist can be gained from a British review of Heim's *Album Lithographique* (75) and *Etiquetten Schatz*:

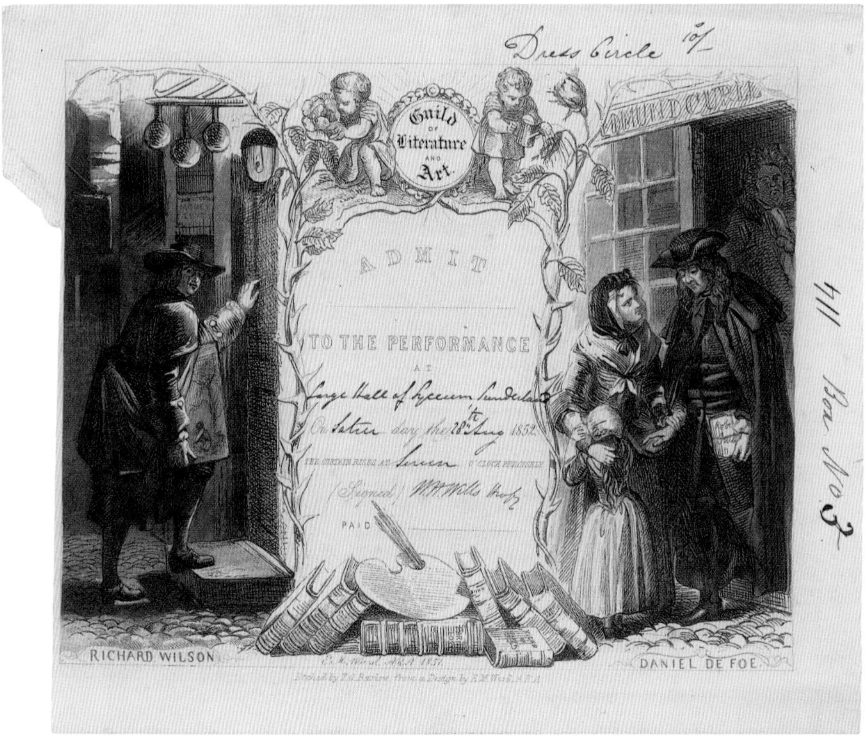

71. Admission ticket, 1852, designed by E. M. Ward, ARA, and etched by T. O. Barlow. The playbill for the same event is shown in illustration 88. The Guild of Literature & Art was formed in 1851 to provide assistance to indigent authors and artists. The illustrations show, on the left the painter Richard Wilson visiting a pawnbroker's, and on the right, Daniel Defoe leaving a publisher's with the rejected MS of *Robinson Crusoe*. Removal of the portion of the ticket on the left presumably served as a cancellation, enabling the ticket itself to be retained as a souvenir. (60%)

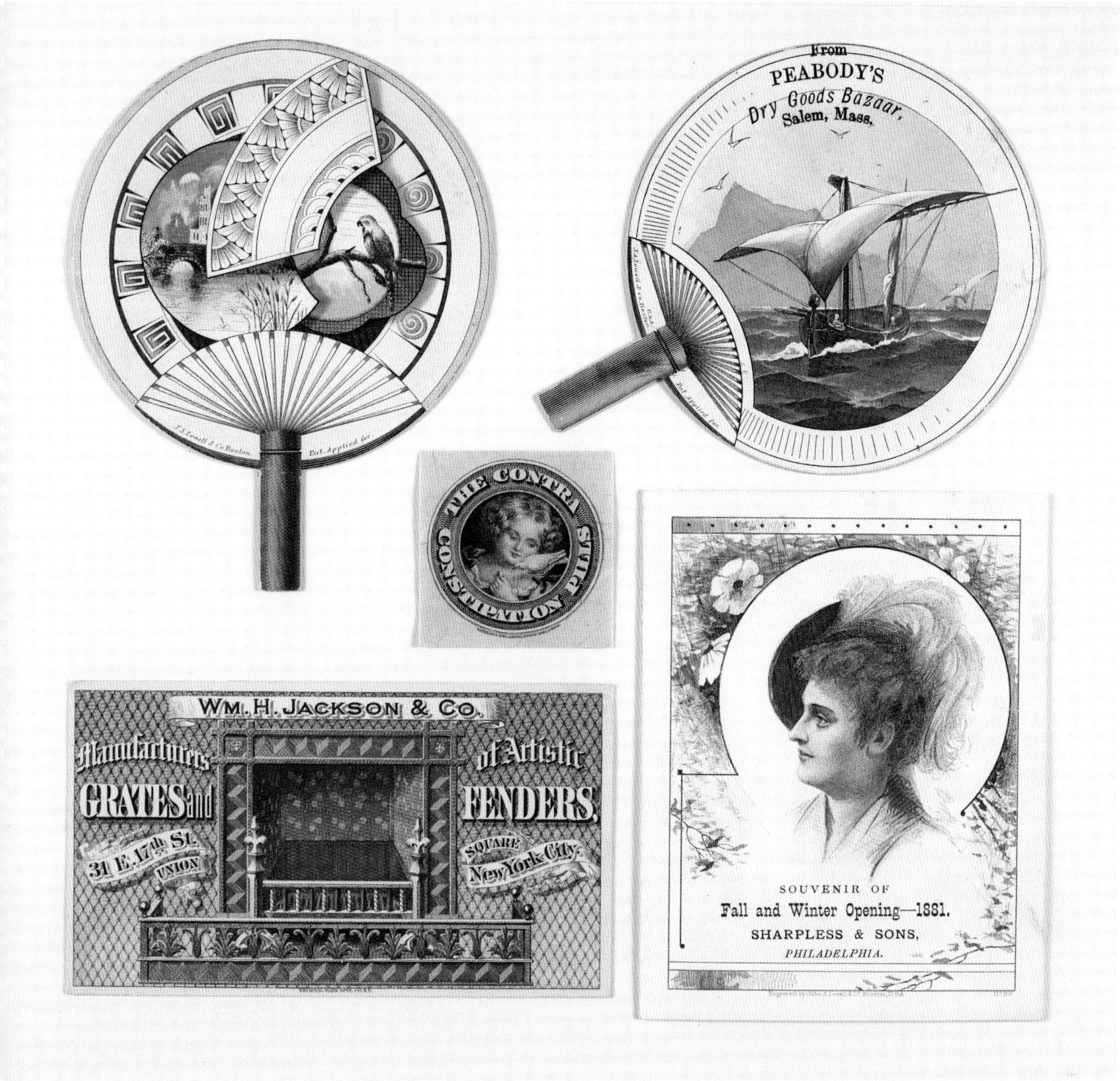

72. Steel-engraved ephemera. *(Top, and bottom-right)* Trade cards by Lowell & Co. of Boston; *(left)* by National Bank Note Co., New York; *(centre)* pill-box label by the security printers Waterlow & Sons, London. (80%)

'The Album consists of specimens of commercial work, in colour and monochrome, by artists and printers of Germany, France, and the United States, and is useful not only for the ideas contained therein but as showing the various styles of work cultivated in each country. [...] The "Etiquetten Schatz" is a collection of coloured designs for labels, many of which also offer suggestions for show cards and other purposes. Every artist will find something worth "lifting" in each part.'[21]

The text of a circular or similar item would be executed by a specialist lithographic writer. When working on transfer paper the skilled writer would use a quill, but the beginner was advised in Richmond's *Grammar of Lithography* to use a steel pen sharpened to an extra fine point. To avoid the pen's snagging the paper the left hand had to be placed behind the sheet to lift the immediate writing area away from the table, which enabled the strokes to be made with delicacy. Double pencil lines were ruled for the writing and further lines at 50° to help keep the correct slope, Richmond helpfully observing 'writing thus kept uniform in size and slope will look very fair, even if the letters themselves are not formed so well as desirable'.[22]

73. American letterpress bill-head and British heading by Crosland & Co. of London printed by lithography, 1840s. The vignette on the Barnes heading is a wood-engraving by Childs, while that on the Warren, Russell design is an engraving on stone drawn in the style of wood-engraving. This heading also illustrates how closely lithographic artists adhered to the lettering and layout styles of the copper engraver at this time. Here, the printed handwriting has been written directly on to the stone rather than transferred. (58%)

74. Engraving on stone. Marriage-license heading by Culver, Page, Hoyne & Co., Chicago, *c.*1870. Though no more than 3⅜ in. (87 mm) across, the vignette is likely to have taken some days to complete. (74%)

Richmond, however, regarded writing directly on the stone as likely to yield the longer print run. Here a pencil layout was prepared on paper and guidelines drawn on the stone using either two brass pins set in a wooden handle or adjustable dividers. The preferred writing instrument was a fine sable brush, Richmond instructing 'both the up and down strokes of the writing must be made with the *down strokes* of the brush: make the down stroke, and then the up stroke. Much practice will be necessary. …' The extra challenge of course was that the script had to be written backwards, and Richmond's instruction here was that the beginner find a good specimen of writing as a model and view it in a mirror.[23]

Once the requisite level of skill had been attained the writer would need neither exemplars nor mirror; and looking at examples of lithographic script today it is often impossible to determine whether they are the results of transfer writing or writing direct to the stone, so perfectly

75. Exemplars for the lithographic artist: specimen designs from Josef Heim's *Album Lithographique*, *c.*1890. *(Top)* stationery heading by Freien Künste of Vienna and Leipzig (1884); *(below)* heading and vignettes by Maverick & Wissinger, New York, 1883. The fine detail indicates use of mechanical reduction as described on page 56. (100%) *St Bride Library.*

could the separate strokes of the latter be joined.

The process of first engraving a copper or steel plate then transferring the image to stone was to continue into the twentieth century (62) with printing from the plate itself becoming less common after around 1850. Intaglio, however, did continue in use for the printing of high-quality fine-art reproductions, thereby maintaining a prestige that some manufacturers sought to associate with their products, and a variety of sophisticated steel-engraved ephemera was produced by this means, particularly in America (72). Among the products of Lowell & Co. were a line of tradesmen's calendars, noticed with approbation by the *British Printer* in 1893: 'Our American cousins have, as it has been gradually allowed to go out of use here, taken up and made their own the beautiful art of steelplate engraving, and in this Messrs. Lowell & Co., of Boston, Mass., have been the pioneers, some of the very finest examples of steelplate work done in the world of recent years emanating from their studios.'[24] Published in a range of new designs each year, such calendars were supplied to letterpress printers who in turn overprinted them with appropriate advertising details for local tradesmen, the

76. Twentieth-century steel engraving. Certificate commemorating the service of a member of the Canadian Expeditionary Force killed in the First World War. The formality of the sculptural flourishes in the heading is offset by the realism of the foliage with its poignant detail of falling maple leaves. The border has been engraved with a rose engine. (45%)

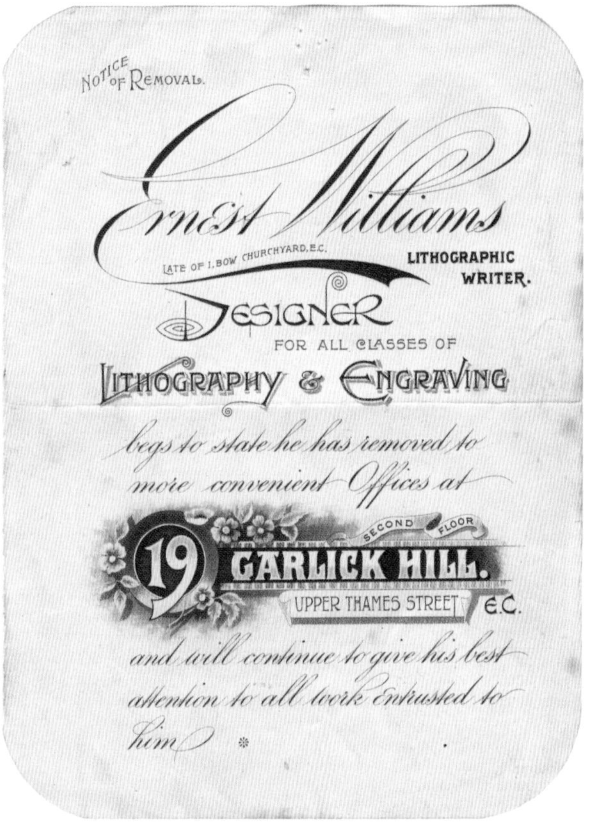

77. Relocation notice of designer Ernest Williams, copper engraving, *c.*1900. Printed direct from the plate rather than transferred to stone, the imagery communicates both the precision of Williams's work and its versatility. Following engraving, the copper would have been steel-plated to resist wear. (60%)

latter distributing the calendars as seasonal gifts to their customers. Although expensive to originate, long print runs kept the unit cost small. Similar calendars were also printed by chromolithography (which will be discussed in the next chapter).

In the general run of ephemera steel-plate printing was exceptional, for by these years the intaglio-engraving trade was much reduced. Writing in 1903, Charles Booth observed 'but little remains of a once important trade … even the printing of visiting cards which formed a large but poorly paid section of [the London] trade is failing the copper plate printer, some of the "card" houses introducing boys for this work, while if more than a few hundred cards or headings are wanted, the impression is transferred to and printed from the stone'.[25]

Those orders that were printed from plates were largely for personal stationery, for here engraved work enjoyed kudos above that of the lithographed, the ink printing in slight relief which the socially conscious would detect with a thumbnail. Apart from this and a limited use in commercial stationery, the chief applications of the process now were for wedding invitations, birth and death announcements and other social ephemera, and commemorative material, to which the intrinsic qualities of engraving imparted an appropriate dignity (76).

4

Advancing technology

Steam power was successfully applied to letterpress printing as early as 1814, when two cylinder machines were installed at the office of *The Times* in London. There they were seen by Andrew Treadwell, who following his return to the United States in 1820 built the first *bed-and-platen* press. Although originally worked with horse power, Treadwell's later models were steam driven. The chief difference in principle between the two systems was that on one the pressure was applied with a revolving cylinder (80), while the other adapted the flat platen of the hand press to mechanisation. Lighter versions of both were also made, particularly in America, where various manufacturers' versatile 'country presses', powered or hand-cranked, were favoured by printers far from the cities.

Such machinery was ideal for the printing of newspapers, booklets, almanacs and similar ephemera, but less appropriate for small jobbing, and here after mid-century the go-ahead American printer would turn to his 'jobbing platen'. British printers were introduced to these machines when New Yorker George Gordon showed his *Franklin* jobber at the International Exhibition held in London in 1862. Affording precise control of 'register', such machines enabled the operator to print successive colour formes with great accuracy, and thereby made possible the Art-printing movement discussed in chapter 6. Many different models of jobbing platen would be produced in both countries (39, 79). The hand press was not made redundant, however, and for the printing of posters and other large ephemera would remain useful for many years.

Steam printing fostered an overall growth in the demand for print, and what had previously been different aspects of the one trade became progressively specialised, eventually to the degree that the journeyman trained in one field – newspaper, bookwork or jobbing – would be well out of his depth in another. One jobbing printer recounted how he had taken on some temporary hands to help with an influx of work. Two whom he set to composing tabular matter quickly gave up; likewise two more who were put to composing auction bills. The largest type that the latter were asked to set was no bigger than 10-line ($1\frac{5}{8}$ in./42 mm) but they had never previously set anything larger than pica, 'and considered such rough work as mine fit only for dray-men or coal-heavers'. Another man put to the auction bills tried his best but he too gave up: 'he was very sorry, he had never been used to jobbing, and did not know Great Primer from 2-line English, as he had never handled such "Millstones" of type before'.[1] It gives an indication of just how unadaptable these compositors had become when one remembers that 2-line English, the larger of the type sizes quoted, was equivalent to no more

78. Playbill seller, a wood engraving from *Punch*, 1862, cut from a drawing made directly on to the wood. The man is saying to the boy, 'Two-pence? Oh, then I won't have a bill; I've only got a penny', to which the lad replies, 'Then pray don't mention it, Sir. Never mind the hextra penny. I respects genteel poverty.' (100%)

than today's 28 point, or approximately $^3/_8$ in. (10 mm) in overall depth.

Effective printing depended as much on clear communication between customer and printer as it did on good composition and presswork, and that problems could arise through lack of it is sometimes illustrated by the labels pasted in the backs of American shelf clocks. The clock factories were located in Connecticut but the label printers could be as far away as New York, and seem to have been poorly briefed as to how the labels would be used. Often a label would display the manufacturer's name in fancy type plus a large wood-engraving of the factory. Seen in isolation the effect was splendid, but when the label was pasted into the back of the case and the clock mechanism set in, part of the typographic display could be obscured (81). The clocks were made from standardised parts, with each operative having his allotted task in the assembly process, but manufacturers had yet to recognise the need to integrate the printer's contribution with that of the rest.

The introduction of printing machines encouraged an increase in cheap illustrated reading matter, and with it came a significant growth in the wood-engraving trade. In 1833, the *Penny Magazine*, circulating in both Britain and America, observed that twenty years earlier no more than about twelve wood-engravers had been working in London, but now there were 'considerably more than a hundred'.[2] A further fillip came in 1842 with the founding of the *Illustrated London News*, followed in America in 1851 by the Boston-based *Gleason's Pictorial*, and numerous others in both countries. When quality counted, the engraver working for these early periodicals would still lower the surface of the block to achieve lighter tones; but long print-runs left no time for the machine man to selectively increase cylinder pressure to enhance the darker tones, as was possible with the tympan of the hand press.

For some years wood-engraving was seen as offering a solution to the perennial problem of the gentlewoman in reduced circumstances and in need of employment. A women's class in wood-engraving was started at the Metropolitan School of Practical Art in London in 1842;[3] and in 1854, in support of similar courses provided at the New England School of Design for Women, the editor of the Boston *Lady's Almanac* enthused that one had 'but to look at the shop-bills thrown upon our door-steps, at the papers sold in the cars, at the books which our children read, in the shop windows, to see everywhere wood-cuts and lithographic prints. So rapidly does the demand for good workmen in these departments increase, that it is very difficult to supply it.'[4] But such hopes were dashed, for as the demand for wood-engraving increased so also did the trade become concentrated in a number of large firms, and into these, according to the mores of the time, women could not be admitted.

A further consequence of the development of these firms was the cutting of large images by *teams* rather than individuals, one man cutting the outlines, another perhaps engraving skies and water, another concentrating on trees and foliage, etc. In 1863 J. & R. M. Wood claimed that by this means (84) they could 'produce engravings with unheard of rapidity, and very much lower in price than is generally charged, no injustice [being] done to the present trade of wood engravers, as the system, not being patented, is open for anyone to adopt it'.[5] In the latter remark, however, the Woods were disingenuous for by this date the practice was well established.

As box was a relatively small tree, the wood blocks themselves were small; thus the block needed for a large engraving had to be made up from several smaller blocks mortised and glued together. Around 1860 the boxwood importer Charles Wells devised a method of assembly and disassembly using steel bolts, facilitating a system in which each man worked on his own constituent block, the whole

79. Jobbing platen by Harrild & Sons, London. The operator is shown placing a sheet of paper on the backward-sloping platen while simultaneously working the treadle. The inking roller descends from *ink disc* (A) to pass over the type forme, then as it returns the platen and type bed swing together and the sheet is printed. Platen and bed then move apart, *friskets* (B) ensuring clean separation of type and paper. (96%) *Printing World*, 2.9 (1892), p. 422A

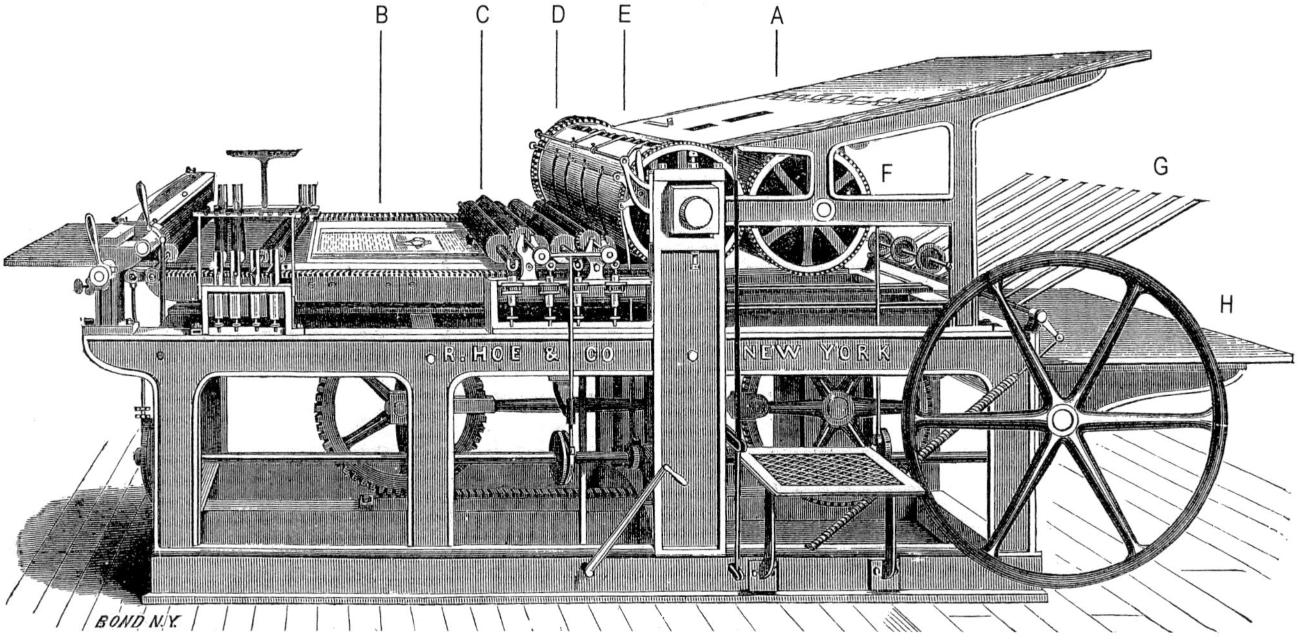

80. Stop-cylinder machine by Hoe & Co., New York. Paper ready for printing was stacked on the *feed board* (A). The type forme (B) reciprocated between inking rollers (C) and impression cylinder (D), which in this view would be rotating anticlockwise. The cylinder briefly halting, the operator slid a sheet of paper down the feed board into the *cylinder grippers* (E). The cylinder then resuming its motion, the sheet was brought in contact with the type and then transferred on to and over the *take-off cylinder* (F); from where it was picked up by the *flyers* (G), which swept it, printed side up, on to the *delivery board* (H). (100%) Ringwalt, *American Encyclopaedia of Printing*.

being reassembled on completion. To ensure that each man's work correctly married with its neighbours, the portions of the image that crossed the joins were engraved by the foreman before the blocks were separated. Today, the fine white lines occasionally seen running across a Victorian illustration are evidence that it was printed from a composite block.

Surprisingly, although seemingly permanently fixed, a wood-engraved image could be altered (85). One method was to drill out the appropriate area, fill the hole with a wooden plug or plaster-of-Paris, then re-engrave preparatory to stereotyping. More extensive changes were achieved by making a plaster mould from the block, carefully scraping the redundant areas deeper, then casting in stereo metal, the surplus where the scraped areas cast higher being skilfully planed down to present a smooth surface for re-engraving.[6]

The more design-conscious printer would prefer to commission an original engraving rather than have recourse to a stock cut; but this was not always economic, so J. & R. M. Wood (and one presumes other firms also) operated a scheme whereby a design likely to have wide appeal would be engraved at reduced charge and the customer granted six months' exclusive use, after which the engraving would be issued as a stock cut.[7] J. G. Campbell & Co. of Sunderland, England, showed similar consideration in the allocation of their stock posters. These came part-printed with colour imagery appropriate to a variety of trades with the greater part of the sheet left blank for overprinting, thus enabling the printer to supply 'at the most reasonable rate, posting bills far more attractive than the ordinary letter-press bills, and in quantities which would never justify printers in engraving blocks for themselves'. A printer ordering a particular design was granted its exclusive use in his own locality.[8]

Stock cuts could be had more cheaply by buying them second-hand from firms such as John Greason & Co. of New York, who besides publishing *The Printer* also dealt in part-used printers' equipment. The following items from their advertisement of 1864 are typical: 'One morticed Eagle, in rays, 5 × 11, \$2.50. One Trotting horse, 6 × 9, \$3. One beautiful fine cut of Liberty, with Constitution in right hand, 6 × 9, \$4. One morticed Steamboat, 5 × 16½, \$5. Lot of 5 small Cuts, each 50c' ('morticed' indicating that there was a slot cut in the block for the insertion of type).[9]

The pages of the Woods' *Typographic Advertiser* abound in stock-cut imagery that has an unmistakable American air, but this was through the plagiarising of American designs not their importation. Some engravings were adapted to suit the British market (86), others were copied line for line; but in neither case did the firm acknowledge the cuts' American origins. In March 1863 the *Advertiser* printed a magnificent 12 in. (304 mm) cut of a black stallion, offered either as a stereotype priced at 15*s*. (then

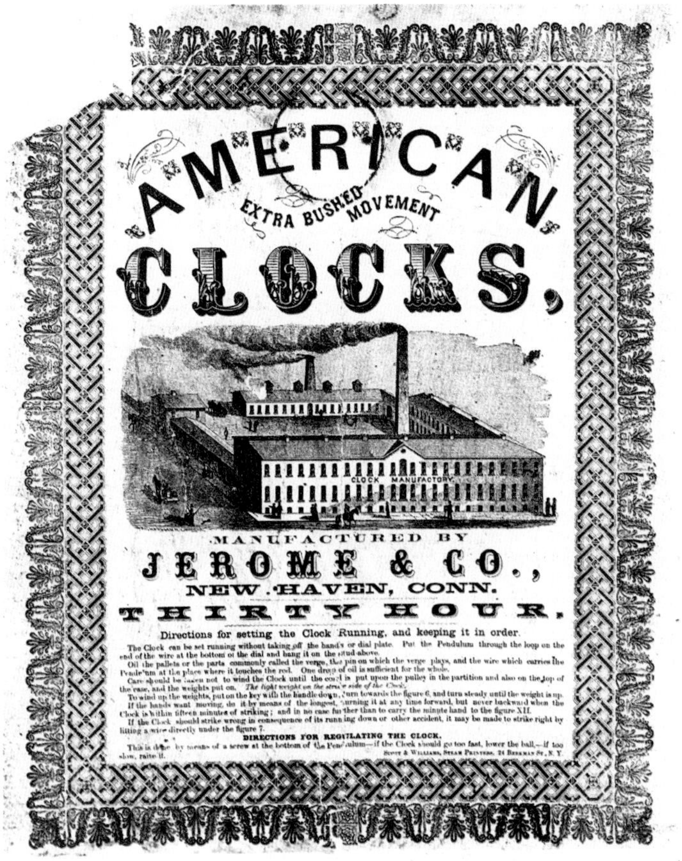

81. Instructions label by Scott & Williams, New York, from a shelf clock by Jerome & Co., New Haven. The circle of discolouration towards the top shows where the chimes of the clock were screwed on to the backboard, thereby unintentionally obscuring the typographic display. (44%)

82. Showman's stock cut by Call Jurss on a handbill by Post-Express Print, Rochester, NY, *c.*1880. Depicting Siamese twins (here being presented to Queen Victoria), the picture is self-evidently not that of one woman with two heads, so the cut probably originated with a different show. (74%)

equivalent to $5.31)[10] or ready-printed on stock posters. The cut was much admired, but prompted the enquiry from one sharp-eyed reader: 'Your stallion is a splendid animal; but I must beg leave to ask where your artist saw a stallion trotting on a flagged pavement?' The Woods admitted, perhaps somewhat sheepishly, 'the stallion is taken from a celebrated American trotter; and the best American roads are formed of logs, covered with gravel, as correctly represented'.[11]

More reckless in its presentation was the cut adapted by the firm for their journal's masthead in April 1864, featuring an eagle crouching on a shield bearing the royal arms (87). Of this the Woods observed: 'We beg to state that mounted casts of the noble design ... are now ready, price 10*s.* [$3.54][12] each. We recommend this cut as being useful for many purposes as a sensation ornament', which drew the response from one angry printer: 'I hope the First of April is the only date on which the *Typographic Advertiser* will make its appearance headed by such a "Yankee notion" as an eagle sprawling over the Standard of England! You speak of the heading as a "sensation ornament". If my "sensations" on the subject are shared by others, you will not find the change generally approved of, nor the "noble design" adopted for many other purposes.' Lamely the brothers replied that the eagle was simply emblematic of their association with a neighbouring printer, the Columbian Press; but truly it was the American bald eagle through and through, and was quietly dropped from the masthead after the next issue.[13]

As commerce increased through the century, so also did manufacturers' premises become larger and more prestigious. These buildings were tangible expressions of their owners' success and thus came to be grandly depicted on a firm's printed stationery (149). In at least one case, however, the industrialist's response was the reverse of what had been expected, as the following anecdote from the *Typographic Advertiser* shows:

We lately engraved a block, from a rough drawing of a factory, for a customer, and, according to precedent, we made the tall chimneys smoking away, to show that the mill was in operation, and to add activity to the landscape, in the same manner that we

83. Two-colour letterpress poster by Goddard & Son, Hull, 1863. Intended to be read close up rather than from a distance, the dark blue and vermilion make a good contrast. The layout is unusual, with the possibility that the elements of the central panel may also have been printed separately as part of a programme. Organised from Hull, this event would have seen a gathering of Druid friendly societies from across the Midlands and north of England. (34%)

always represent a stylish carriage and pair at a tradesman's door, a few fashionably-attired figures in the street, and a little frisky dog in the distance, to lend enchantment to the view. Our customer's customer, upon seeing a proof of the block, said, 'Take away the – – smoke, I'll have none of it in the sketch; haven't I just paid upwards of two hundred pounds [then equivalent to $1,416][14] to have the smoke consumed?'.

To this the Woods dryly added, 'We request our friends, when ordering engravings of mills, to ascertain if the gentleman giving the order "consumes his own smoke".'[15]

How a building of bricks and mortar was translated into a vignette is indicated by the Bristol printer Heber Mardon, writing of a time in the 1860s when many customers wished to have views of their premises on their billheads, bags and tea papers. The drawings were executed by the firm's artist Henry Whatley (lately returned from Philadelphia 'where he had been learning the lithographic artist branch'). Many of these jobs came via the firm's traveller in south Wales where, Mardon recollects, 'I often went to make the sketches for orders he had taken.'[16] Thus it was normal practice for the studio artist to 'work up' someone else's sketches rather than seeing the buildings with his own eyes. An artist might also have to adapt his design to an imaginary bird's-eye view (58) or suit his drawing to a less-than-ideal format (92), while figures were regularly

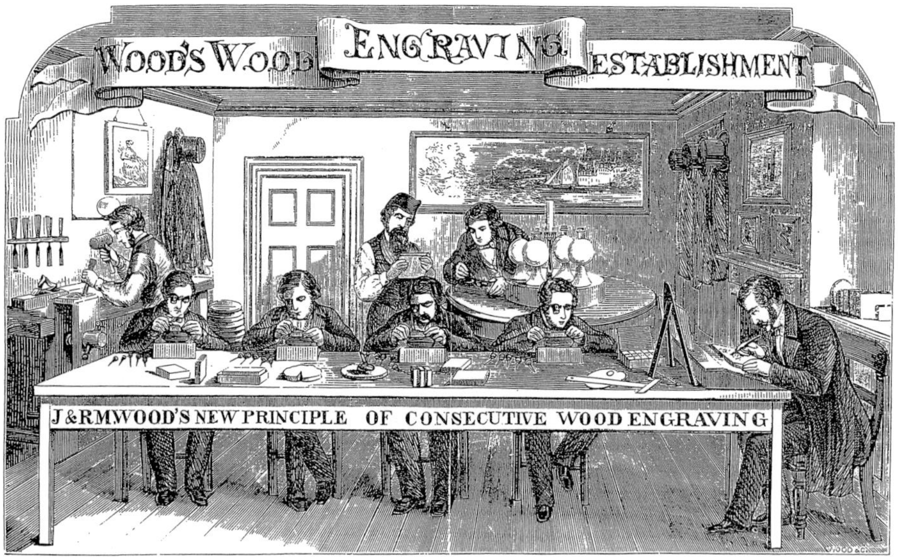

84. J. & R. M. Wood's wood-engraving team, 1863. From right to left: *artist* drawing on the wood block following the design on the easel before him; *outliner*, cutting round all areas intended to print white; *tint hand*, engraving evenly toned areas; *finisher*, engaged on crosshatch work and general touching up. The fifth man gouges out the portions indicated by the outliner, while the foreman engraves faces and similar fine work. At night, each man would use one of the water-filled globes to direct the light of an oil lamp on to his work. (68%) *St Bride Library.*

85. Stock cut for auctioneers' printing engraved by the Johnson foundry, Philadelphia, and the same cut adapted for a different purpose. That the lower image is the modified version is evident from the raffish clientele, who are clearly more at home at the horse sale than when bidding for domestic furniture. (65%) Clarence P. Hornung, *Handbook of Early Advertising Art.*

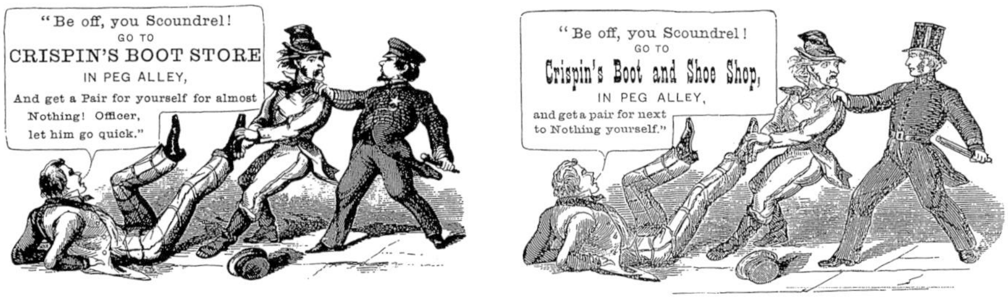

86. Trans-Atlantic plagiarism. American stock cut *(left)* with British adaptation advertised in Woods' *Typographic Advertiser* in November 1862. (American) Hornung, *Handbook of Early Advertising Art*; (Woods') *St Bride Library*. (75%)

87. American-eagle mortised cut from the Johnson foundry, and below it the same eagle adapted in April 1864 as the masthead of the Woods' *Typographic Advertiser* – 'sprawling over the Standard of England!' as one British printer protested. (xx%) (Johnson) Hornung, *Handbook of Early Advertising Art*; (Woods') *St Bride Library*. (100%)

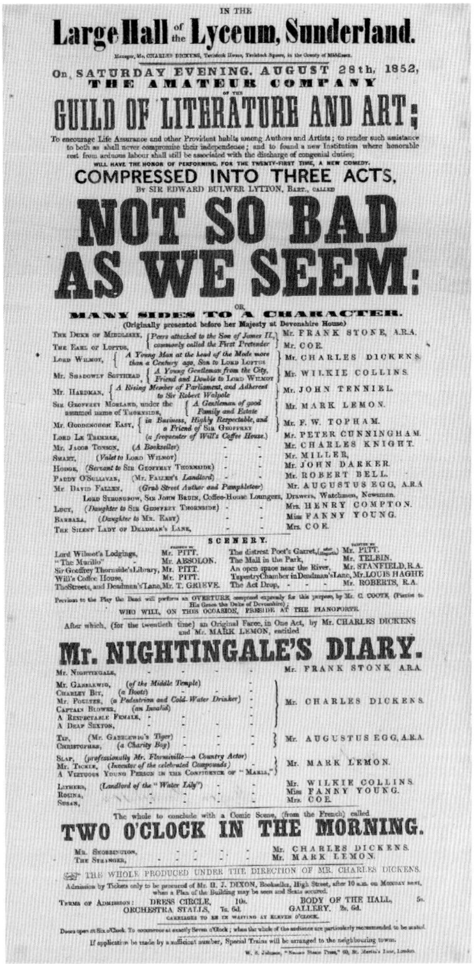

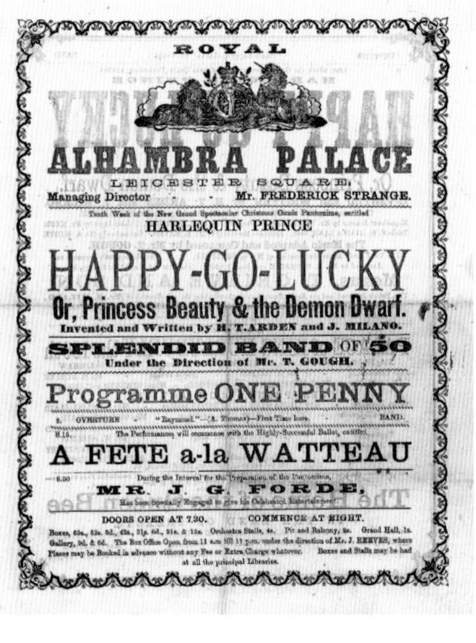

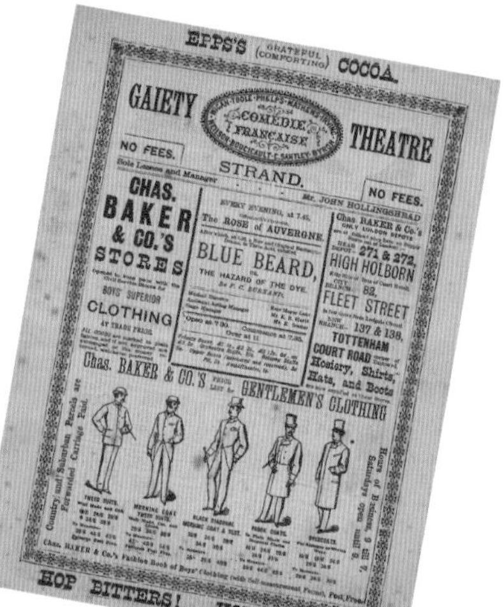

88. Suggested evolution of the theatre programme. *(Top left)* Playbill, Nassau Steam Press, London, 1852. Charles Dickens was the manager of this production, appearing in the cast list with Wilkie Collins, the illustrator John Tenniel and other supporters of the Guild of Literature and Art (see also illustration 71). *(Right)* Double playbill by W. S. Johnson of the Nassau Steam Press, 1865, illustrating the excessive amount of text that necessitated a bill intended to be folded. *(Bottom left)* Early booklet-style programme by Elliott, London, 1871 adapting the typographic style of the playbill to the more convenient four-page format. *(Right)* Eight-page programme by R. Wilson & Co., London, 1883: here only the centre two pages are devoted to the performances, the rest being given over to advertising. (25%)

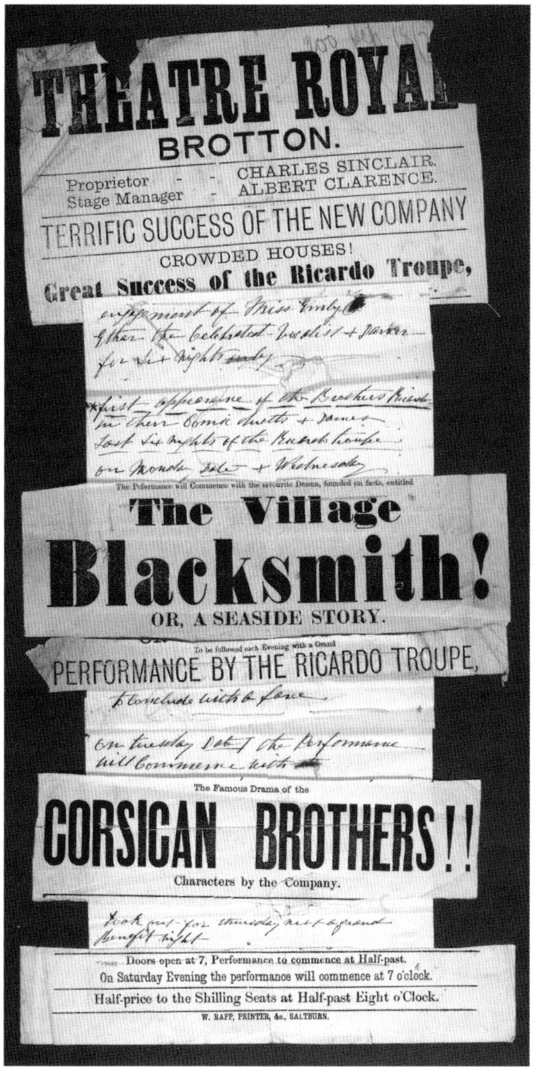

89. British compositor's instructions for setting a playbill, *c.*1870 – portions of old bills interspersed with hand-written copy. As the pieces are stitched together with needle and thread it seems likely that the assembly was done by the stage manager's wife. (27%)

90. Theatre poster, Birmingham, 1871. It is possible that the two-column matter was also used with a different heading for a separately printed double playbill: the text is replete with witticisms and stanzas of verse, clearly indicating that it was to be read at leisure. (19%)

miniaturised to make buildings appear all the grander, and it was not unknown for one factory to be pictured twice, from widely different angles, suggesting ownership of additional premises.

In the manufacturer's catalogue, however, accuracy was essential. An artist working from a sketch of a simple tool would draw it directly on the boxwood, but a complicated machine called for the intermediate stage of a detailed drawing on paper. The average charges for engravings of agricultural equipment quoted by Jabez Hare in 1847, were 30*s.* [then equivalent to $3.60][17] for the initial sketch and a drawing made directly on to the block plus 30*s.* for engraving the wood, but with an additional charge of 15*s.* if the subject were sufficiently complicated to need a precise drawing on paper to be made first for transferring to the block.[18] (The drawing would be secured face down on the block with a slip of paper rubbed with pencil lead laid between the two; careful scribing of the lines visible through the back of the drawing would then transfer the main lines of the image.)

The theatre was a significant user of stock cuts. Until the early 1880s the American and British stages shared a considerable repertoire, and there was scarcely a melodrama, burlesque or pantomime not represented by commercially available cuts. Theatre managements would keep a selection corresponding with the dramas, etc. most frequently played, and touring companies, lecturers and showmen would also have their own engravings (82),

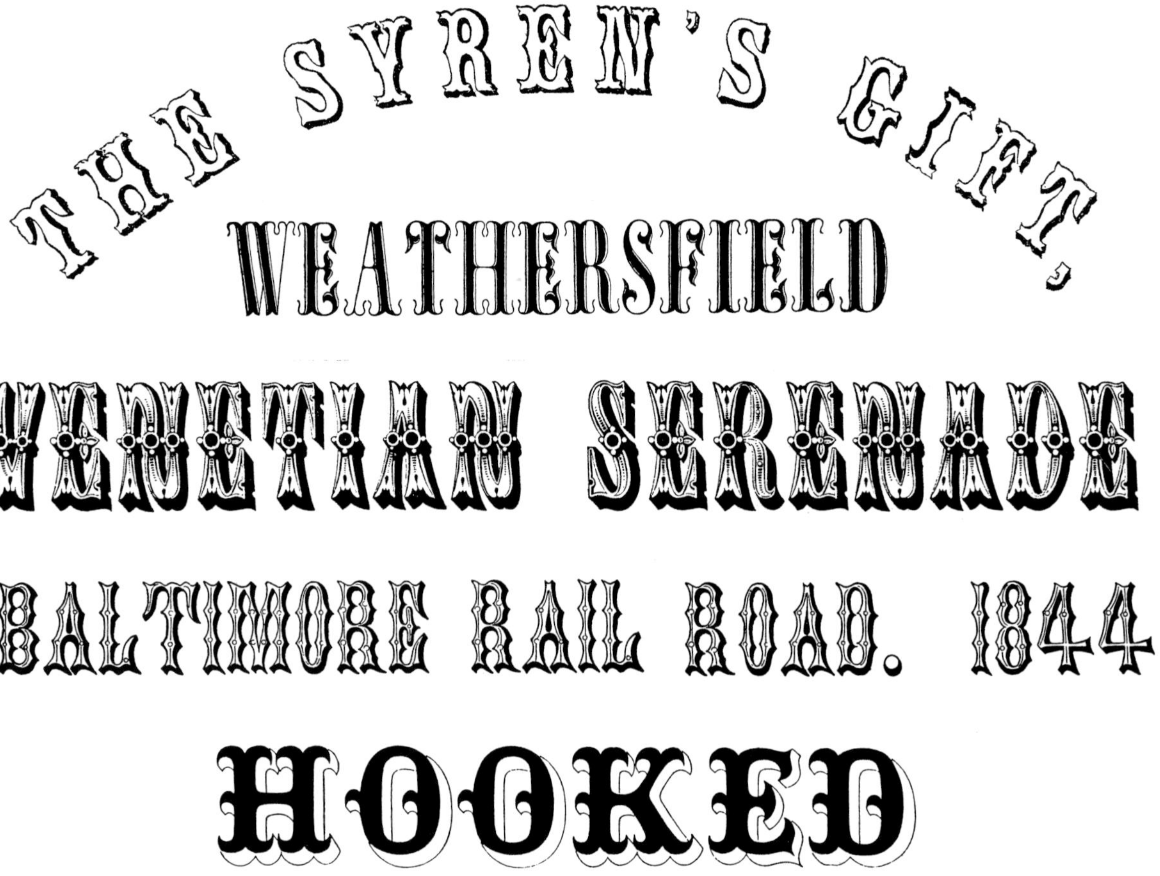

91. Some mid-nineteenth-century decorative types. Defying more detailed classification, such letterforms were collectively known as 'ornamented', the individual naming of typefaces not becoming common until later in the century. (100%)

which they would post on ahead of them from printer to printer along their circuit. Some printers specialised in theatrical work and kept extensive stocks of cuts suitable to a wide range of productions. E. J. Bath of Whitechapel, London, held over 1300 separate images, which Bath claimed would 'be found adapted (or nearly so) for every Play, Pantomime, or Burlesque, on record'. Besides imagery specific to given dramas, Bath also had cuts of a generic application, such as 'full length figure of a sailor', 'a forest; a man in the act of stabbing another, who is on the ground' and 'five Engravings suitable for Highwaymen's Pieces'. Bath printed everything theatrical from tickets to four-sheet posters, and with the sizes of his cuts ranging from a modest 3 × 3 in. (76 × 76 mm) up to quad-crown (30 × 40 in./763 × 1010 mm), his catalogue relied on detailed description rather than illustrations.[19] By contrast, the Ledger Job Printing Office in Philadelphia offered for sale an extensive series of stock posters in sizes from single-sheet up to four-sheet, printed in black or colours ready for over-printing of theatre and performance details. Such large posters would have been cut on the plank face of pine or basswood boards rather than on boxwood.[20] Catalogued in *Specimens of Theatrical Cuts Being Fac-Similes, in Miniature, of Poster Cuts* (*c.*1875), each poster was illustrated with a corresponding electrotype which could itself be purchased.[21]

It may be in the familiar long format of the playbill that one finds most clearly reflected the influences of technology and function on the design of ephemeral printing. The iron press, and then the printing machine, made possible the printing of increasingly larger sheets, and this in turn encouraged theatre managements to add more and more copy to their bills, often of a dramatic or humorous nature; for playbills were produced both to advertise a performance and as programmes (80). Thus the playbill became an entertainment in its own right, to be pored over by the audience before the performance began as well as consulted during it. In the tight confines of a theatre seat or the jostling crowd of the gallery a sheet of conventional proportions would have been unwieldy, hence (the present writer conjectures) developed that characteristic narrow format, which could be read from top to bottom without much movement of the elbows. The same format is found utilised for orders of procession, where the press of a

92. Image and actuality. Pelham Crescent, Hastings, depicted on a steel engraving by Rock & Co., London, 1855, and the Crescent photographed in 2005. To include the adjoining range of Pelham Place in the vignette the artist has squeezed the Crescent almost beyond recognition. (92%)

watching crowd would similarly have restricted movement; but ephemera of similar surface area to the playbill and partly set in comparably small type, such as auction notices, adhere to conventional sheet proportions.

Sometimes the amount of copy to be got on to a playbill was excessive and thus printers devised the double (88) and triple forms. These were designed to be folded, but even so must have been awkward to handle, while the cheap ink also dirtied the hands; and it may have been for both these reasons that in the 1850s smaller, simpler bills began to replace them, followed by booklet-style programmes. The long format was old-fashioned by 1875, though for promotional purposes it was to persist well into the days of the cinema; indeed so closely had it become associated with entertainment that its use extended to ephemera intended solely to inform, such as notices of race meetings and other outdoor events.

The melodrama can have held few surprises for its patrons, for plot synopsis was almost standard on theatre bills. On posters the story of the play might be presented in a series of images (93) but on playbills the sequence of events would be spelt out in words. Thus on an unillustrated bill for a performance of *Crime and Retribution* at San Francisco's Turn-Verein Hall in 1881 we have: 'Scene 1. – Harry Fairfield's Farm – The Harvest Feast – Wm. Brierly's insolent conduct chastised by a blow from Harry Fairfield – Brierly swears revenge. Scene 2. – (Six months later.) – William Brierly's office – Commands Josiah Nibb to avenge his wrongs and fire the farm of Harry Fairfield', and so on.[22] But melodramas were highly predictable and such 'giving away'of the plot was of little significance. The audience wanted glamour and spectacle, and for these their appetites were amply whetted.

Printers whose customers included travelling players and other entertainers could find themselves called on as their local agents. In 1852 the north of England printer John Procter received an enquiry from the itinerant lecturer William Richardson, then in Northallerton, asking Procter about the hiring of Hartlepool town hall, followed a few days later by:

93. Theatre poster by Maurice & Co., London, 1841, printed in red and black. The twelve wood engravings present highlights of the plot, thus whetting the public's appetite to see the same events enacted in the flesh. In this, such posters served a function similar to that of the modern cinema trailer. *Victoria & Albert Museum.* (32%)

I sent you the woodcut from here yesterday and hope you have got it safe. I should think 300 syllabuses will be enough, and from 70 to 100 large posters, the form of poster I sent on Sunday from home which you would no doubt get. Please get the poster to post two together side by side in the most conspicuous places, and get a few into the most respectable shop windows.[23]

The instructions a printer received as to the setting of a bill could be very informal. He might receive no more than an old playbill, its printed text heavily amended and a letter on the back combining updated copy with domestic matters – 'I hope you have done the needful about lodgings for us' – and typographic guidance limited to single and double underlining showing where emphasis was expected.[24] Alternatively, copy might comprise merely bits of old bills and new copy tacked together (89).

The further development of display types was promoted in 1845 with the invention by the Philadelphian T. W. Starr of a means of making type matrices without steel punches.[25] The original for each character was cut in

94. Minstrel show poster printed on yellow paper, 1846. The first minstrel troupe to visit Britain were the Virginia Minstrels, who had appeared at the Adelphi Theatre, London, three years earlier. *Punch* reported in March 1847 that there were then no fewer than twenty-four 'sons of Ethiopia' (probably five troops) performing in London, with numerous others touring the provinces. (47%)

type metal and the matrix made by electroylysis, the softer alloy facilitating the cutting of more finely detailed decorative types (91). At that time American type designs either copied or closely imitated the British, but from the late 1860s American founders began to take their own line.[26] Previously, highly ornamented though they might be, the traditional configurations and proportions of the letters had been maintained, but from the late 1860s these too became subject to fanciful alteration (130).

With the continuing influx of decorative types, however, a compositor could be increasingly tempted to use whatever novelties came his way, resulting in something more akin to a synopsis of his employer's stock than a pleasing design. Nevertheless there still were those to whom well-considered composition was important. Writing of the display work carried out at the Ashtabula, Ohio, *Sentinel*, in the 1850s, W. D. Howells recalled 'we enjoyed our trade as the decorative art it also is. Questions of taste constantly arose in the arrangement of a title-page, the display of a placard or a handbill, the use of this type or that'.[27] A letter in the *Printers' Register* from the Sussex printer Karl Burg in 1866 also instances one who cared, Burg writing 'it is not unfrequently that one hears even practical printers pooh-pooh the idea that any art is required, or can possibly be displayed, in the getting up of a showbill; and perhaps this somewhat general impression is the cause why we see so many tasteless bills about'. The key to setting a good bill, Burg continued, was first to spend five minutes thoroughly reading the copy to decide which lines should be emphasised, followed by thought as to which mode of display would best suit the subject. For church, parochial and municipal announcements he recommended the *light and open style*, where plenty of space was left between the lines. For auction and general business work the *close and full-line* approach was best, i.e. each line set full out and minimum line spacing. The most attractive style of layout, however, was where full and short lines alternated down the sheet, which he advocated for shipping and insurance announcements, entertainments and other better-class work. But Burg gave little advice on type choice, observing 'no art should be thus fettered, but allowed to move freely, with full and independent scope as to originality'.[28]

Further understanding of the typographic thinking of the period is gained from Theodore Lowe De Vinne (1829–1914), who addressed the New York Typographical Society on the subject of display just a year or so later. Contrast was an important element, De Vinne observed, and in large-scale work it could be strong, but 'the finer, more artistic, and more elegant the class of work, the less need of contrast and the greater need of harmony'. He also stressed that the chief purpose of display was clear communication, 'not to show a large and varied stock of types'; but even so this was still the 1860s, and it is clear that De Vinne envisaged successful display as embracing a far wider range of types than would be customary today. Thus he instructs that harmony was to be achieved by selecting faces that were 'in contrast to and yet in agreement with' those immediately above and below, while cautioning that setting two successive lines in precisely the same size and style was to be avoided. Yet even the most beautiful types would produce dull monotony if a setting consisted of them only, but 'remove some of the Ornamental lines and put plain Romans, Antiques, or Gothics in their place, and the effect will be quite magical'. Successful display would also include 'one leading line, superior to all others in size, clearness, and effect', this giving a focus to the design.[29]

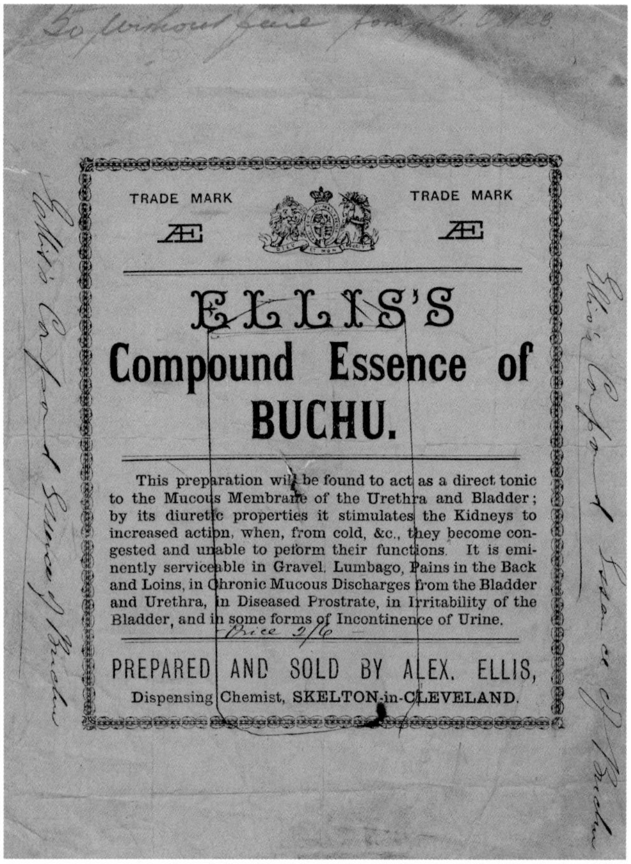

95. Compositor's instructions for adapting the wording of an existing label to the smaller format of a patent-medicine bottle. The shape of the intended label and the wording for the side panels are roughly penned in while a note at the top reads '50 without fail tonight'. (39%)

Further insight into attitudes to display in the 1860s is provided by a design competition set by the *Typographic Advertiser* in February 1865. The challenge was to set the copy for a lecture admission card, with prizes of new composing sticks for the three best designs. The response was excellent, thirty-two entries being reproduced in the April issue and a further thirty-two in May. Publishing the entries entailed resetting each one line by line, and such were the journal's resources that only two competitors complained of wrong types being used. Following the closing date for entries the editor gave his own thoughts on how the copy might best have been approached, and it is interesting to note that in this period when fancy types were the norm he made no reference to type styles, discussing the words solely in terms of their degrees of importance in the message. It also says much for the trade's concern for design that no less than forty-one master printers were willing to devote time to judging the entries (96).

Printer 'CW' commented that '"this rearing the tender plant" to teach "the young idea how to shoot", may bear good fruit', while 'RL' was sure that 'many of the unsuccessful competitors will be much benefited by the varieties given'. Opinions as to the overall standard of the entries, however, were mixed. 'WA' saw 'many good specimens of our art' but the word used by both 'WT' and 'M&C' was 'lamentable'. Particular ire was directed towards competitor 'RP', whose design '[presumably] sent as a foolish attempt at a joke', drew the comment from one fellow entrant that its perpetrator 'deserved to be kicked'. The first-prize winner was James Smethurst, compositor with John Barnes, Manchester. It was an interesting choice, for of all the entries Smethurst's was the most restrained, only a single roman being used throughout and variation restricted to italicisation and changes in type size. The choice did not go without comment, 'JTD' admiring the design but querying whether a setting entirely lacking in fancy letter could qualify *as* display typography, while

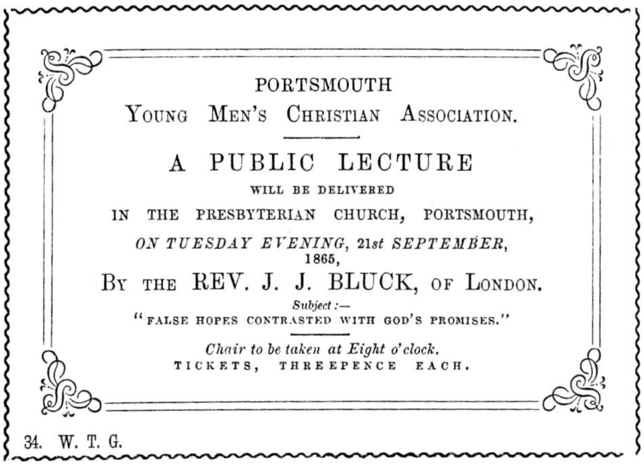

PORTSMOUTH
YOUNG MEN'S CHRISTIAN ASSOCIATION.

A PUBLIC LECTURE
WILL BE DELIVERED
IN THE PRESBYTERIAN CHURCH, PORTSMOUTH,
ON TUESDAY EVENING, 21st SEPTEMBER,
1865,
BY THE REV. J. J. BLUCK, OF LONDON.
Subject :—
"FALSE HOPES CONTRASTED WITH GOD'S PROMISES."
Chair to be taken at Eight o'clock.
TICKETS, THREEPENCE EACH.

34. W. T. G.

A

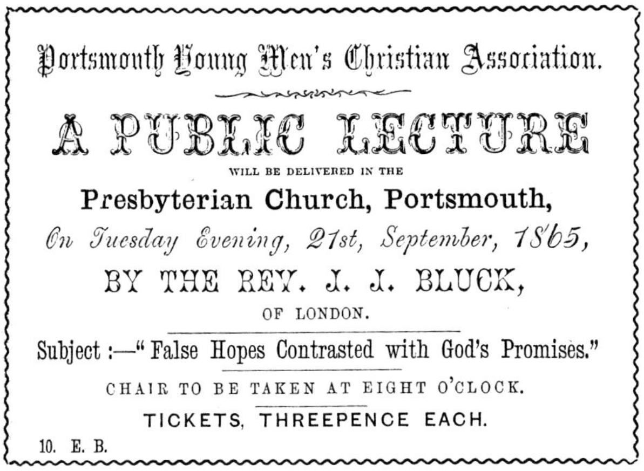

Portsmouth Young Men's Christian Association.

A PUBLIC LECTURE
WILL BE DELIVERED IN THE
Presbyterian Church, Portsmouth,
On Tuesday Evening, 21st, September, 1865,
BY THE REV. J. J. BLUCK,
OF LONDON.
Subject :—"False Hopes Contrasted with God's Promises."
CHAIR TO BE TAKEN AT EIGHT O'CLOCK.
TICKETS, THREEPENCE EACH.

10. E. B.

B

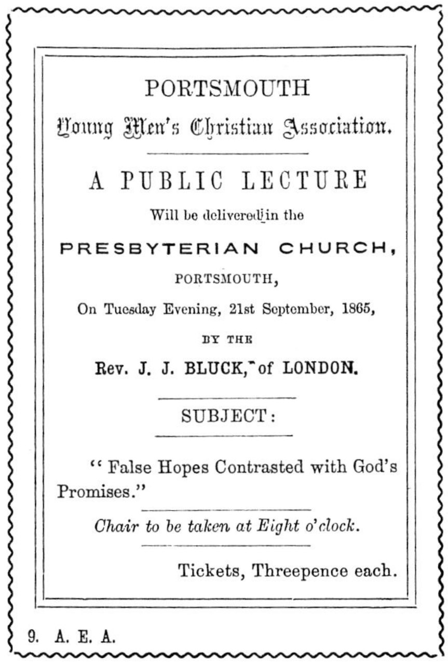

PORTSMOUTH
Young Men's Christian Association.

A PUBLIC LECTURE
Will be delivered in the
PRESBYTERIAN CHURCH,
PORTSMOUTH,
On Tuesday Evening, 21st September, 1865,
BY THE
Rev. J. J. BLUCK, of LONDON.

SUBJECT:

"False Hopes Contrasted with God's Promises."
Chair to be taken at Eight o'clock.

Tickets, Threepence each.

9. A. E. A.

C

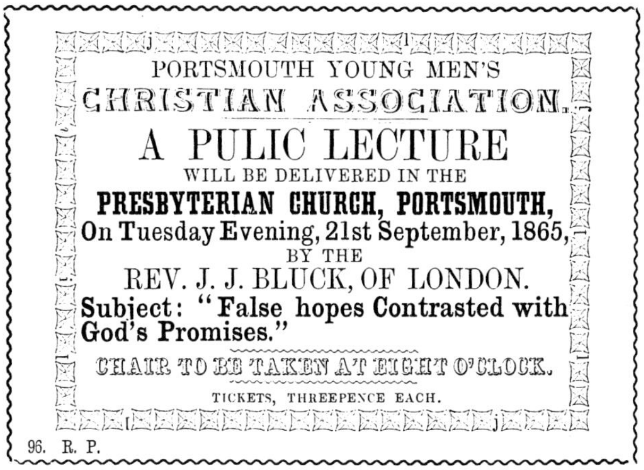

PORTSMOUTH YOUNG MEN'S
CHRISTIAN ASSOCIATION.
A PULIC LECTURE
WILL BE DELIVERED IN THE
PRESBYTERIAN CHURCH, PORTSMOUTH,
On Tuesday Evening, 21st September, 1865,
BY THE
REV. J. J. BLUCK, OF LONDON.
Subject: "False hopes Contrasted with God's Promises."
CHAIR TO BE TAKEN AT EIGHT O'CLOCK.
TICKETS, THREEPENCE EACH.

96. R. P.

D

96. Entries for J. & R. M. Wood's design competition, 1865. A,B,C are the first-, second- and third-prize winners respectively, as judged by a panel of forty-one master printers. It is interesting to note, however, that the first-prize winner attracted some criticism for *not* using decorative type in display work. Of all the entries, D was the most criticised, drawing the observation from one fellow contestant that its perpetrator deserved to be kicked for sending in so stupid a piece of work. (89%) *Typographic Advertiser, St Bride Printing Library.*

another 'CW' felt it raised the whole question of what good taste actually was:

If good taste means uniformity and consistency without embellishment, then you have it in the 1st Prize Card; but what if it be a consistent and agreeable contrast of various kinds of type, of uniformity in proportions, rendering it pleasing and captivating to the eye – 'a thing of beauty, and a joy for ever?' then your pattern card is no pattern. The taste of modern times is certainly of the latter character; and I protest against this card as a model for young printers, as by many it may be taken.[30]

Regrettably, there was no subsequent discussion.

5

Colour and special processes

In his *Mechanick Exercises*, 1683–4, Moxon informs his readers: 'Yea, any Colours that are used in Oyl-Painting [may] also be used to Print withal'.[1] Red was the colour most commonly used both then and later as it provided the richest contrast with black. Yet for many decades most printing was to be done in black only: on suitable jobs colour might be added by hand (102), but printing in colour remained uncommon until well into the nineteenth century.

In Britain the ten years up to the last government lottery in 1826 did see the production of lottery bills printed in up to three colours by firms such as Branston & Whiting and Gye & Balne, the latter (from 1829 continued by Balne alone) also printing colourful bills for London's Vauxhall Gardens,[2] while John Parry's watercolour of 1835 suggests that London fly-posting sites were bright with colour. But just as he exaggerated the scale of the posters, so also may Parry have overstated the contemporary use of colour, for writing in 1841 the printer Thomas Hansard regretted that jobbing printers were then making so *little* use of it.[3] Even so, the printing of *pictures* in colours was by this time well established (as will be discussed), and in his *Printer's Every-Day Book* published in that same year Thomas Houghton provided the trade with information on colour pigments and how to grind and mix them. Subsequent to this, entertainment bills printed in up to three colours began to appear, the British jobbing printer receiving further encouragement when ready-mixed colours became available from ink manufacturers a few years later. In America coloured inks were introduced *c.*1830 and again *c.*1840, but with scant success as they proved difficult to work. Further efforts from 1850, however, 'making colored inks upon scientific principles' were eventually fruitful, the resulting 'brilliant hues rapidly [finding] favor' with both printers and their customers.[4]

The first practical advice on the *use* of colour appears to have been given by Karl Burg in his letter of 1866 noticed in the last chapter. Burg observed that the two-colour

97. Chromolithographed promotional leaflet for the actors Mr & Mrs George S. Knight, by the Forbes Litho Co., Boston, 1880s. The portrait figures are a mixture of hand stippling and Ben Day tint wok. (69%)

98. Billheads in colour.
(Top) Single-colour copper engraving in use 1843, a period when stationery printed in colour was unusual.
(Below) Two-colour American design of the 1890s illustrated with what appears to be a cut down wood-engraving rather than a commercially produced stock cut. The same heading is also known printed in black only. (51%)

combination most commonly seen on letterpress posters at that time was red and blue, but this he felt to be a mistake owing to the colours blending into each other when seen from a distance: for a strong contrast red and black were preferable. With any three-colour combination, the third should be analogous to the lighter of the others and even lighter in tone; and if a border were introduced into a job it would be best printed in a neutral colour. Burg also noted that if a two-colour bill was set with alternating full and short lines (i.e. for better-class work) 'a pretty effect' could be achieved by printing the full lines in the darker, and the short lines in the lighter colour.[5]

Printers in Birmingham, Nottingham, Manchester and Leeds were to become noted for their colour posters, one writer in *Printing World* in 1891 claiming that they far outclassed the London men, who by that date appear to have been largely limited to the red-blue combination earlier criticised by Burg. The five- or six-sheet posters produced for the annual Birmingham Musical Festival were much admired. Speaking of Birmingham work, the same printer was to recall:

> I have not forgotten a pilgrimage I made in the year (I think) 1859, in company with a typographic enthusiast who has since made his mark in the United States. We walked twelve miles on a dusty country road for the purpose of seeing, and in our little way criticising, a coloured poster issued by a Birmingham firm for the dog show of that year. And well we were repaid. It was to us a feast indeed, and I have reason to believe that the effect of that poster on the mind, especially of my companion, will never be effaced.[6]

In this we have a further reminder that quality in design could be as important to the Victorian printer as to his counterpart today.

Guidance as to the most appropriate typefaces to employ in colour work was published in the *Modern Printer* in the 1880s. The journal advised that the best faces were those 'strong and decided in character' for those would withstand the lightening in tone consequent on printing in colour. 'Shaded' types were to be avoided. The surface of this class of letter was engraved over with fine lines, which produced a nicely contrasting grey when printed in black, but when printed in colour were too pale to be effective. Even more to be eschewed were extra-condensed letters, which when printed in black had 'character, grace and elegance', but in colour were 'almost useless'.[7] Not mentioned by the journal but certainly in use by this time was *chromatic* type, where each individual letter comprised two, sometimes three, separate pieces (103, 104), bringing rich colour contrasts into the letters themselves.

Printing a two-colour job usually entailed its going through the press twice. The most common method was to set the whole as one forme then transfer the colour lines to a second forme, careful spacing ensuring that the two settings would print in exact register (83, 93). An alternative was to make two stereotypes then cut away the unwanted matter from each. A method suited to short-run jobs on a hand press and which also enabled the job to be printed at a single pull, was to take out the colour lines, ink them and the material remaining in the forme in their respective colours, then replace. There was also *rainbow printing*, where either the colours were rolled out side by side on the ink slab then carefully transferred to the forme (or litho stone) with a hand roller, or the inks fed through

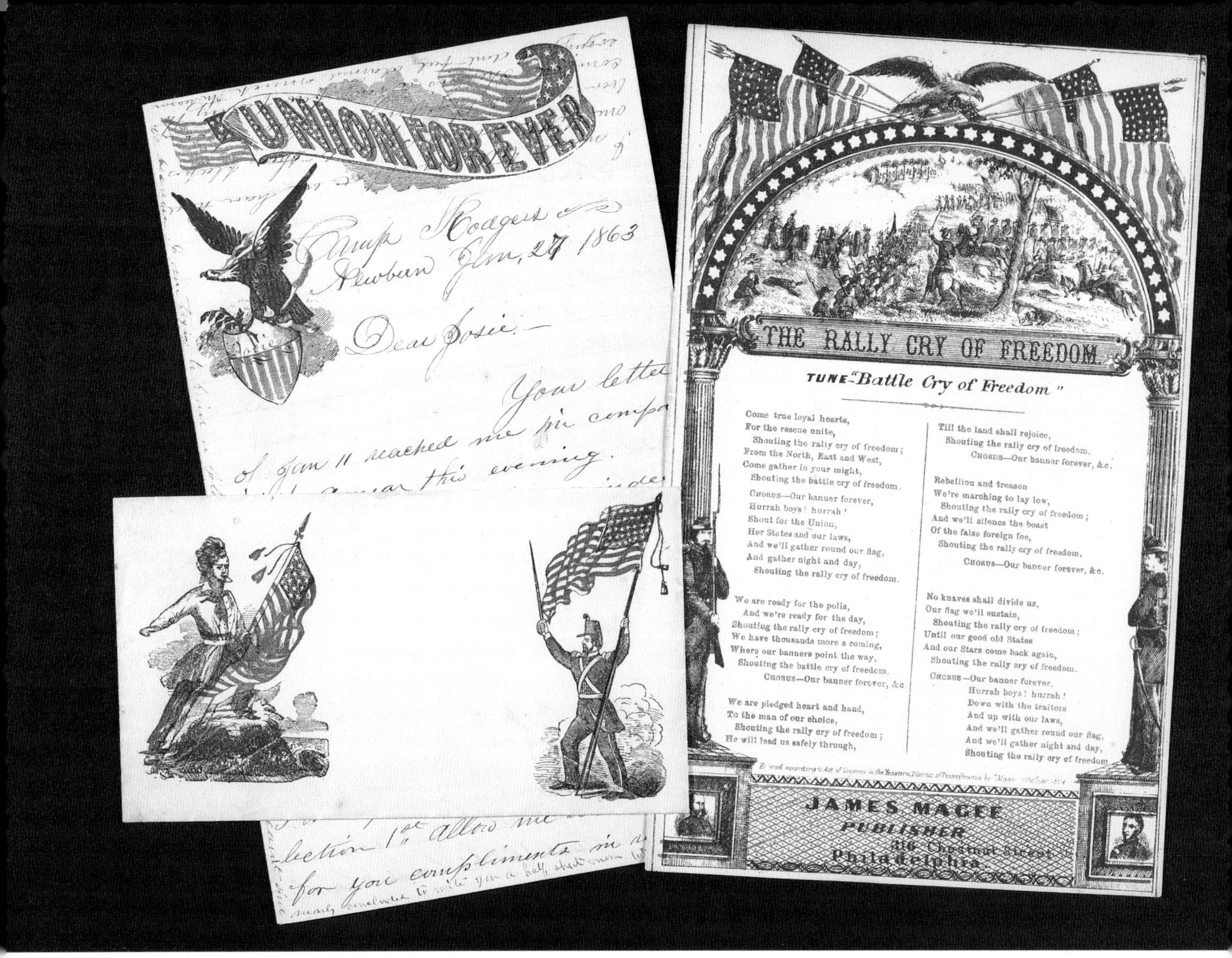

99. Two-colour printing. *(Right)* Song-printed front of folded sheet of Civil War writing paper lithographed by James Magee of Philadelphia, 1864. *(Left)* Writing-paper heading and an unused envelope, both printed from two-colour stock cuts. The dark tone of the eagle has been achieved by accurate overprinting but the images on the envelope are noticeably out of register. The writer of the letter was Henry Weeks, a private in the 43rd Infantry, writing from Newberne, NC, in January 1863. (68%)

a special ink duct on the machine. The printed effect was of each colour merging into the next (101).

Compound-plate printing was patented in 1820 by Sir William Congreve. Here the plate was actually two plates together, the surface of one having various shapes in relief which fitted through corresponding voids in the other to make a single printing surface. In printing (for which a special press was used), the plates were separately inked in contrasting colours then brought together for the impression, the resulting print exhibiting a pattern of interlocking colours. Invented for security work, and consequently often engraved with a *rose engine*, with which an almost limitless variety of patterns could be cut (57), the quality of the results also led to the process being applied to less exalted forms of printing, such as lottery bills and the labelling of blacking and other commodities (105). Compound-plate printing was not introduced in America.

In addition to the above, the Victorian printer's repertoire embraced a number of special processes, and these were more often employed on ephemera than on any other form of printing.

First demonstrated in 1817 and becoming familiar on ephemera in the 1830s, *medal engraving* was developed by inventors in America, Britain and France. Here the image was created with a ruling machine which had two points linked by a form of pantograph, one point moving back and forth over a low-relief original, the other drawing a corresponding wavy line on an etching plate, litho stone or similar surface. The result was a drawing in apparent relief. Developed for the reproduction of medals, the process was also used on billheads, showcards and other ephemera (119).

100. British valentines showing a variety of Victorian colour and other techniques. *(Top left)* Hand-coloured wood engraving *c.*1870, making fun of both the velocipede craze of the period and the rational dress for women advocated by Mrs Amelia Bloomer, here taken to its extreme. *(Centre)* Hand-colouring on crayon-drawn lithography: a more sophisticated comic valentine of approximately the same period. *(Right)* Hand-colouring on crayon-drawn lithography within a frame of embossed lace-paper work, 1850s: pushing up the tab raises the girl's skirts to reveal crinoline and ankles beneath. Bearing in mind the mores of the period, this valentine is more likely to have been sent by one young miss to another than by a gentleman to a lady. *(Below left)* Embossing with pink background tint plus chromo-lithographed scraps and gold lace-paper work. The front is hinged to lift away from the panel to create a three-dimensional effect. *(Centre)* With colour print 'The Hairdresser' by Baxter-licensee Joseph Mansell, set within a frame of embossed lace paper by Kershaw & Son, *c.*1850. *(Right)* Gold lace-paper work fringed with blue silk: the flower-basket scrap swings aside on its ribbon to reveal the verse beneath and the front of the card is designed to lift away from the background. (49%)

101. *(Left)* music cover *c.*1850. Title and illustration are wood-engravings overprinted on grey-into-brown rainbow printing, the yellow, red and blue being added by hand. Included in the background scene are Edinburgh Castle and the Scott Monument, the latter completed in 1844. (49%)

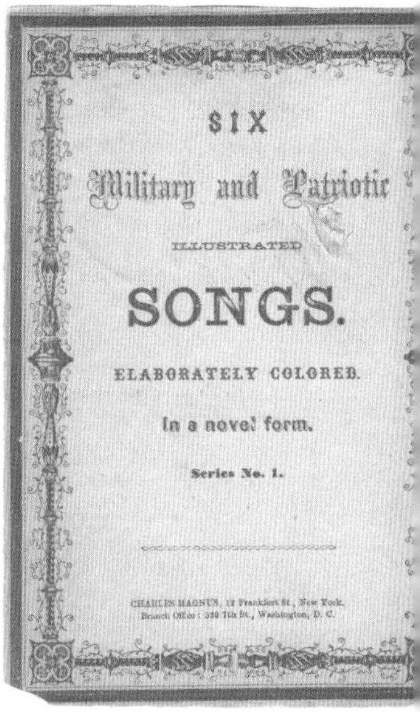

102. Cover and *(right)* set of Civil War songs lithographed by Charles Magnus of New York and hand coloured with seven different tints. The mixed styles of the illustrations indicate that the songs were originated as separate items (27%, 47%)

Embossing, in which paper or card is stamped between male and female dies to create a design in relievo, was patented by John G. Hancock in 1796. For work in light relief the female die would be cut in steel by hand, but the quality and depth of modelling required on much Victorian embossing was such that the form had first to be modelled in plaster and the female die then cast from this in brass.[8] In both cases, the male die was moulded from the female in gutta-percha, plaster or other substance. Leaders in the field were Dobbs & Co. of London and Dickinson & Co. of Boston (44), the latter initially importing their dies from Dobbs then subsequently making their own. Often employed with embossing was *lace-paper* work, invented by Dobbs employee Joseph Addenbrooke in 1834, where the dies were made to fracture and virtually detach the paper, which with a little hand finishing transformed into a decorative filigree (100). In *blocking* only a single die was used, this being chiefly employed on book bindings either 'blind' or printed with inks and/or metal foil, but occasionally also on trade cards (108). *Gold printing* (108) was usually achieved by printing in a yellowish colour then dabbing fine bronze powder over while the ink was still tacky. Alternatively, actual or imitation gold leaf could be used.

In the field of illustration, means were sought of bypassing the wood-engraver and giving the artist direct control of the finished image, for as a lecturer addressing the Royal Society explained, 'the cleverest engraver, with the utmost exercise of his skill' could at best produce only an approximation to the original, too often 'losing entirely

the points which the artist has laboured most successfully to reproduce'.[9] One ingenious alternative was Edward Palmer's *glyphography* patented in 1842, in which a metal plate was coated with a layer of wax through which the design was engraved, this intaglio then being used to make a relief-printing electrotype. Equally inventive was *graphotype,* introduced by the New York wood-engraver De Witt Clinton Hitchcock in 1865. Here the drawing was made on a block of highly compressed French chalk using an ink that hardened the chalk immediately beneath it, the unaffected chalk then being brushed away to leave the lines of the drawing in relief, from which a stereotype was made.[10] Both processes had initial success but ultimately their effect on the engraving trade was negligible.

What did affect wood-engraving was the discovery that the surface of the wood-block could be treated with light-sensitive chemicals and the artist's drawing printed on to it photographically for the engraver's guidance. This process came into use in the 1860s, though so habituated had artists become to drawing *on* the wood that for some years many continued to do so, their drawings then being photographed and printed on to further blocks, which were the ones actually cut. The more rational process of drawing on paper superseded this odd procedure during the 1870s, and this also enabled an artist to work at any convenient scale, the drawing being photographically reduced or enlarged when printed on the block.

In 1835 George Baxter patented a method of printing pictures in colour, in which a detailed intaglio or lithographed image was printed in a neutral tone then over-printed in transparent inks from a series of wood-blocks. The result was an image of great subtlety, but one calling for the careful engraving of between eight and a dozen blocks (and occasionally many more). Being relatively expensive, the process was chiefly used for collectable prints and high-quality book illustrations, but Baxter did produce some more ephemeral work including pictures in ladies' pocket books, music covers (107) and pictorial

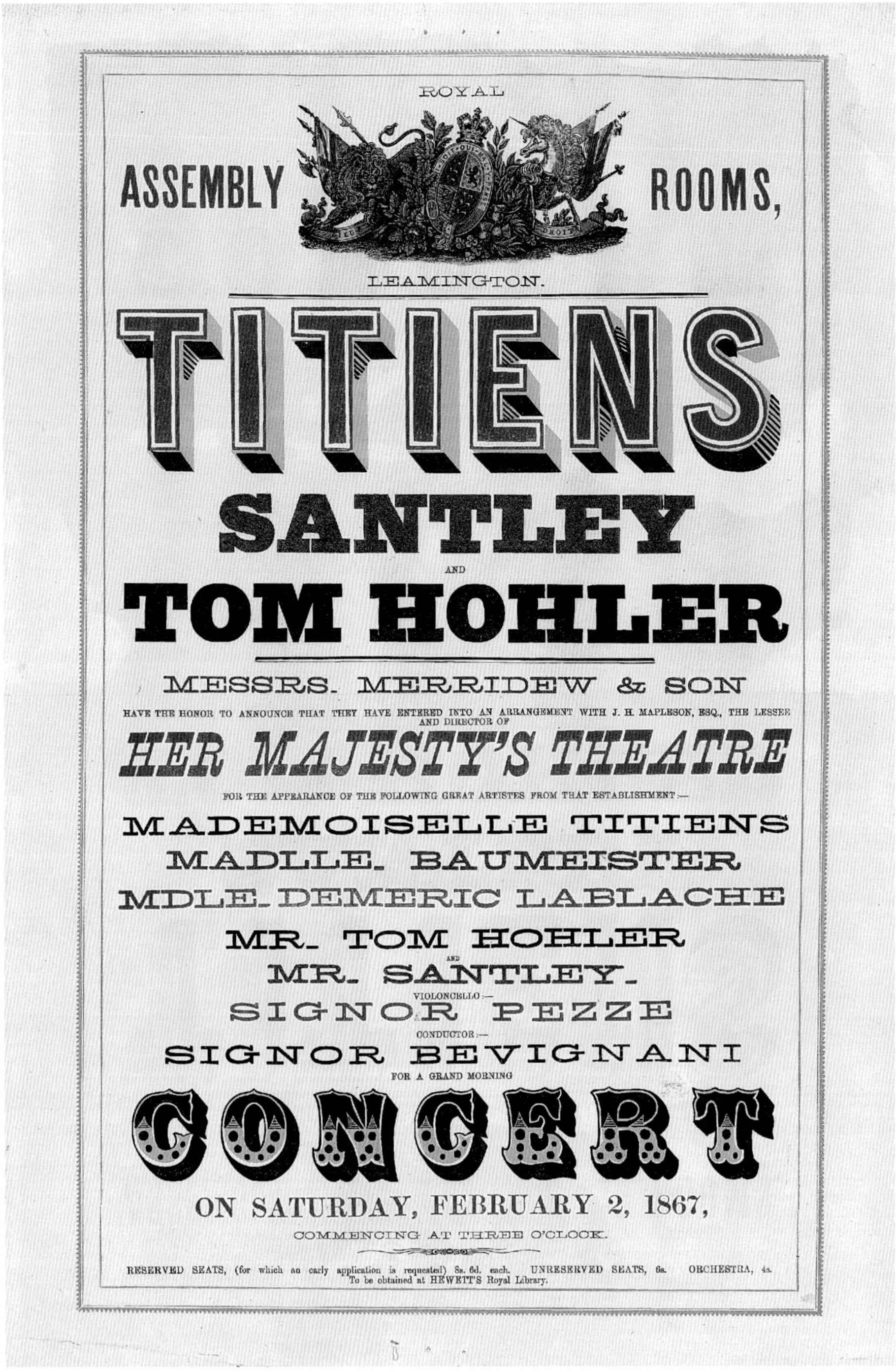

103. Chromatic type. Concert bill, Leamington, England, 1867 printed in five colours. 'Titiens' and 'Concert' are printed in three and two colours respectively. The finely engraved royal arms is a stock cut printed in yellow, red and blue with the green achieved by overprinting. (36%)

needle-box labels. From 1849 Baxter issued licences to other printers (100), but there is no evidence for the process being used in America.

Chromoxylography – colour printing by wood-engraving alone – was developed in the second half of the century. Baxter's patent protected only his intaglio-printed base image, and an unsuccessful challenge to the patent by one of his ex-apprentices prompted the realisation that effective work could be achieved without it. The image would first be cut in outline (for subsequent printing in black or dark brown) and proofs of this transferred while wet on to the respective blocks to serve as guides to their engraving. By varying the treatment, e.g. cutting with fine or broad parallel lines, cross-hatching or leaving solid, a variety of further colours could be achieved in the overprinting.

These developments in letterpress colour printing were paralleled in lithography. In the *tinted* style, introduced into England from Germany early in the century, a black-printed drawing was enhanced with a second printing in fawn, with the white of the paper utilised to create highlights. In the 1830s a third working in pale blue was often added, and from this it was a natural progression to printing in several colours or *chromolithography*. This was developed both on the Continent by Godefroy Engelmann

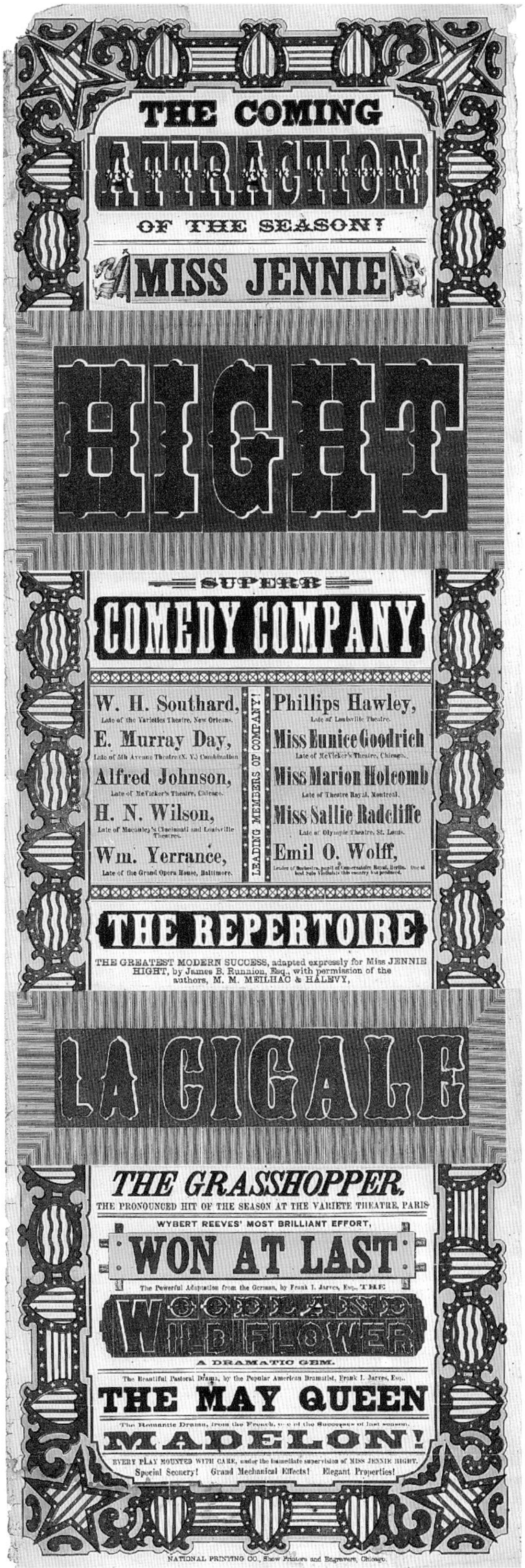

104. Show printing in colour. *(Left)* Menagerie bill in nine colours by Crabbe of Plymouth, with colour panels backing the black-printed type and cuts. A blank space is left below the main display line for insertion of date and venue. *(Right)* Show bill by National Printing Co., Chicago, printed in red, yellow and blue with the fourth colour, violet, achieved by overprinting. The main display lines and the stars-and-stripes border are set in chromatic characters. *Menagerie bill courtesy Heather Walker.* (20%)

105. *(Above)* Compound-plate printing: labels printed in three colours and two. With its rose-engine patterning, the blacking label seeks to achieve the authority of security printing, the central panel also showing how the compound plate enabled patterning to continue from one colour into another. *Centre for Ephemera Studies, University of Reading.* (90%)

106. *(Below)* Chromoxylography. Window bill *c.*1840, each of the three colours representing a separately engraved wood block. The creasing down the centre results from the original shopkeeper having used the card for the cover of a homemade account book. (59%)

107. Baxter printing, detail from music cover 'Paul and Virginia' printed from one steel intaglio plate and twelve colour blocks, 1850. Illustrating the adventures of the eponymous pair on their desert island, the print is flush mounted on to the cover and set within a wood-engraved frame printed in gold. (68%)

108. *(Top to bottom right)* Gold printing with embossing on friendship cards of the 1860s (writing on the back of the left-hand card suggesting that it was sent by a girl to her soldier brother during the American Civil War). (61%, 52%) Gold-printed needle packet, *c.*1870, featuring Eugenie, wife of Emperor Napoleon III. (59%) Gold-blocked trade card, late nineteenth century, the costumed figure indicating that decorator Thomson was an adherent of the Aesthetic movement. (62%)

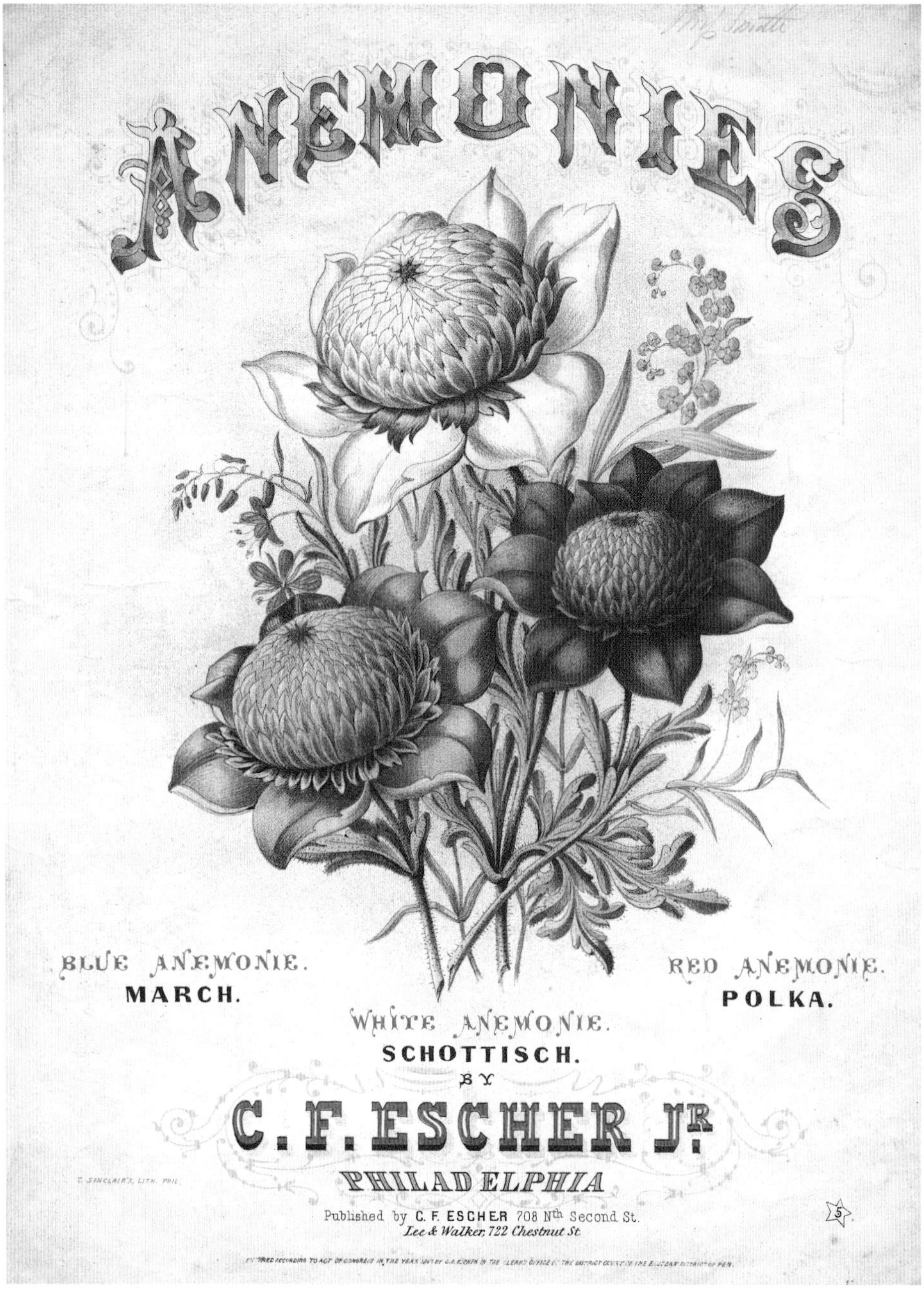

109. Music cover, 1867, chromolithograph in five colours by Thomas Sinclair of Philadelphia. The inventive three-dimensional lettering is typically American. The Scots-born Sinclair was a pioneer of American chromolithography, starting his Philadelphia business in 1838. (48%) *Michael Twyman.*

and in Britain by Charles Hullmandel and introduced in America by the English immigrant William Sharp in 1840.

Chromoxylography and chromolithography were rival processes, and it was lithography that was to prevail, for engraving in wood was manually more demanding and took longer than the equivalent work on stone. Chromoxlography was to find its greatest application in book illustration (memorably in Edmund Evans's reproductions of Randolph Caldecott's and Kate Greenaway's illustrations) but it was also employed in the printing of trade cards, showcards, and other ephemera (106, 111). In Vienna from 1868 the wood-engraver Heinrich Knöfler and his sons produced chromoxlographs of great quality printed from as many as thirteen blocks; but these were essentially fine-art prints sold individually and had no application in commercial printing.[11]

The simpler form of chromolithography is typified in the music cover, which was often in essence a black line and/or crayon drawing *enhanced* with colour, i.e. if the colour were taken away the image would still 'make sense' (109, 169). This was also one of the few areas of Victorian colour printing where the artist who originated a design could work on the stone himself, though in most cases all but the black stone was probably left to assistants. Usually no more than four or five colours were used, with their effect extended both by overprinting and by varying the crayon work, lighter or heavier crayoning producing lighter or more intense tones. Occasionally, touches of colour, a plume or a scarf for instance, would be put in by hand.

110. Chromolithography on Liebig cards (four of a set of six). *(Top left to bottom right)* Designer working in watercolours. Lithographic artists preparing the individual colour stones. Proofing the stones on hand presses. Machine printing, the girl sliding a partly-printed sheet into the cylinder grippers during the moment the cylinder is briefly halted. Note here also the large machine stone on to which some dozens of images have been transferred. Published in 1906, this set of cards was printed in twelve colours, the portrait of Baron Liebig demonstrating successive stages in the overprinting. (87%)

Music-cover artists were usually artists in others spheres also. In America, Benjamin Champney was an exponent of the Hudson River School of painting and a president of the Boston Art Club, while Lewis T. Voight drew fashion plates for *Godey's Lady's Book*.[12] In Britain, Alfred Concanen designed both music covers and theatre posters, while the ballet prints of John Brandard were admired by the painter Degas.

The great period of Victorian chromolithography commenced in the 1870s when the technology of colour printing was well established and cylinder-printing machines began to be widely adopted (110). At its most sophisticated, the process was capable of commercial work equalling that of a Baxter or Knöfler print; but this form of chromolithography was significantly different from that employed in the production of music covers.

The first step was for the foreman in charge of a team of chromolithographic artists to analyse the colour content of the design. With greetings cards and other

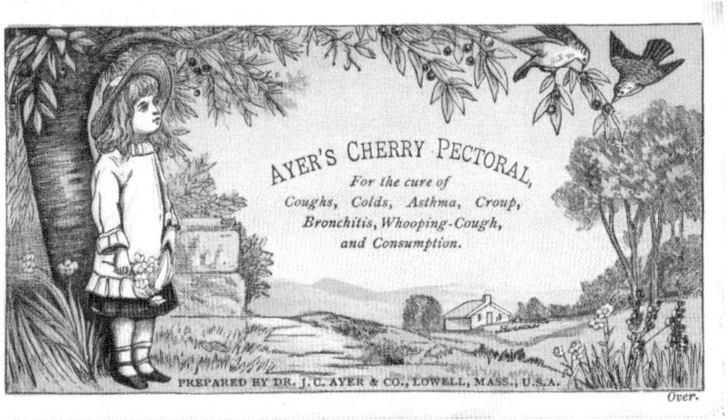

111. Chromoxylography. American advertising trade card, *c.*1880, printed in eight colours. Printing in colour from wood-engraved blocks was relatively uncommon in America. (91%)

112. Cigar-box labels by Schumacher & Ettlinger, New York, 1893, showing chromolithography of the highest quality. The 'blank flap' design is printed in black and grey enriched with gold embossing, but the number of colours used on the other designs is impossible to determine. Inset: detail of stippling on Miss Daisy's lips and cheek. (61%; inset 350%)

ephemera he would work directly from designer's original, but where fine art was to be reproduced – as for example Millais's Royal Academy picture 'Bubbles', reproduced in 1887 as a poster for Pears' Soap – a studio copy had to be made (in the case of 'Bubbles', with the addition of lettering and a bar of soap). As well as keeping the original safe from the hazards of the print works, this facilitated the image being scaled to reproduction size. From this, an intricate 'keyline' drawing was traced indicating the boundaries between each discernibly different colour area, defining with equal clarity, for example, the line between a girl's lips and teeth and the softer boundary where cream turned to pink on her cheek. This keyline was transferred as a non-printing image on to each of the stones required.

Each stone was the responsibility of an individual chromolithographic artist, his job being to ink-stipple all parts of the keyline that were to print in his designated colour. Writing in 1905, the Belfast printer S. Leighton took as his example a man responsible for a yellow-printing stone, who would appropriately stipple every part of the image that included even a trace of yellow – the greens, the oranges, yellow browns, buffs and other hues – Leighton observing, 'and in doing so he has to imagine the effect that the yellow he puts on the stone will have when the other ten or twelve colours are printed on top of it'. Clearly a very demanding task, and made the more difficult by most jobs being printed in not one but *two* yellows – one cold, the other warm – *two* blues, *two* reds, etc. The stippling technique was necessary because the polished surface of the stones required for machine printing was unsuitable for crayon work. It was a tedious process, though much alleviated in the 1880s with the introduction of *Ben Day tints* – gelatine sheets with a variety of stipple and other textures in relief, which could be inked and rubbed down on to the stone. With this form of chromolithography no single stone contained the image, which instead gradually

113. Twentieth-century chromolithography. Cigar-box label by the American Lithographic Co., New York, commemorating the first transatlantic flight between New York and Paris, flown by Charles Lindbergh, 20–21 May, 1927. The colours are entirely worked in Ben Day tints. (54%)

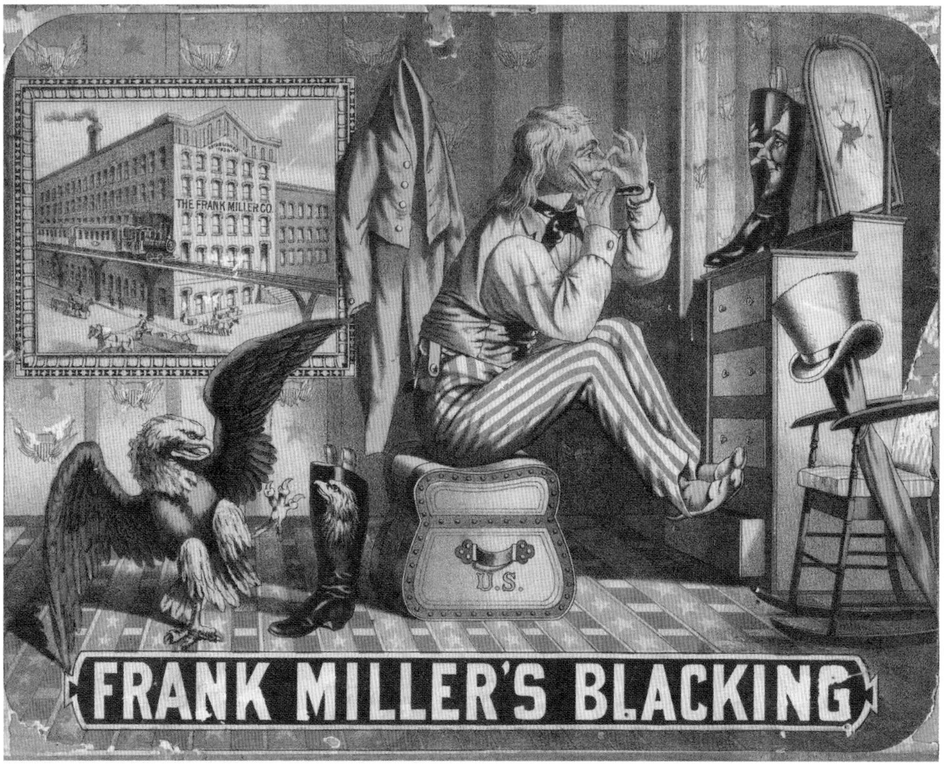

114. American blacking-box label, a chromolithograph printed in either five or six colours from crayon- and ink-drawn stones. The theme of a polish so high that one could see one's reflection in it was used on blacking advertising on both sides of the Atlantic. (51%)

built up as the successive colours were printed, each subtly adding to and modifying what had gone before. As many as sixteen colours might be needed even for commercial work.[13] Louis Prang is known to have published Christmas cards printed in as many as twenty colours, and for fine-art reproductions the number could be considerably more.

Prang's chromolithographic artists were among the best, though not always beyond the criticism of the designers whose work they reproduced. Having seen a print of the Christmas card he had designed, Will Low wrote in 1885, 'I am afraid that my design will be anything but popular ... the head of the Virgin is almost missed. The eyes are too big, too staring and too blue [also] the border around the design strikes me unfavourably in color.' The Canadian artist Henry Sandham evidently had a good working relationship with Prang, writing that same year regarding two designs returned for amendment 'I have been hard at work all day sharpening and defining the drawing in these two pictures till I think I have got it so that your artists will clearly see what is meant and be able to reproduce it'.[14]

The separation between the activities of the artist who designed and the artists who reproduced was not always clear cut. Apropos the latter, Leighton observed, 'The best men are those who can draw well, who have studied painting in water-colours or oils and who have a well-balanced

115. American chromolithography, *c.*1870s–90s. The top items are novelty calling cards – a form of social exchange unknown in Britain. The left-hand one is a printer's sample and the others are of the 'hidden-name' variety, the givers' names being concealed beneath the lightly attached scraps. The example in the centre is an unused stock design. Bottom-right is a reward-of-merit card, inscribed by teacher Laura J. Smith to pupil Bennie Sanborn. The remaining items are advertising trade cards, the example at bottom-left being a printer's sample stock card printed in two colours, the white tablecloth providing space for overprinting. (67%)

116. British chromolithography – insets from popular magazines of the 1890s. Inserted at the binding stage, these were the only practical means of introducing full-colour advertising into periodicals, which at that time were predominantly printed in black and white. Bottom left and centre are designs by leading illustrators of the day Tom Browne and Lawson Wood, and it is likely that in both these cases the artists' original line drawings were transferred on to the stone (or possibly zinc) printing surfaces photographically, the colour stones then being prepared by chromolithographic artists. The work on the other insets is entirely that of the latter, the original designers remaining unknown. (57%)

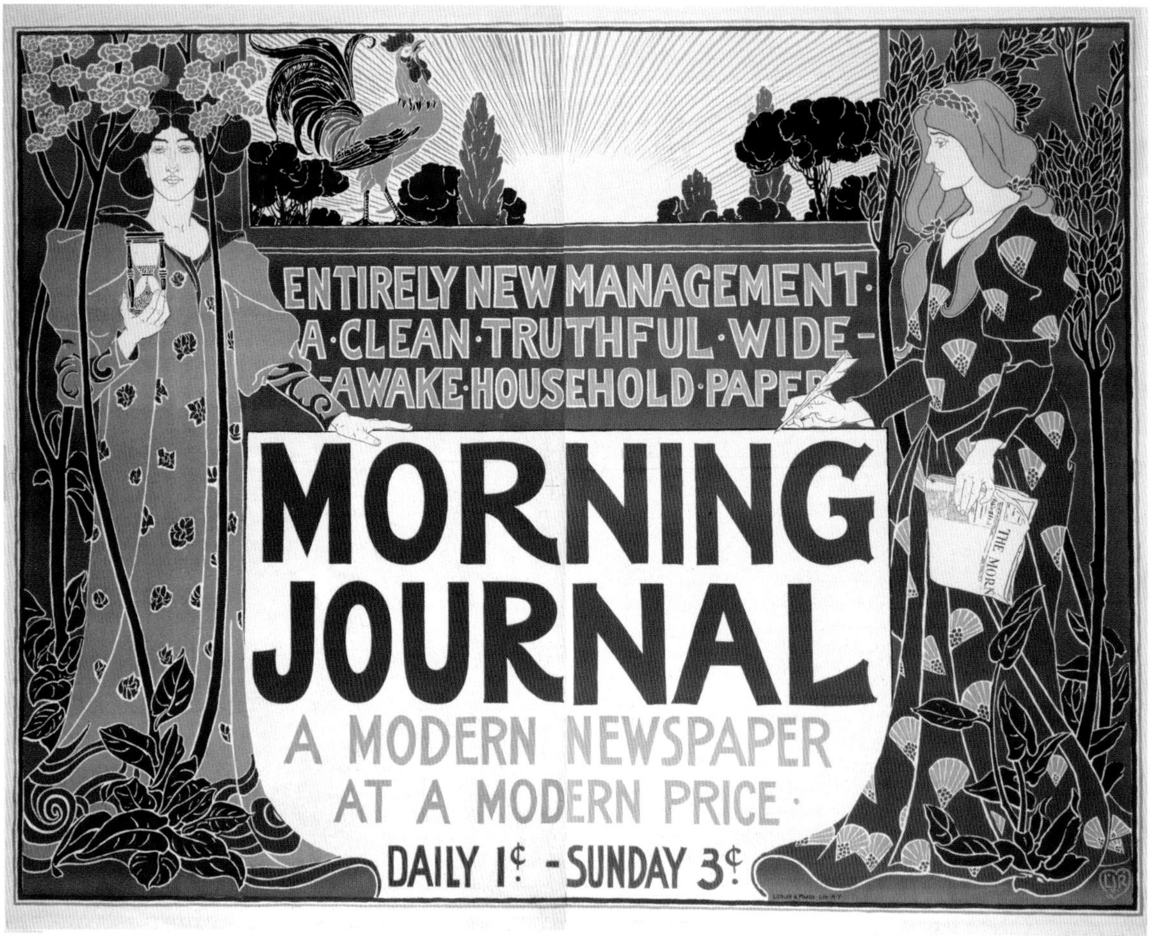

117. Contrasts in poster design. *(Top)* Art poster by Louis Rhead, printed in four colours by Liebler & Maas, New York, 1895, showing maidens apparelled in the loose-fitting aesthetic dress adopted in artistic circles. *Metropolitan Museum of Art, New York.* (13%) *(Below)* Theatrical stock poster by David Allen & Sons, Belfast, 1895, designed in the 'full stage, crammed, jammed full of figures' mode. At least four separate incidents of the play are presented in this one picture. (17%)

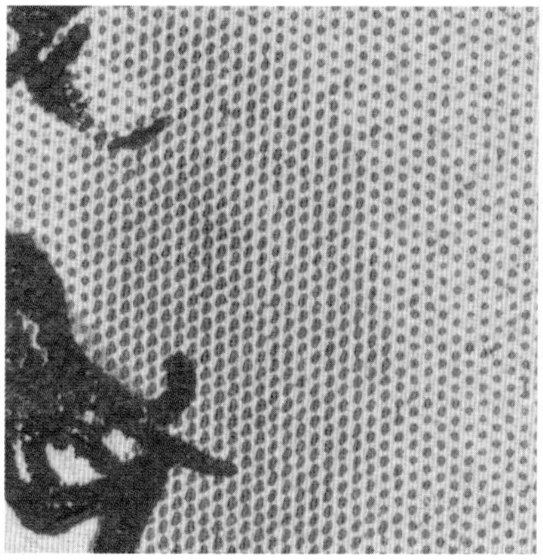

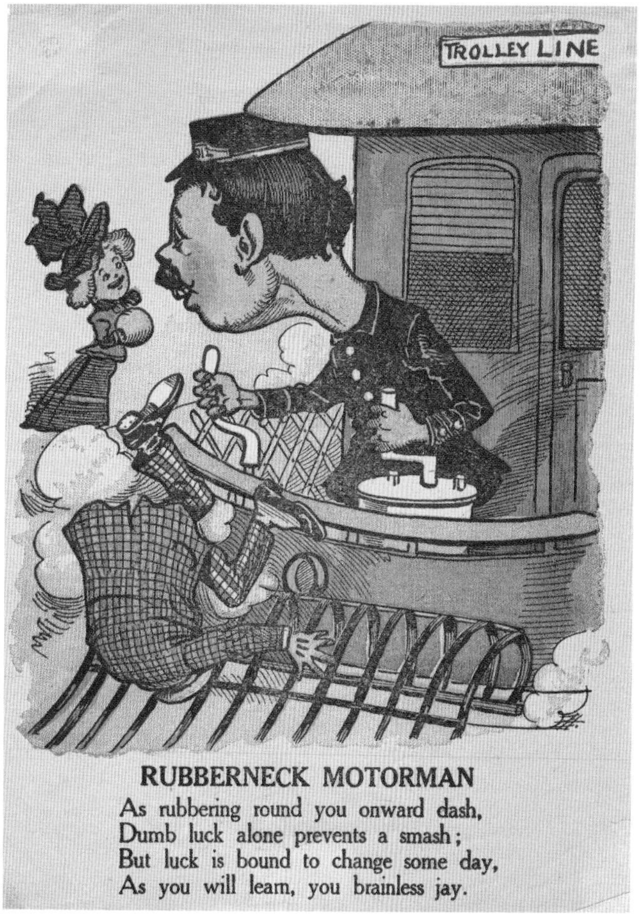
TROLLEY LINE
RUBBERNECK MOTORMAN
As rubbering round you onward dash,
Dumb luck alone prevents a smash;
But luck is bound to change some day,
As you will learn, you brainless jay.

118. American comic valentine, chromolithographed in yellow, red, blue and black, *c.*1900. The colour tones are achieved entirely with Ben Day tints, the detail above showing how the blush on the motorman's cheek has been achieved by the artist applying increased pressure to the tint to increase the size of the dots. (51%, detail 350%)

eye for form and colour generally';[15] which was equally the case for any artist. Sir Alfred Munnings, President of the Royal Academy 1944–59, began his career as a junior chromolithographic artist at Page Bros. of Norwich, where his talent took him from artist's bench to designer's studio, thence into a career in fine art.[16]

Chromolithography also enabled the letterpress jobbing printer to introduce colour inexpensively into his posters, menus and other ephemera, lithographic firms supplying stock designs for cattle and poultry shows, football, cycling and other sporting events, as well as colourfully bordered sheets and cards of general application.

A form of ephemera particularly associated with American chromolithography is the advertising trade card, 'advertising' distinguishing this form of ephemera from the tradesman's card of the eighteenth and early-nineteenth centuries. The one developed from the other, but as will be seen by comparing the illustrations (16, 17, 115), the younger form was clearly different from its ancestor. Produced in their tens of thousands to be inserted by storekeepers among the grocery orders or in the wrappings of hardware goods, etc. or simply left on the shop counter to be picked up, these colourful ephemera were avidly collected from the 1870s until the end of the century. Trade cards were already circulating on the Continent when Louis Prang visited the Vienna International Exhibition in 1873, and it may have been through his seeing such cards there that prompted Prang to begin producing them himself. Prang did distribute his firm's own florally decorated cards at the exhibition but these appear to have been essentially business cards. Among the more celebrated of the European card-issuers was the meat-extract company LEMCO, whose first sets of Liebig cards (110) were published in France in 1872. Advertising cards were produced in Britain also, though to a lesser extent than on the Continent or in America.

In the 1890s chromolithography also took colour into magazine advertising. The rise of mass-circulation periodicals brought advertising into every home, but sans colour, for magazines were printed by letterpress and thus largely in black and white. The answer was the separately-printed *inset* collated with the magazine at the binding stage (116, 122). With their colourful imagery and brief advertising messages these were virtually posters in miniature. Insets were also printed by letterpress, in black only or occasionally in two colours or on coloured paper. The use of insets as an advertising medium was more limited in America than in Britain.

International exhibitions and improving communications brought exchange of business between Europe and America. In 1884 the *Printers' Register* commented on some huge chromolithographic posters advertising *In the Ranks* then running at the Adelphi Theatre, 'drawn and printed with a style and finish far above the level of ordinary pictures from the hoardings'. Displayed in London's West End, these posters were printed in Cincinnati.[17] In 1876 Heber Mardon visited the Philadelphia Centennial, taking with him a set of designs his firm had used on a range of tradesmen's calendars; he sold them on to Bufford Bros.

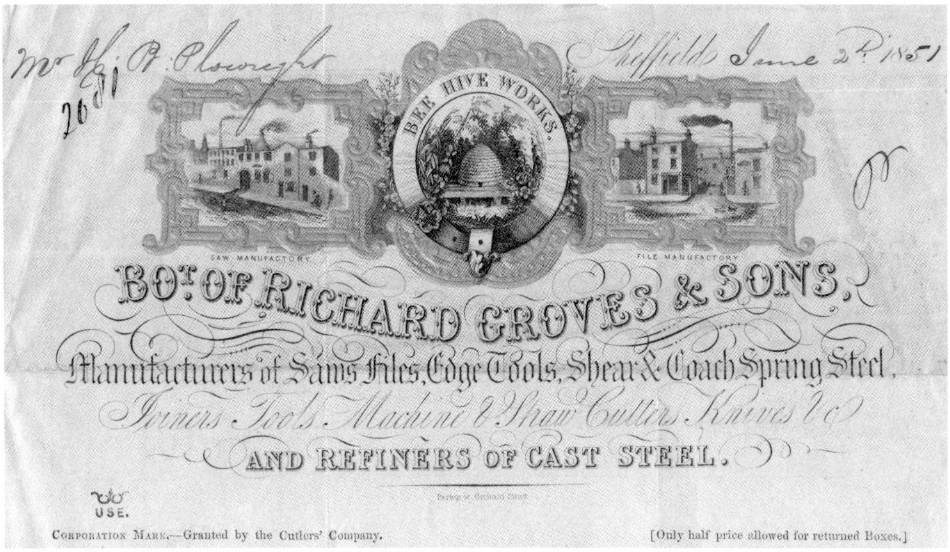

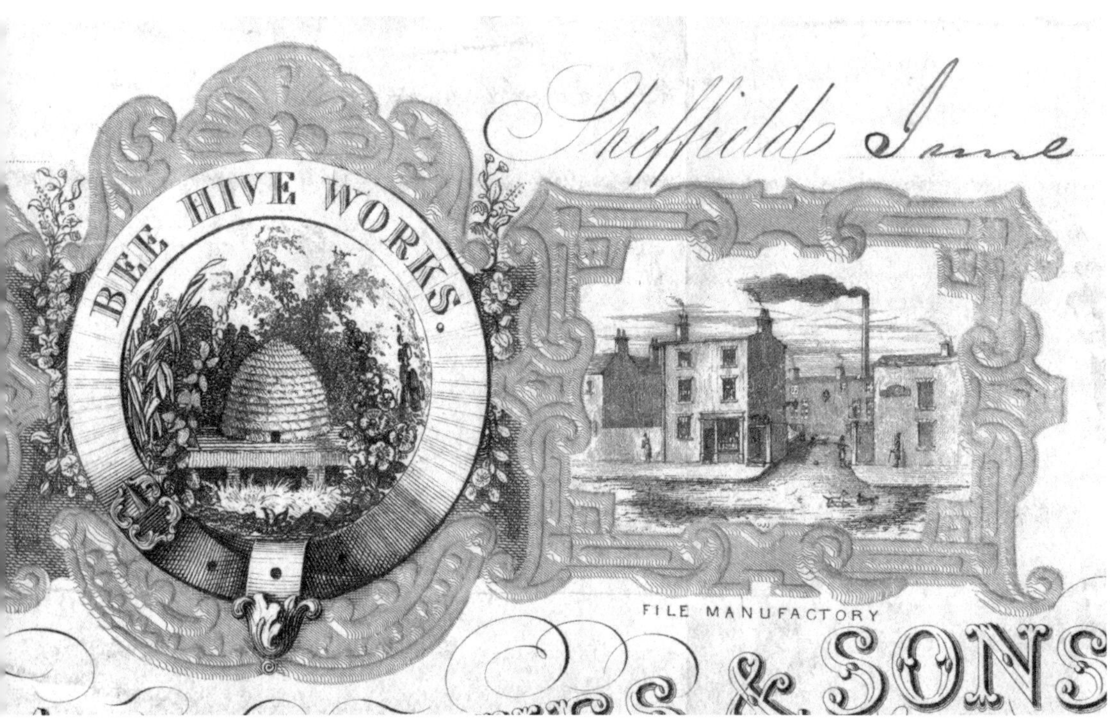

119. Copper-engraved billhead by Parkin of Sheffield, in use 1851, its beehive motif emblematic of industry. The frame to the vignette, here shown in enlargement, is an example of medal engraving. At this period it was not yet usual to glamorise a building on business stationery, and here the premises look virtually Dickensian. (62%, detail 162%)

120. Fabric labels embossed in silver foil. The beaver and bald-eagle motifs show that these designs were for the labelling of British cotton fabrics exported to America. Spaces are provided on the circular frame around the eagle and the arc beneath the beaver for noting stock number and length. (73%)

121. Monochrome lithographic music cover by G. & W. Endicott, 1847. The vignette of the river steamer *Baltic* is drawn in crayon while the lettering is pen-drawn. A pioneer of American lithography, George Endicott opened his shop in New York in 1828. (48%)

of Boston; subsequent to this he commissioned designs for corset-box labels from an artist in Paris, the designs proving of such quality that his firm had to take on a better class of chromolithographic artist for their reproduction.[18]

Through its production of large colourful posters, chromolithography brought a new visual interest to the urban scene. In 1884 the *Art Age* remarked how 'Every … lithographer who sends out well drawn, well colored, well composed … posters to adorn the streets of a large American city is materially assisting in the art education of a Nation'.[19] In this the journal was reflecting ideas stemming from the current Aesthetic movement, which sought to make appreciation of art a part of everyday life; but it is unlikely that many of the posters then to be seen in New York or London would have found favour with the art cognoscenti as, designed for the most part in the lithographic firms' own studios, their pictorial treatment was directed more towards literal representation than expression of artistic values.

Then in Paris in 1891 Toulouse-Lautrec's first poster appeared, and with it was initiated the decade of the 'Art' poster. Prominent among a new wave of young designers were Edward Penfield, Will Bradley and Louis Rhead in America (117), and in Britain, Dudley Hardy, John Hassall and the Beggarstaffs, all of whose work was characterised by a new awareness of design and draughtsmanship. In his preface to *Les Maîtres de l'affiche* in 1896, the art critic Roger Marx wrote 'Advertising has called upon art for help … and its beautiful appearance has bestowed upon it, with unexpected efficiency, the indefeasible right to the

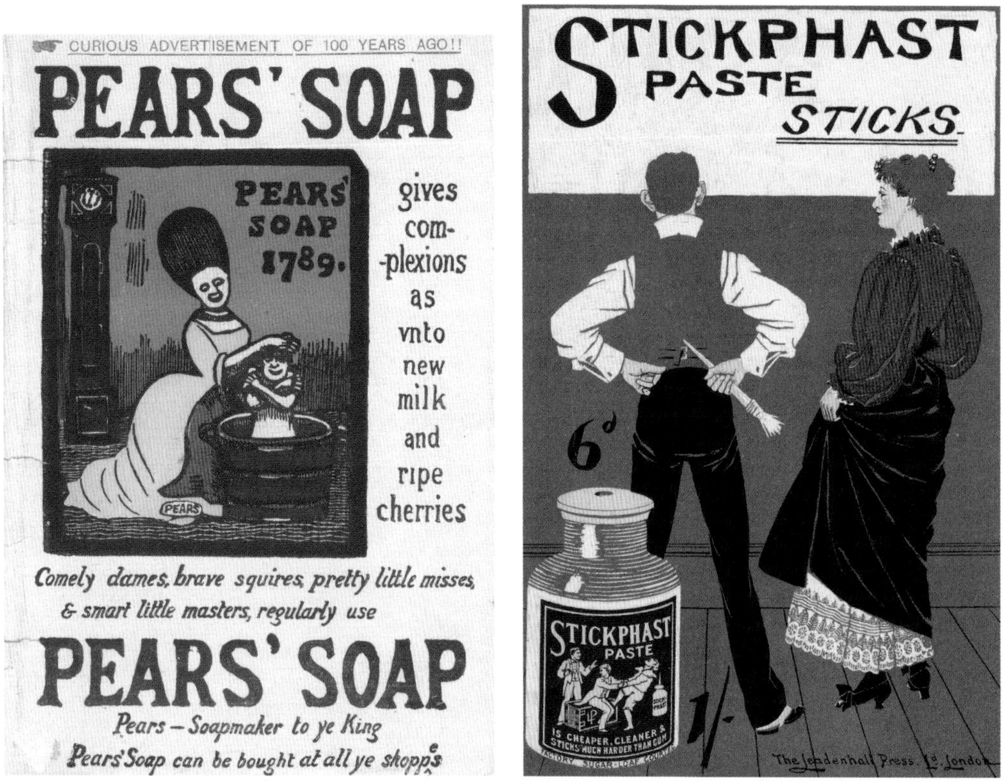

122. Contrast in 1890s magazine insets. *(Left)* Chromoxylograph in the antique style by the Newcastle wood engraver Joseph Crawhall, printed by Andrew Tuer at the Leadenhall Press. *(Right)* Showing the influence of contemporary French and American poster art, designed by the cartoonist Phil May and reproduced by chromolithography. Insets were a more popular form of advertising in England than America. (44%)

esthetes' attention';[20] and in 1898 the British journal *The Poster* wrote, 'In the future we hope that London will be one vast national picture gallery, open day and night, free to all ... to observe the passing glory of the work of great artists.'[21] It became common now for an aspiring artist to produce speculative posters – aesthetically pleasing imagery without wording, the latter to be added when and if an advertiser had been found to buy the design. Thus the Art poster was seen by its practitioners primarily *as* an art form, with the needs of the advertiser met simply through the name of his product being associated *with* Art – an attitude little removed from the 'art for art's sake' attitude of the thoroughgoing aesthete.

But artistic or not, the posters of the 1890s still had to be drawn on stone or zinc by teams of wage-earning chromolithographic artists. Designer artists would on occasions complain of the lithographers' ineptitude, but so skilled were the better class of chromolithographic artists that they could capture not only the qualities inherent in the original but virtually the designer's very brush strokes. Those designers who drew on the stone themselves were few, but among them were Jules Chéret, himself a lithographer, and Toulouse-Lautrec, to whom the milieu of a chromolithographic works was initially unfamiliar: working there in 1891, Lautrec wrote to his mother, 'I had a feeling of authority over the whole studio.'[22]

Much poster design, however, remained less than artistic. The Belfast firm of David Allen & Sons published a large range of stock theatrical posters and kept a foot in both camps, offering both artistic designs and others of the type elsewhere described as 'blood-stained meloramatic [...] full stage, crammed, jammed full of figures' (117).[23] One major firm advertised that it would 'buy and pay for at once rough designs conveying a good idea ... under various tradesman-like heads, such as watches, perambulators, corsets, and so on.' Even sketched on cardboard by an amateur, a suitable idea could be worked up by the firm's own artists, rewarding its originator with 7*s.* 6*d.* (at this time equivalent to $1.83)[24] per notion.[25]

In England, America and elsewhere Art posters were for a while avidly collected, but the craze faded as the century ended. So too did their commissioning, manufacturers becoming less inclined to pay for designs that were more Art than they were advertising. The new awareness of design that these posters brought into the world of commerce was, however, to continue into the twentieth century, albeit with more attention now paid to the needs of the advertiser.

6

Artistic printing

THE PROBLEM for the letterpress printer of the 1860s was that there were too many fancy types. Pleasing results might be achieved where text was limited and only one or two lines required emphasis, but where copy was extensive and a variety of topics vied for attention the outcome could be a jumble. Recognising this, in the second edition of his *Printer's Manual*, 1864, Thomas Lynch of Cincinnati promised a supplementary publication showing specimen settings of title-pages, cards and other job work.[1] The book was never published, but it was probably Lynch's unfulfilled promise that prompted another Cincinnatian, Oscar Harpel, to bring out his own design manual, *The Typograph or Book of Specimens*, in 1870.

The International Exhibition held in London in 1862 had demonstrated a new-found confidence in British design, with the artistic design of furniture, ornament and other aspects of domestic life becoming a topic of everyday middle-class conversation in the 1870s. In post-Civil War America also, influenced by the writings of John Ruskin and growing familiarity with developments across the Atlantic, there was similar quickening of aesthetic awareness. Thus began the Art or Aesthetic movement, in which milieu Harpel's *Typograph* played its part, Harpel acknowledging in his preface the now 'cultivated tastes' of the printer's clientele.[2]

The *Typograph* was the first printers' manual to devote itself wholly to matters of typographic design, with specimen settings a major feature. These included several in up to five colours, some of which were credited to their individual designer-compositors. But Harpel's chief purpose was to demonstrate how the printer could achieve quality in more everyday work, thus the majority of his specimens are invitations, labels, flyers and other ephemera printed in black or a single colour (124).

123. Billhead of Brunt & Fisher, San Francisco, printed in gold and seven colours with the dark green produced by overprinting blue on yellow. Discussed in the *American Art Printer*, 1.5 (1887), the editor remarked that further economy in working could have been achieved had the dark blue also been used for printing the lighter-blue areas, with the strength of the impression reduced by engraving the tint block with fine lines. (88%)

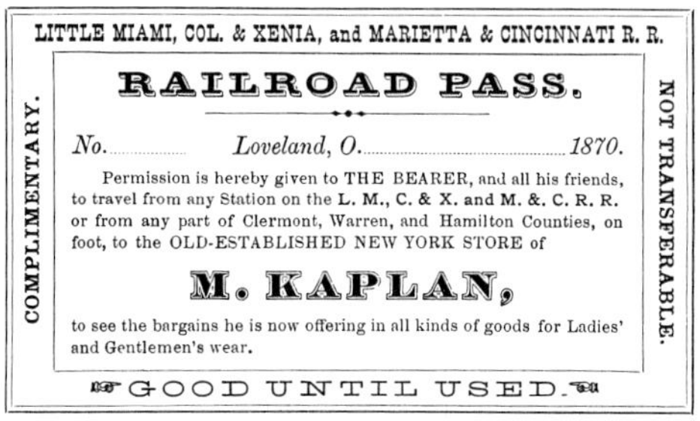

124. Trade card, labels and 'rail road pass' advertising novelty shown in Oscar Harpel's *The Typograph or Book of Specimens*, 1870. With items such as these Harpel demonstrated how even the humblest ephemera could be designed with care. (66%)

Advising as to the equipping of a printing office, Harpel warned against purchasing 'a large, incongruous collection of type, bought without regard to its harmony or application',[3] thus echoing De Vinne's paper of a few years earlier. Types should be selected that would work harmoniously together, either because they were sufficiently similar in character or were among the few then available in series – the same face in a range of sizes.

As to design, Harpel dryly observed 'rules that will teach the producing of original ideas, and gracefully avoiding perceptible sameness in arranging the multitude of subjects that fall into the compositor's hands, have not yet been discovered, so far as we know'.[4] However, there were some general principles that could be borne in mind, thus (taking as given that the display would be arranged on a central axis) 'a long line should be placed between two shorter ones neither of the same length, and these again harmonised to others longer or shorter than themselves', while 'lines of large, heavy letters need to be relieved with smaller light ones in the same manner'.[5] Should the customer's copy not easily lend itself to such an arrangement, Harpel advised that the wording be slightly amended, adding 'it not infrequently happens that patrons expressly desire and expect this'.[6] Harpel also recognised how seductive ornamental border units were to the compositor: 'ornaments', he cautioned, 'should be used to *improve* the appearance of work, and not merely because they are at hand, or to fill it up'.[7]

Harpel was but one of several American printers who sought to improve the standard of jobbing printing, others of note including William Kelly of New York, Andreas Haight of Poughkeepsie (125, 134) and John Earhart of Cincinnati (152). Among British printers of similar mind was Thomas Hailing of Cheltenham, who was inspired by Harpel's *Typograph* and in 1877 commenced publication of *Hailing's Circular* (129) with the aim of informing both fellow printers and the public as to 'what really constituted good work'.[8] Another British enthusiast was Andrew Tuer, active partner in the Leadenhall Press and proprietor of the *Paper & Printing Trades Journal*. American and British, they had a common aim: that of bringing Art into the composing room; and thus inspired, they inaugurated that offshoot of aestheticism known as Art or Artistic printing.

In 1879 William Kelly published the first number of his *American Model Printer*, announcing his intention of showing the craft and its patrons that letterpress was capable of work 'such as they have hitherto believed quite impossible, save in lithography and engraving'.[9] The Art-printers' intention that letterpress should now match lithography in both design and colour quality is clear. Included in every number of Kelly's journal was a colour page of specimen jobs (in the earlier issues each compositor credited as

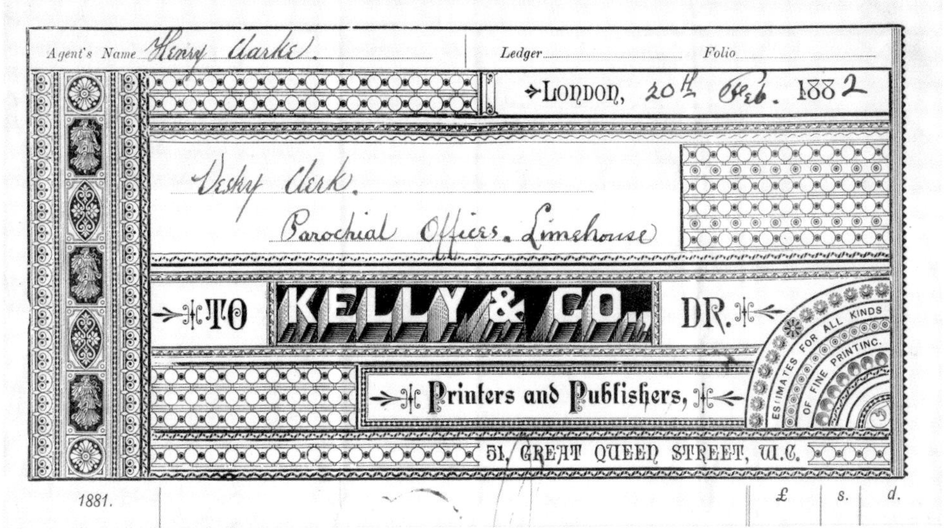

125. Letterheadings, *(top)* by Andreas Haight of Poughkeepsie, NY, and *(below)* by Kelly & Co., London, in use 1882, showing how similar American and British typography could be in the 1880s. Originally published in his *Specimens of Printing*, 1884, Haight's design is here reproduced from George Joyner's *Fine Printing*, 1895. (64%)

'artist') where the aspiration was amply fulfilled, many printers finding it difficult to believe that the specimens were not chromolithographs (134).

Elaborate in colour and complex in setting, the new typography manifesting among these American printers was wholly different from what was usual in Europe. Opinion at the Paris Exhibition in 1878 was that such work represented 'liberty gone mad',[10] and when Kelly's agent for the *American Model Printer*, M. P. McCoy (133), did the rounds of English firms in the following year, the response in some composing rooms was 'that kind of thing might do for America, but it won't do here, you know'. The doubters, however, appear to have been in the minority, McCoy adding 'still, the majority have their eyes open, and are not ashamed to take a hint from others'.[11]

In Britain, Andrew Tuer favoured a mode of typography having cultural parallels with Pre-Raphaelite painting and the archaic diction of William Morris's prose. Known as antique printing, this approach was characterised by old-fashioned types, quaint illustrations and, in severe cases, a pseudo-Chaucerian form of spelling (132, 136). Also working in antique style was the wood-engraver Joseph Crawhall, whose deliberately naïve engravings echoed the crude cuts on old ballad sheets (122).

It was recognised that the best means of improving one's work was by seeing what others were doing. Informal

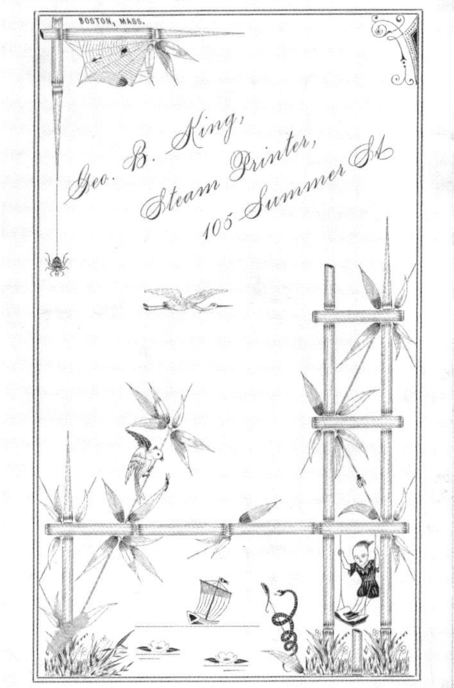

126. 'Not engraved but printed from type': trade card of printer George B. King of Boston, MA, *c.*1885, demonstrating the versatility of his newly acquired 'Chinese' border units. (72%)

127. Some of a miscellany of British and German ephemera discovered at an Ephemera Society fair, presumed to be a personal study collection assembled by an aspiring young typographer/compositor of the 1890s. (44%)

128. *(Left)* American ball invitation printed in red and green, 1873, the lines of type neatly occupying the lightly embossed frame and the absence of black giving an appropriate lightness to the design. *(Right)* American programme, 1887, a stock design printed in gold, green and light blue on to which details of the production have been overprinted in black. The stock image is in the Artistic style of the period but the centred layout of the typography is wholly conventional. (60%)

A PRINTER'S PROTEST

BY A TYPO.

WHY don't people form their *a*'s,
And finish off their *b*'s—
Why do they make such crooked *c*'s
And such confounded *d*'s?

Why do they form such shocking *e*'s
And *f*'s with ague-fits?
Their *g*'s and *h*'s are too much
For any printer's wits!

What a human eye is without sight
Is an *i* without a dot;
J's are such curious, crooked things
We recognize them not.

K ought to stand for kussedness
But comes in well for kick,
L's and *m*'s are mischievous,
While *n*'s just raise Old Nick.

O's are rarely closed at all,
And *p*'s are shaggy things;
Q's might as well be spider legs,
And *r*'s mosquito wings!

Some people make a passing *s*,
Who never cross a *t*,
Others use the self-same strokes
To form a *u* or *v*.

W's get strangely mixed,
X's seem on a spree,
Y is a skeleton on wires—
Zounds, how we swear at *Z*!

& yet, just think, what typos get
From drivers of the quill—
They call us such a careless set
And scribble on at will!

Well, they will scribble, and we must swear,
And vainly try to please,
Till they go back to school and learn
To make their *a, b, c*'s!

Albany Press and Knickerbocker.

129. Specimen setting in red and olive from *Hailing's Circular*, 1.10 (1882). The title panel is built up with units of Zigzag border from founders MacKellar, Smiths & Jordan, Cincinnati, while the columns of decoration is composed chiefly with border units of German origin. As evidenced by the poetry, Victorian compositors were often skilled versifiers. (59%)

exchanges were arranged between individual printers; and Tuer's journal ran a popular 'Specimens' column to which both American and British printers sent material, but production limitations meant that little of what was reviewed could be illustrated. The need for a more systematic means of exchanging specimens was discussed in the American journals, but it was Thomas Hailing who came up with a workable proposal. Each half-year, he suggested, each printer joining the scheme would send a hundred copies of one job to a central clearing point, there to be bound into sets and annually distributed, thereby uniting 'a few of us together in the bonds of fellowship and in the worship of the beautiful'.

Giving full support to the idea, Tuer announced that the *Paper & Printing Trades Journal* would manage such an exchange provided it received a hundred or more subscribers. The subscription would be one shilling (24c). As to the specimens, 'Subscribers would not be expected to print special work, but might work off one hundred copies in excess of any artistically arranged and carefully worked job passing through their hands'.[12] Tuer regarded printing as closely allied to the fine arts and believed that

130. Artistic Type, decorative material and vignettes. From the top, the types are Spiral, Kismet, Modoc and Mikado, their unorthodox shapes characteristically American; below them are the Aesthetically inspired British Sunflower initials. The border units are just a few from the extensive Holbein series supplied by Schelter & Giesecke of Leipzig. (100%)

131. Picture-making in brass rule – images perhaps better understood as demonstrations of ingenuity than as serious attempts at illustration. *(Left)* By John F. Harner, 'one-horse' job printer of Taylorville, Illinois, reproduced in *Paper & Printing Trades Journal* 26 (1879). *(Below)* Printing-machine composed by a London apprentice, shown in *Printers' International Specimen Exchange* 10 (1889). (93%, 67%)

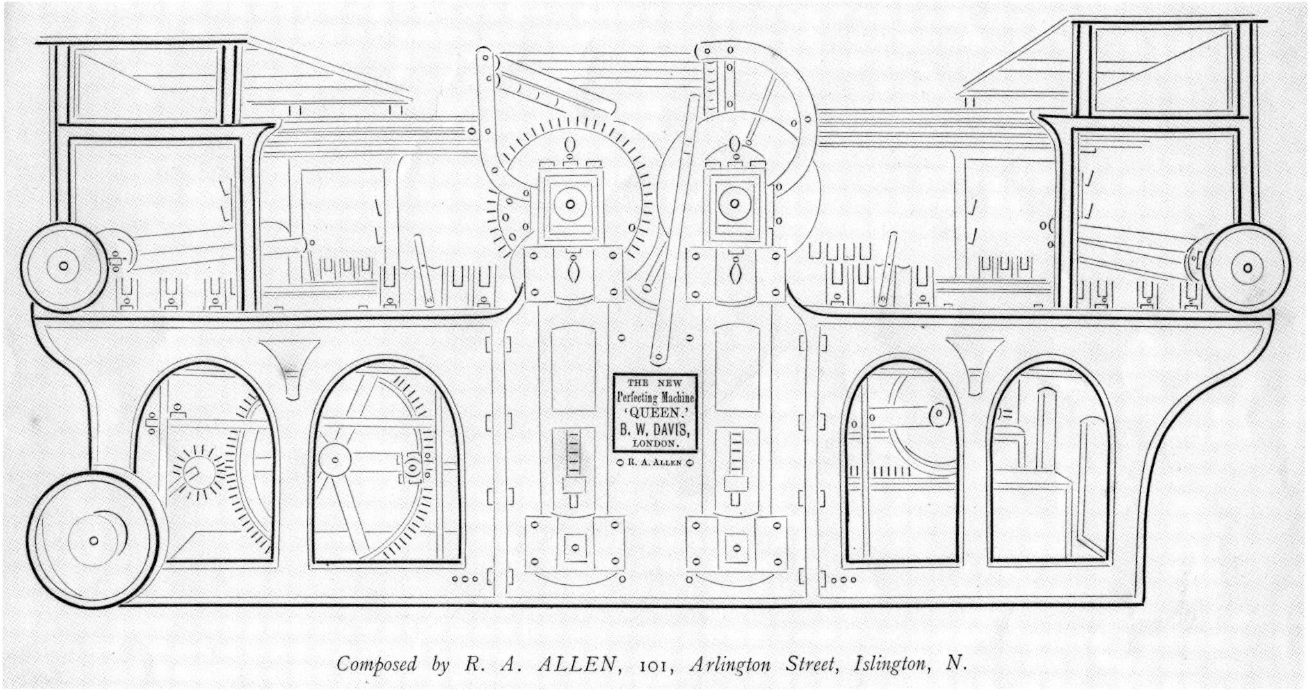

through the raising of its standards national taste would be elevated and society at large benefitted, and in pursuit of this he twice wrote to John Ruskin about the exchange. Ruskin responded, 'I assure you again how gladly I hear of an association of printers who will sometimes issue work in a form worthy of their own craft and shewing to the uttermost the best of which it is capable. [...] I have the most entire sympathy with your objects.'[13]

The proposal was well received generally, one Yorkshire firm declaring that a thousand subscribers would easily be found (Tuer saw this as perhaps *too* optimistic); but in America William Kelly was cautious, envisaging the outcome as either 'a very valuable volume – or a moderately worthless one', the latter through the inclusion of work from inferior printers who would join simply to get their hands on the specimens. Kelly proposed vetting panels in London and New York,[14] but Tuer declared that this would have nearly all the English subscribers resigning, and 'if I can see there are evidences of painstaking and conscientious care – in other words, that subscribers have done their *best* – I shall be very chary about excluding contributions ... there will be many gems of art, but it is impossible that they should all be gems',[15] which Kelly accepted.

In the event, the number of subscribers actually rose to 230, but through illness or pressure of work not all were able to send in specimens. Of the 178 who did, only a few had their jobs rejected, one by fulfilling Kelly's prognostication and sending in a cheap handbill ('he might have saved himself the trouble'), and two or three for 'unmitigated bad work'; but true to his principles, where Tuer felt that subscribers would benefit from encouragement, the weaker specimens were admitted.[16]

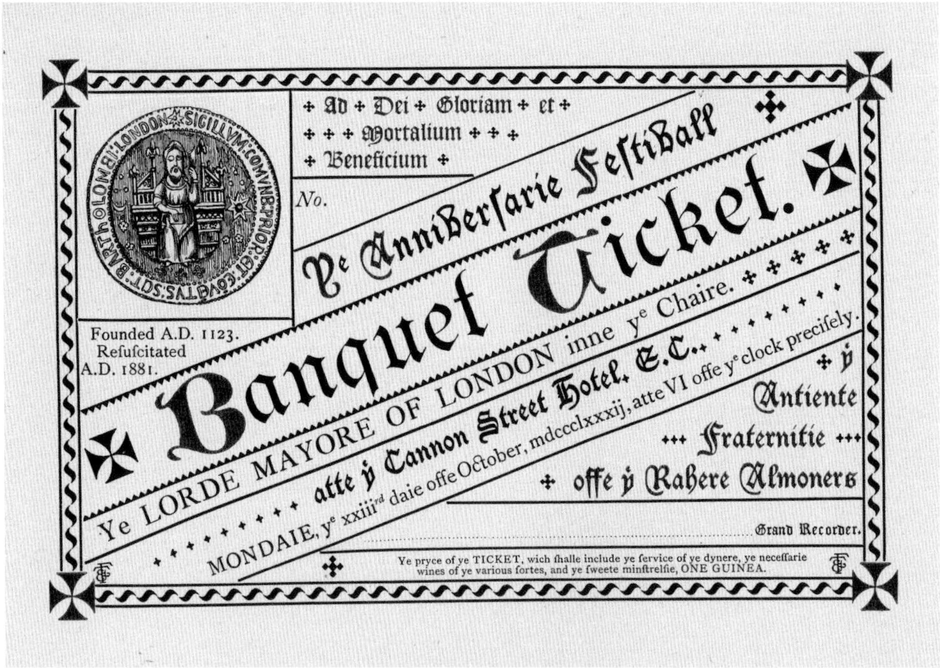

132. Banquet ticket in the Antique style, 1882, set by John Burnett, compositor with Field & Tuer at 'ye Leadenhalle Presse', London. *Printers' International Specimen Exchange*, 1, 1883. (93%)

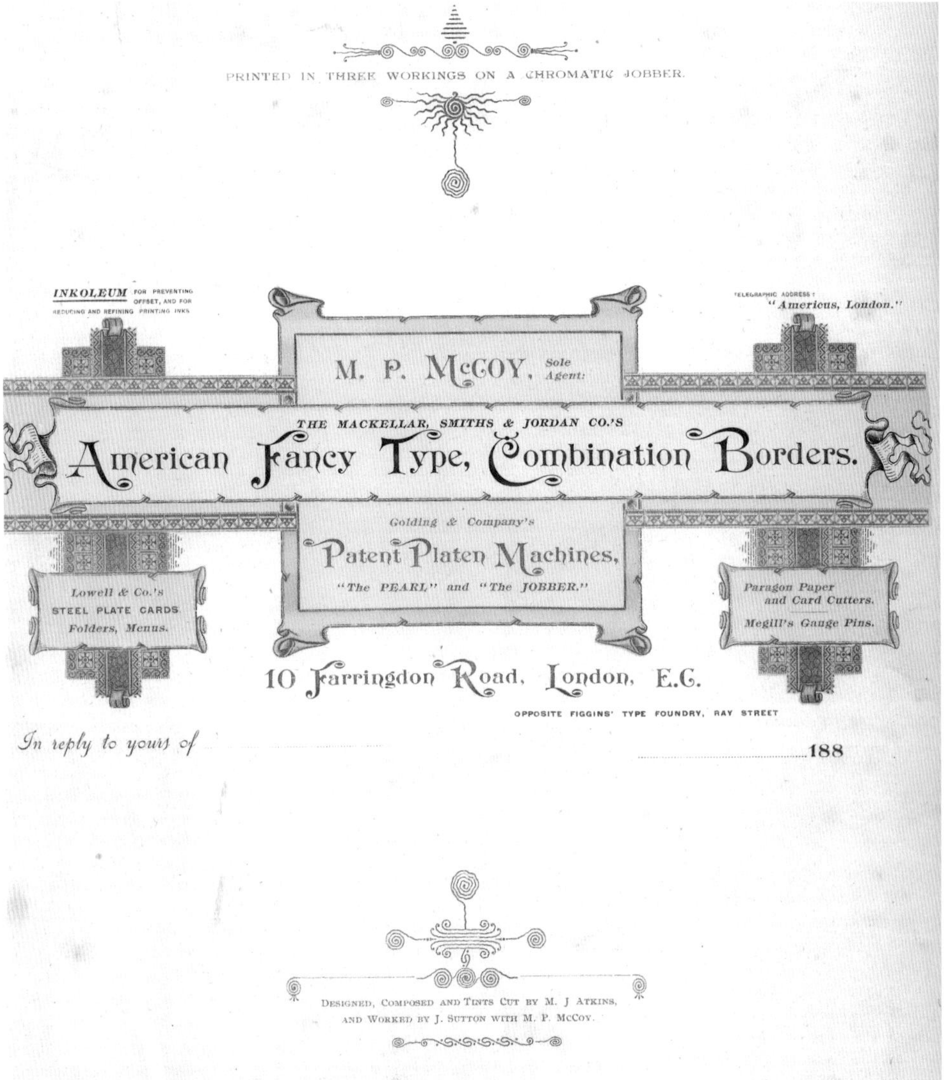

133. Letterheading of M. P. McCoy, shown as a specimen in *Printers' International Specimen Exchange*, 8, 1887. The heading is composed entirely with types and ornaments from the MacKellar, Smiths & Jordan foundry of Philadelphia, for which McCoy was the British representative. Although McCoy was himself an accomplished typographer, in this case design and composition were by M. J. Atkins and, as credited on the specimen, the job was printed by J. Sutton with McCoy acting as his assistant. (67%)

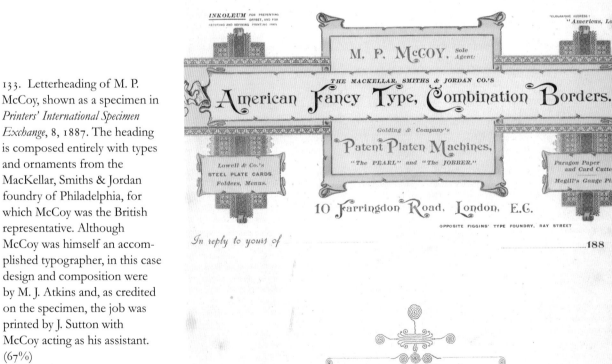

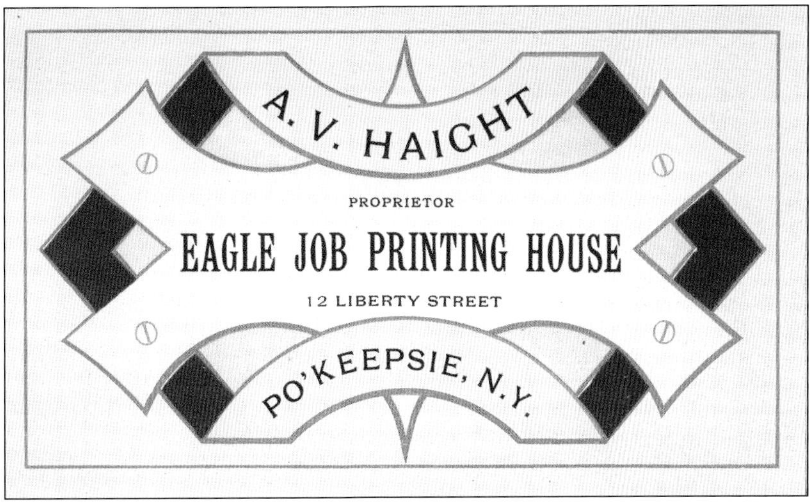

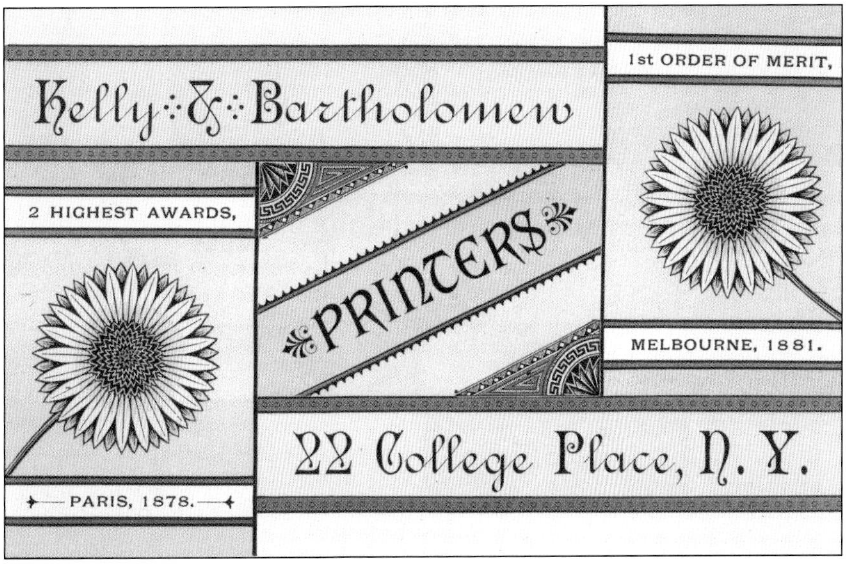

134. Rivalling lithography. Settings from Kelly & Bartholomew's *American Model Printer*, vol. 1 no. 1, 1879, and no. 12, 1881–2: *(top)* by Andreas Haight, whom the editor ranked as 'on the top rung of the ladder of printerdom'; *(centre)* by foreman William Lambert in six colours, the Japanese scene entirely made up from combination units and fine rule; and *(below)* in four colours by junior partner William Bartholomew, 'an exquisite aesthetic design which cannot fail to entrance the typographic soul of dreamy critics'. Each design combines brass-rule work with ornamental motifs, the latter including the screw heads on Haight's card. On Bartholomew's setting the sunflower stems have been ingeniously contrived by the compositor.

The printing – and thus the designing – of work of this richness and complexity was made possible by the development of jobbing platen presses (78), such machines affording an accuracy in register and precision of impression far superior to those of the hand press. *St Bride Library*. (78%)

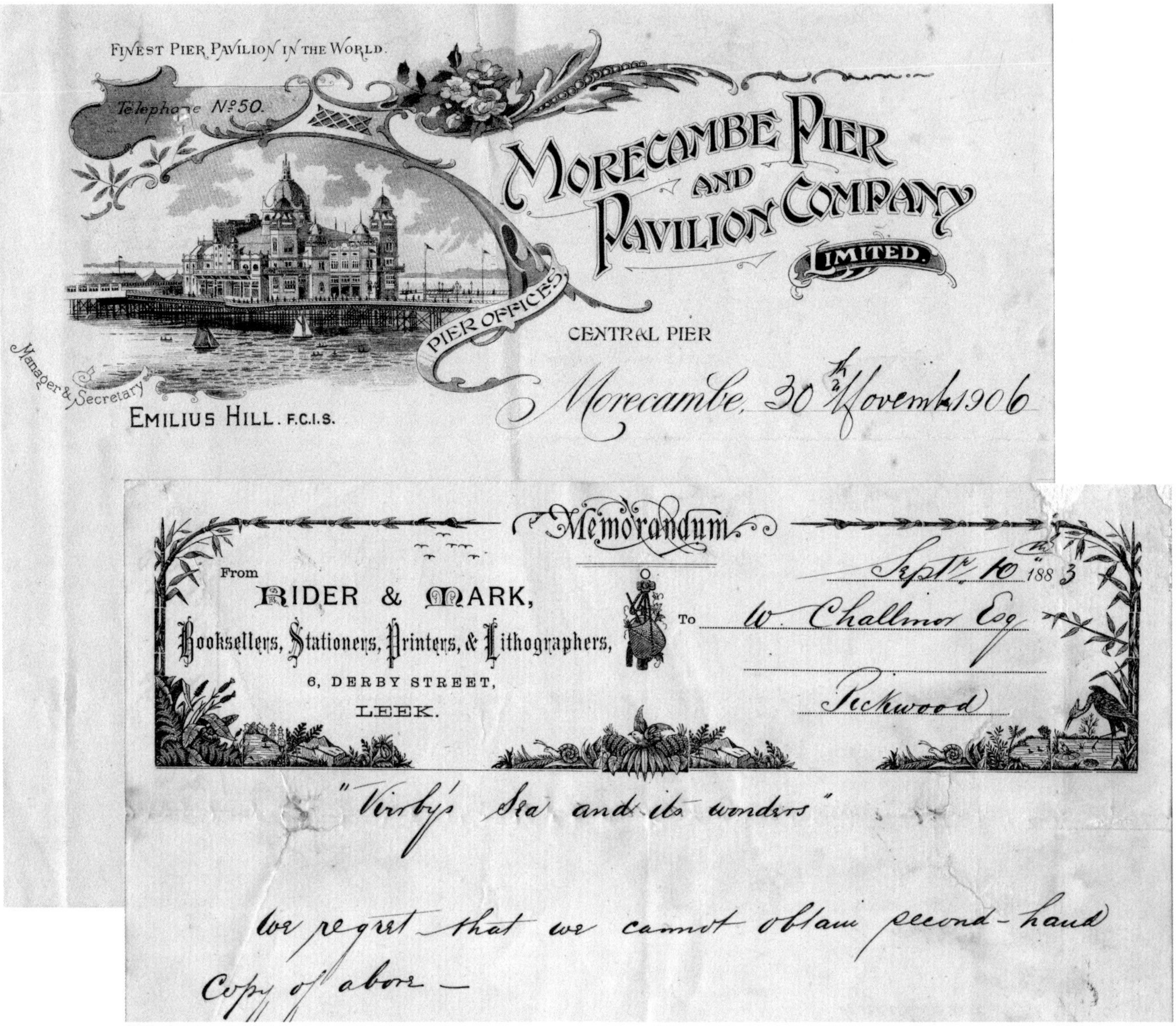

135. Decoration in lithography and letterpress. *(Above)* Letter-heading engraved on stone, exhibiting the freedom in design characteristic of lithography. *(Below)* Letterpress heading utilising 29 separate units of MacKellar, Smiths and Jordan's Orient border to create a Japanese scene framing the design. The calligraphic treatment of 'Memorandum' shows that it was cast as a single unit, such complex interweaving being impossible with individually set types. (79%)

Volume 1 of the *Printers' International Specimen Exchange* was distributed to its subscribers in September 1880. The editorial matter was set in *Old Style* (a derivative of Caslon introduced in 1860) and, for an extra five shillings, the otherwise loose specimens were half-bound in antique mode in gold-blocked white parchment and vellum. The work was generally well received, the *Printers' Register* reporting its surprise at finding a desire for fine printing widespread throughout Great Britain, the editor commenting 'cities which rival London in their activity, and little towns in which the hum of business is as strange as the sight of rent to an Irish landlord, vie with one another in work betokening the possession of artistic genius as well as of most perfect practical skill'.[17] Hailing was delighted. 'The gem of our library', he enthused, and 'there still remains a small body of men who greet each other, across vast continents and mighty seas, with cheering words and helpful advice'.[18] The volume included work from Britain, America and Canada, and one specimen from an English-speaking printing shop in Antwerp.

Over the following years the *Specimen Exchange* became part of the jobbing-printing establishment, its subscribers increasing in number and work included from as far abroad as Vienna, Milan and Rangoon. Similar schemes started in France and Germany, and in 1886 in Buffalo, NY, Ed McClure commenced his *American Printers' Specimen*

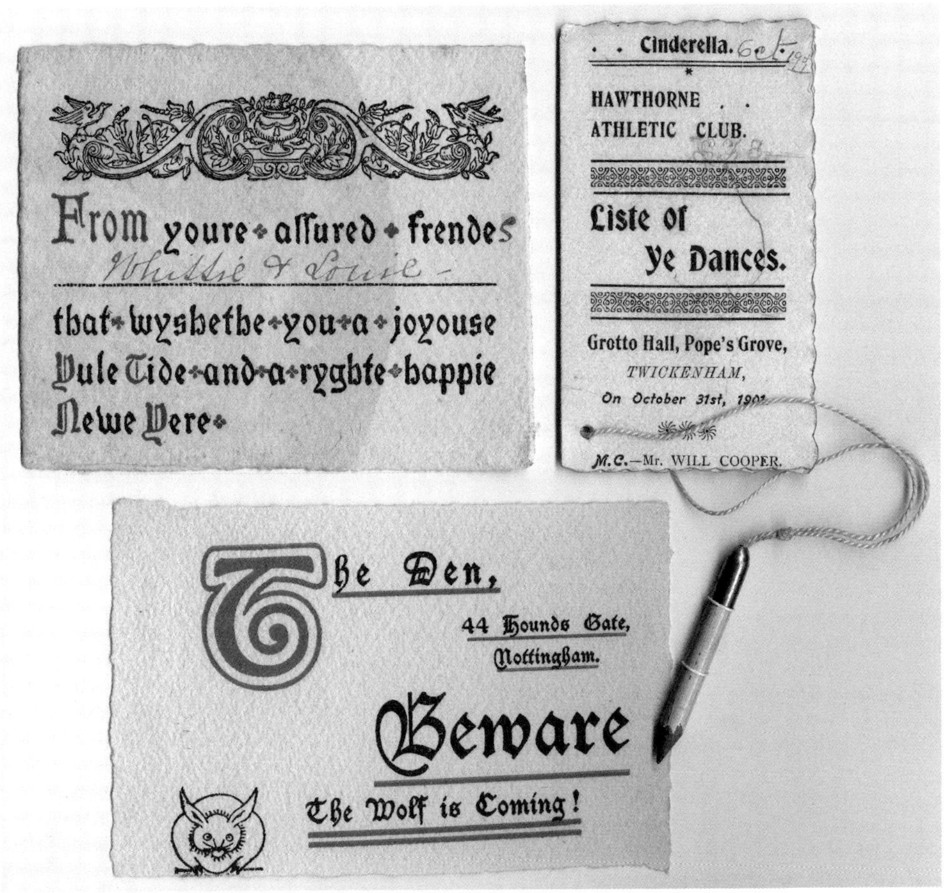

136. Greetings cards and a dance programme in the Antique style, the first card adopting the pseudo-Chaucerian spelling espoused by the more committed adherents of the style while the other items adhere to the conventional. The purpose of the 'Beware' card is obscure, but the little beastie is an 'art-fake', one of a series of eccentric ornaments introduced by John Earhart of Cincinnati *c.*1887. This card is one of the many items found in the study collection shown in illustration 128. (65%)

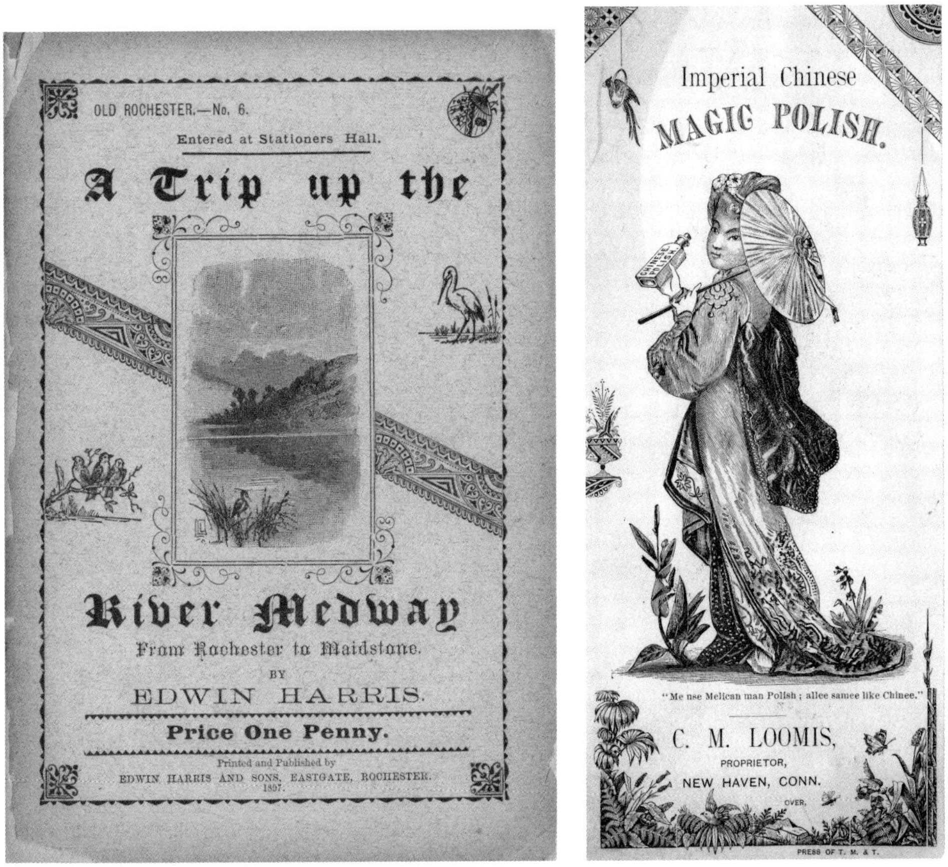

137. Booklet by Edwin Harris of Rochester, Kent, 1897, and American trade card of the 1880s by 'Press of T. M. & T.' Both the diagonal band on the booklet and the decoration on the card are composed with units from MacKellar, Smiths & Jordan of Cincinnati. (61%)

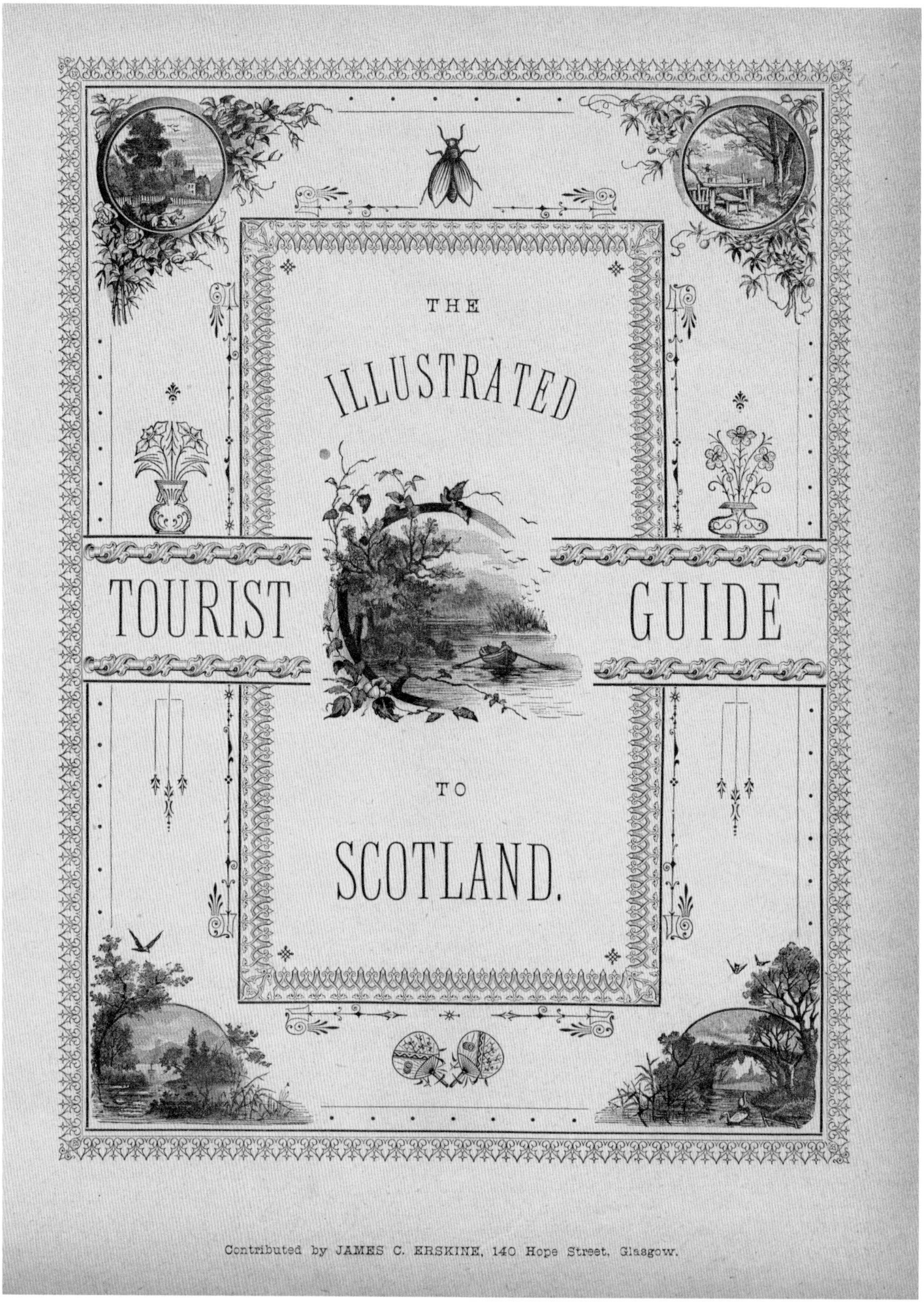

138. Guide book cover contributed by James Erskine of Glasgow to *Printers' International Specimen Exchange* 10 (1889). The utilisation of imagery for its purely Aesthetic values is clear, neither the fly, Japanese face screens nor all but one of the vignettes having relevance to Scotland. The design itself is skilfully organised, the central vignette providing a focus and its tone echoed by the smaller vignettes from the same series in the corners; the decoration also harmonises well with the type, which Erskine has wisely restricted to one face and size. (97%)

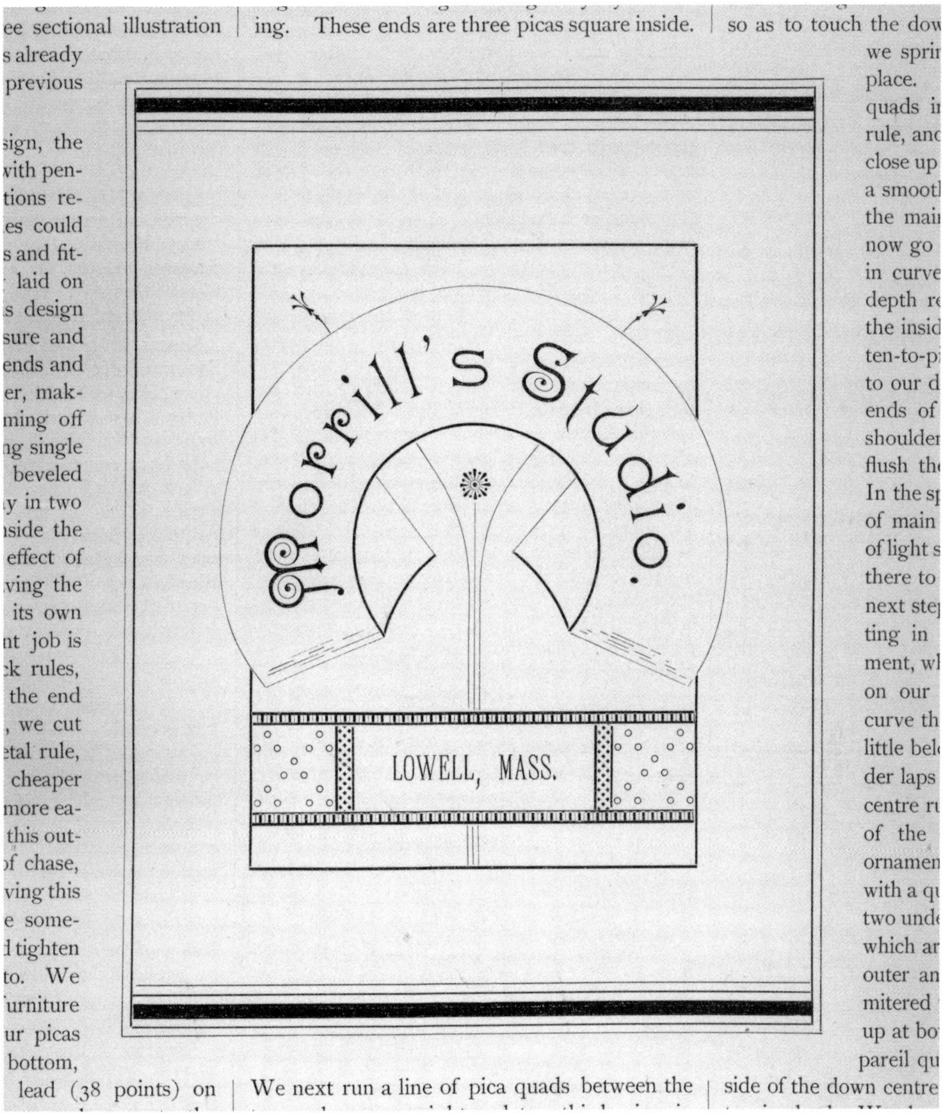

139. Intricate setting in brass rule by Clarence E. Rice of Hall & McChesney, Syracuse, NY, as featured in an instructional article in *American Art Printer* 1.4 (1887). This is the black-printing keyline of a job designed to be printed in several colours, the colour scheme being decided with the aid of watercolours or crayons once the structure had been established. The journal stressed that with this sort of work it was always necessary to start with an accurately drawn layout. (91%)

Exchange. Kelly planned his own strictly-vetted *World's Specimen Album* (submissions from as far afield as China were envisaged), but this grand scheme never materialised.[19]

Art-printing in the 1880s was characterised by colour and complexity, American compositors, and the British too who received the American journals, utilising 'every appliance of type, rule, flourishes, ornaments, and … every possible product of the typefounder and rule-maker, and every conceivable combination of those products'.[20] Colour was used not only for type and ornament but in light backgrounds of plain or patterned tints printed from leathers, cork, lace and other surfaces, tint blocks also being engraved in boxwood or built up with border units. Also exploited were the textures of *Owltype*, *Chaostype* (152) and other techniques, involving procedures such as dabbing acid-resistant ink on to a zinc plate then etching or hazardously pouring molten stereo metal on to damp blotting paper.

In Germany great ingenuity was shown in the design of *combination borders* – type ornaments produced in founts of many characters combinable into a variety of different arrangements (130, 142). German borders began to enrich British typography from 1880 but were less often seen in America where the home foundries sufficiently met the compositors' needs (137).

As early as the 1830s compositors had occasionally employed brass printing rule for decorative effects, but it was during the 1880s that this medium came to be exploited to the full. Aided by devices such as Kelly & Bartholomew's 'Curving Machine' the compositor could structure his tinted display on perfect circles and serpentine curves, or with Earhart & Richardson's 'Wrinkler' crimp and spiral his brass rule into virtually any shape he might fancy. In America, and to a certain extent in Britain also, some compositors went as far as making actual pictures in brass rule – animals, portraits, even in one case a cylinder printing machine in intricate detail (131). These

140. Plate in the Aesthetic Japanese style by Gildea & Walker, 1881–5, and trade card in gold and five colours by George Seaman of Haight & Dudley, Poughkeepsie, NY, both designs based on similar angular and curving divisions and with some similarity in the choice of motifs. Every line in Seaman's card, reproduced here from *American Art Printer* 1.6 (1887), has been achieved with brass printing rule. (75%)

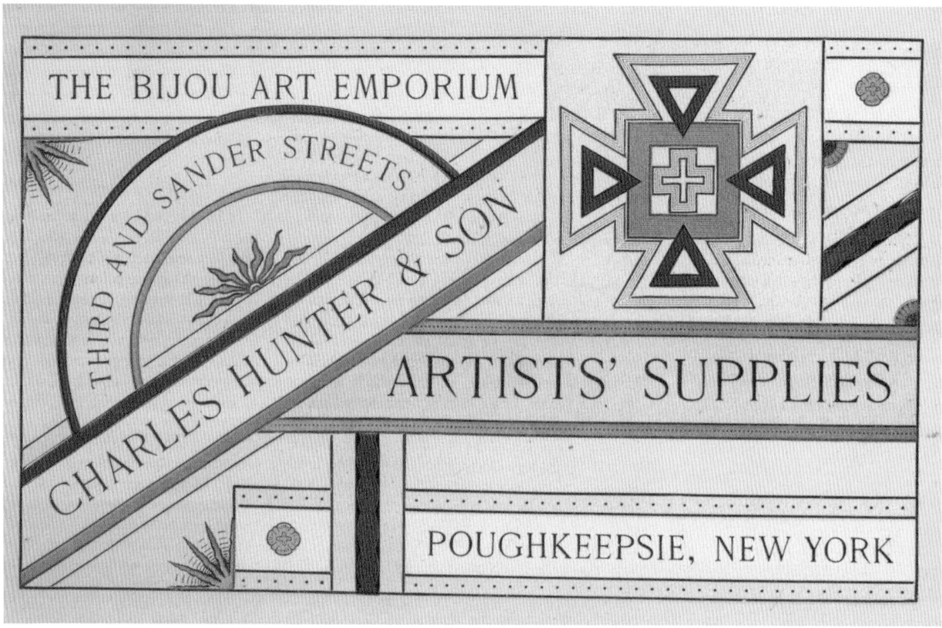

were looked at askance by Tuer who questioned whether such work was not 'talent prostituted and ingenuity gone astray',[21] yet one suspects that such tours de force were intended more for enjoyment within the trade than for serious commercial consideration.

During the 1870s American type design began to take its own line, no longer content merely to decorate letters of more or less conventional proportions but often distorting the letterforms themselves (130). In 1880 the *Scientific American* observed that it had become 'as difficult for a really good printer to see a nice new face of type without buying a font of it as it is for a fashionable lady to do without the latest style of bonnet',[22] while the *Pacific Specimen* two years later urged the printer to keep abreast of the type-foundries' output but to 'buy little and use it while it is the rage, for style and fashion are dominant in the printer's realm as elsewhere'.[23]

The wide choice of faces available in a well-equipped printing shop demanded a high level of self-denial. William Kelly's advice was to avoid too much variety 'or, in plainer words, a too liberal "peppering" from every font in the office'. Kelly also emphasised the importance of the 'grouping of all the sizes used so as to form some satisfactory design',[24] i.e. the arrangement of lines should create an aesthetically pleasing shape.

Within the Aesthetic movement there was great interest in Japanese design, and this manifested in typography when MacKellar, Smiths & Jordan of Cincinnati brought

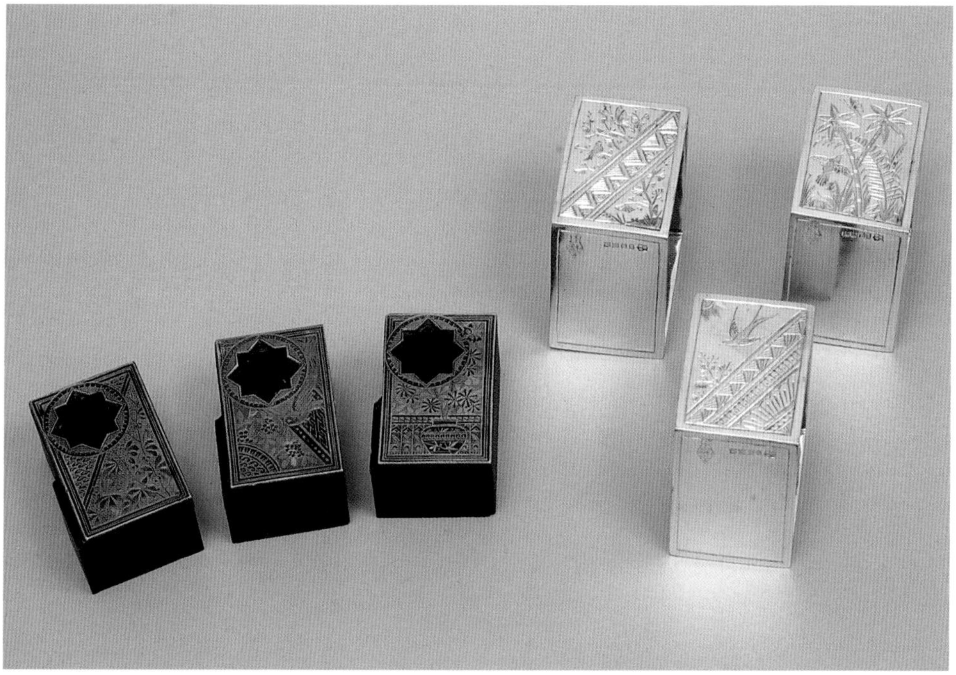

141. Electrotype factotum cuts in the Japanese style from the Reed foundry and three of a set of six napkin rings possibly by Hukin & Heath of Birmingham, *c.*1880, decorated with similar Aesthetic motifs. Proofs of the factotums are shown below. *Napkin rings by courtesy of Geffrye Museum, London.* (100%)

out their first Japanese combination border in 1879. Subsequently Chinese (126), Egyptian and Assyrian borders were created by various American foundries. Sunflowers, lilies, peacock feathers, Japanese fans and other emblems of the Aesthetic movement were among the design elements of jobbing composition, while angular 'Japanesque' patterning found like expression on domestic ware and in the print shop (140, 141). Yet Art-printers were always to remain more aware of the Aesthetic movement than that movement ever was of Art-printing. There were books and articles on dress and ornament and how to artistically furnish the home, but no printer thought to write a lay person's guide on what to look for in well-designed printing – a surprising omission when one considers the articulacy of these printer-designers, their constant censure of bad work, and the abundance of circulars, certificates, bazaar posters and other ephemera the Victorian public was endlessly requiring from them.

William Morris declared that 'to give people pleasure in the things they must perforce *use*, that is one great office of decoration; to give people pleasure in the things they must perforce *make*, that is the other use of it':[25] and these too were the sentiments of the Art-printer. Elsewhere Morris wrote of the need to combine 'clearness of form and firmness of structure with the mystery which comes of abundance and richness of detail',[26] in this paralleling principles commended by Hailing some six years earlier: '[first] we must have our construction – the lines of type that have to be used properly laid down. Then let us begin to ornament them.'[27]

The 1880s was a decade of great enthusiasm. In Sheffield, England, apprentice George W. Jones rose at 5 a.m. to work on his entry for the *Specimen Exchange*,[28] and it was reported of Andreas Haight that often he had 'stolen from his hours of sleep to work out an idea that gave him no rest until completion'.[29] In Selkirk, Scotland, John Lewis slept with work beneath his pillow, and was sometimes 'lucky enough to *dream* a "brilliant" idea in type, which was carefully put on paper in the morning'.[30] A demonstration piece shown by an enthusiast at the 1883 London Fine Printing Exhibition ran to 53 colours.[31]

'Artistic Printer' became a familiar attribute on printer's

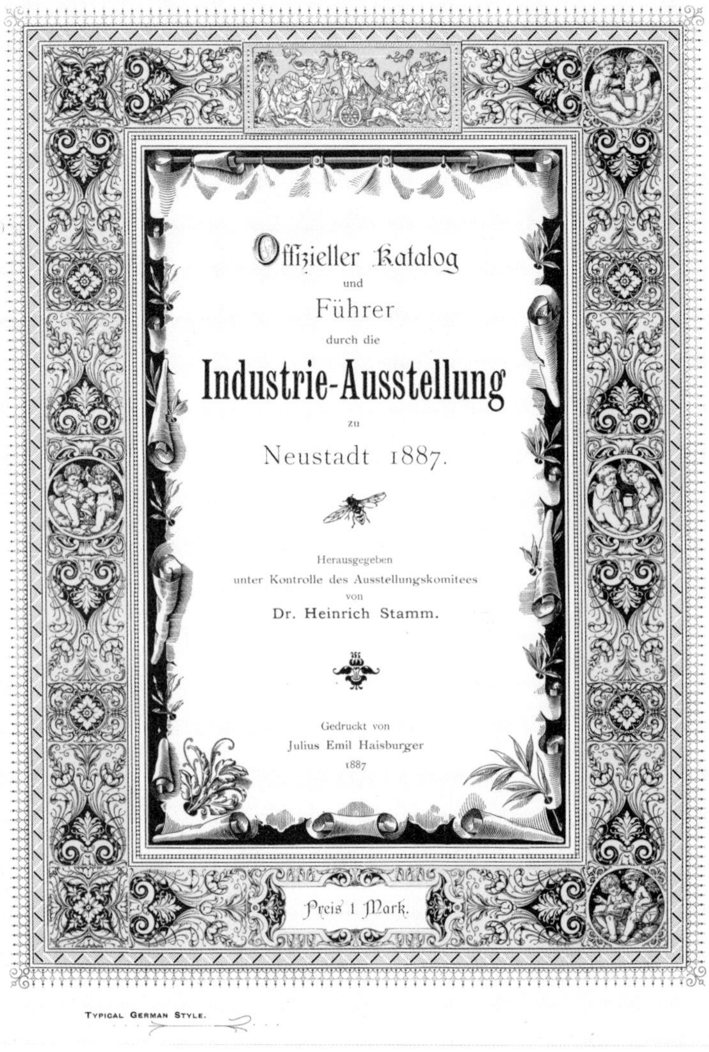

142. Art printing in Germany. Catalogue cover in four colours by Julius Haisburger, 1887. German printers excelled in their sensitive use of the combination borders produced by their native foundries. Here even the decoratively ragged *Curtain* border is composed from separate units. Compared with American and British printers, however, German typographic display was noticeably conservative. From Joyner, *Fine Printing*, 1895. (59%)

letterheads; but it was always easier to adopt the phrase than fulfil the promise. Occasionally, it was said, one would encounter a printer content merely to pick up a few aesthetical phrases: 'lightening up a job with a touch of the not-severely-plain', and 'a proper appreciation of the artistically correct' were among his stock phrases, but as the *Inland Printer* observed, 'his customers have no idea of what they mean, and he has still less'.[32] And 'Alas!', wrote George Joyner in 1895, 'far too many are the examples sent broadcast, heedlessly branded "Artistic Printing," which not only do not possess any attribute approaching artistic merit, but do not show even an acquaintance with the elementary principles of typographic production'.[33]

The contrast between the worthy and those content merely to climb on the Artistic bandwagon was keenly felt by the trade journals, which could receive whole parcels of work for appraisal in their columns. Good endeavour earned its reward, as in a review of specimens sent in by William Hoefgen of San Antonio, Texas, aged twenty-one:

> Our young correspondent possesses the stuff of which first-rate printers are made ... most of his jobs are fresh and unconventional in style, and all ... redound to the credit of a young man situated in such a far away place, where the usual emulation of large centres can hardly be said to exist, and where facilities for procuring novelties in type and ornaments are extremely few.[34]

But where he felt it necessary, an editor would not spare a printer's blushes, as in this response to a batch of work from Wales:

> Mr. Jones evidently has a well-stocked office, but his employés sadly require more taste and originality. Above all, they cram into a job all and more than it will stand. The specimens are too showy. [...] Mr. Jones must forgive our criticism, which, however, seems invited when he so ostentatiously proclaims his character as an 'art printer'.[35]

7

The Leicester free style

In 1884 Thomas Hailing wrote: 'printing is an art, certainly, in every proper sense of the term, and in its cultivation demands and admits all elements of beauty, form, figure, proportion, drawing, design, light, shade, color, relief [and] is justly entitled to be ranked among the Fine Arts'.[1] Likewise, in 1888 the *Inland Printer* could aver 'the job printer especially has advanced in his profession, until he now justly ranks among the most prominent and cultured of artists'.[2] Odd though such notions may sound today, they accorded with some Victorian ideas of art, William Morris defining the artist as 'a workman who is determined that, whatever else happens, his work shall be excellent',[3] while the designer Christopher Dresser described his own approach to the decoration of textiles, wallpapers and other surfaces as 'ornamentation considered as high art'.[4] By such tenets, genuine Art-printers were justified in considering themselves artists, for their technical skill was of the highest and their feeling for composition and colour equalled that of designers in any other field.

The skills and sensibilities necessary for fine printing were recognised as those that also informed fine art, with drawing ability seen almost a *sine qua non* for the aspiring compositor. Reviewing two entertainment programmes, Tuer's editor declared 'the merit lies in the design, which is evidently that of a printer possessing a knowledge of drawing – an almost indispensable qualification to any one who aspires to do real "artistic" work';[5] while the Manchester *Typographical Circular* urged 'a knowledge of drawing, and the cultivation of the other faculties which it carries with it [...] and an appreciation of truth and elegance of form, which generally follows it, would preserve us from the typographical monstrosities we too frequently encounter'.[6]

Drawing was both useful in its own right and valuable as an aid in finding ideas for typographical arrangements. The London *Printers' Register* recommended the compositor keeping a scrapbook, either of actual specimens or, if spare prints could not be procured, by making pencil sketches of their salient features: for 'every printer, with a love for his trade, ought to be able to sketch sufficiently well to do this'. Faced with devising something new, the compositor might find an item in his collection to strike an idea, thereby producing 'by a combination and a little alteration, a piece of work the novelty and beauty of which will be limited only by his ideas of harmony, skill in execution, and attention to detail'. Drawing would also enhance the artistic sensibilities generally, thus equipping one to look for inspiration in lithographs and engravings, even the painted window blinds of private residences.[7] M. P. McCoy similarly recommended the study of stained glass, church architecture, fancy work in omnibuses and trains and the 'frescoes, settings, suggestions of form and colour for close and distant effects' of the theatre.[8]

It was within the Art-printing movement that the practice developed of the compositor working from a prepared design. In the late-eighteenth century Luke Hansard had effected economies in the setting of complicated parliamentary reports by this means,[9] but the first reference to the use of a layout in job work appears in the *Typograph* in 1870, where Harpel observes 'a good way to get up a design, is to sketch it out first on paper'.[10] The chief concern of Harpel's manual was relatively simple work, so his 'sketch' may have been just that, a general indication of what went where; but something far more precise was needed for the complex rule patterning of the 1880s. With a proper layout, the *American Art Printer* told its readers in 1887, 'there is no groping in the dark, no fishing for the indefinite; on the contrary, you go straight on with your work, measuring on sure lines, and finishing as you go', with the brass rules 'fitted to a hair'.[11]

It is evident also that in America by this date it was not unusual for a compositor to work to someone else's layout for, discussing the difficulty that many found in knowing where actually to *start* on a piece of complicated artistic setting, the *American Art Printer* said that this could be so 'even when the design is furnished them'. But the advice in the trade press could be conflicting. Reviewing that year's contributions to the *Specimen Exchange*, the editor wrote in 1883, 'it is evident that in most cases the commendable and time-saving plan of first sketching the job out on paper has been resorted to, instead of letting it "grow up" haphazard as one line or ornament suggested another';[12] but in the

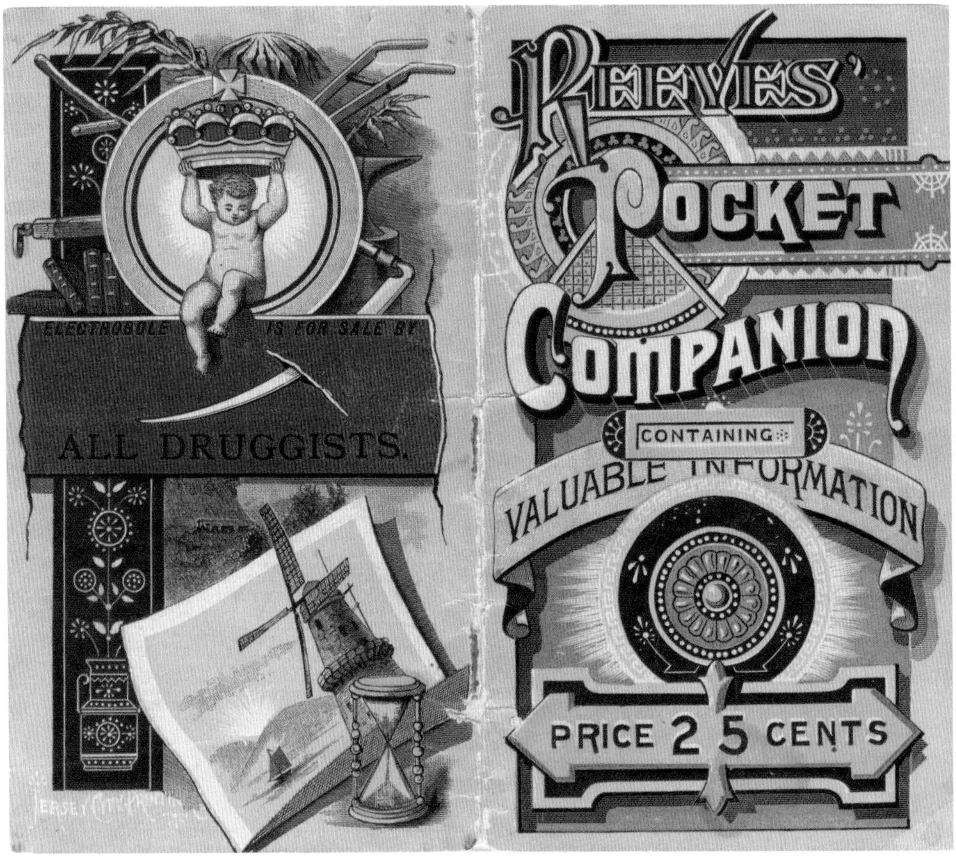

143. Booklet cover, chromoxylograph in four colours by the Jersey City Printing Co., 1896. The shadowed three-dimensional design is in the gaslight style more familiar from lithographically-printed stationery. The fading of the red on the front cover is a result of light exposure. (74%)

same year, after inspiring readers with the idea that they truly were 'artists, not mechanics', the *Inland Printer* advised: 'the whole work should be clear *to the mind's* eye before a line of type is set'[13] (author's italics). The *British Printer* recommended much the same procedure a few years later, though with a different metaphor: 'a sort of mental photograph of the job as it will appear'.[14]

Nevertheless, the practice of working to a layout became more customary, and from this developed the role of the specialist designer. In 1888, George W. Jones, by this time head of the Art-printing department at the Darien Press, Edinburgh, was reported as devoting himself exclusively to designing,[15] and in 1894 John Lewis was described as being the designer for his family's firm.[16] In 1880 or 1881 Daniel Berkeley Updike began working as a designer of books and ephemera at Houghton Mifflin of Boston; but his circumstances were different from the above in that he was appointed from outside the industry – a successful designer of print who had never been a compositor.[17]

It was also during the Art-printing period that the old convention of designating sizes of type by name began gradually to give way to the point system of today. Supposedly there were six picas to the inch but in practice no two founders' picas were exactly alike, nor any of the other nominal sizes. This began to matter as type styles proliferated and type, ornaments and spaces from different foundries came to be composed in the same jobs. Nothing was done towards rationalising the situation until Marder, Luse & Co. lost their foundry in the great Chicago fire of 1871, and in re-establishing it devised a system based on twelve 'points' to the pica, with all type sizes related to standard point measurements. In 1887 all US founders agreed to adopt the point system and in England it was actively promoted by the *British Printer*, but it was to be many years before the new system completely replaced the old. When in 1892 Mrs Jane Pyne of William Morris's Kelmscott Press became the first woman granted a union card by the London Society of Compositors, they commemorated the event in verse with a refrain running:

> Then room for the Type-setting Girl!
> Shall we call her our 'Ruby' or 'Pearl'?
> For it's each comp.'s opinion, he'll soon be the 'Minion'
> Of the up-to-date Type-setting Girl![18]

Respectively, the corresponding point sizes are 5½, 5 and 7 points, – but they have not the same magic.[19]

It was also in 1887 that the *Specimen Exchange* changed hands. Although nominally under Tuer's editorship, the work on both the *Exchange* and the *Paper & Printing Trades Journal* was done by Tuer's assistant, Robert Hilton. In January 1887 Hilton was accorded a generous testimonial by his British and American confreres, and this seems to have embittered Tuer for the testimonial made no mention of him. Some time later Hilton began negotiating to buy the rights to the *Exchange* with the threat of starting his own if Tuer did not accede. Had Hilton done so, that would certainly have led to the demise of the original. Thus Tuer had little option, and late in 1887 he signed the *Specimen Exchange* over to his erstwhile assistant, now working for Messrs Raithby & Lawrence at Leicester. Under Hilton's ownership both volumes 9 and 10 appeared in the familiar antique-style binding, but with volume 11 (1890) a more workmanlike dress of red cloth half-bound in red leather was adopted.

Hilton also brought out a new trade journal, the *British Printer*. Printed by Raithby & Lawrence with design and production overseen by their then works manager George W. Jones, the first number was published in January/February 1888. The journal's aim was 'to help the average printer combine the artistic with the practical on a paying basis',[20] and this it was to successfully achieve over the coming years through its technical articles, competitions, supplementary pages printed in colours, and 'designs and suggestions for job work'.

In 1892 John Southward observed that Art-printing 'designates a new department of the printing business' – that is, that it was a significantly different *class* of printing from what had gone before.[21] Thus what one might term ordinary rule-of-thumb jobbing continued as the norm (45); as is clearly demonstrated by Joseph Gould's *The Letter-Press Printer*, published in Middlesbrough in 1876, for in none of its editions – the second in 1881 and the sixth in 1904 – is there any reference to Art-printing. Concerning 'display', Gould observes no more than 'all depends upon the proper arrangement of lines of various lengths, and the proper selection of different faces and sizes of type, which, by harmoniously blending, will produce the best effect',[22] the author eschewing further explanation

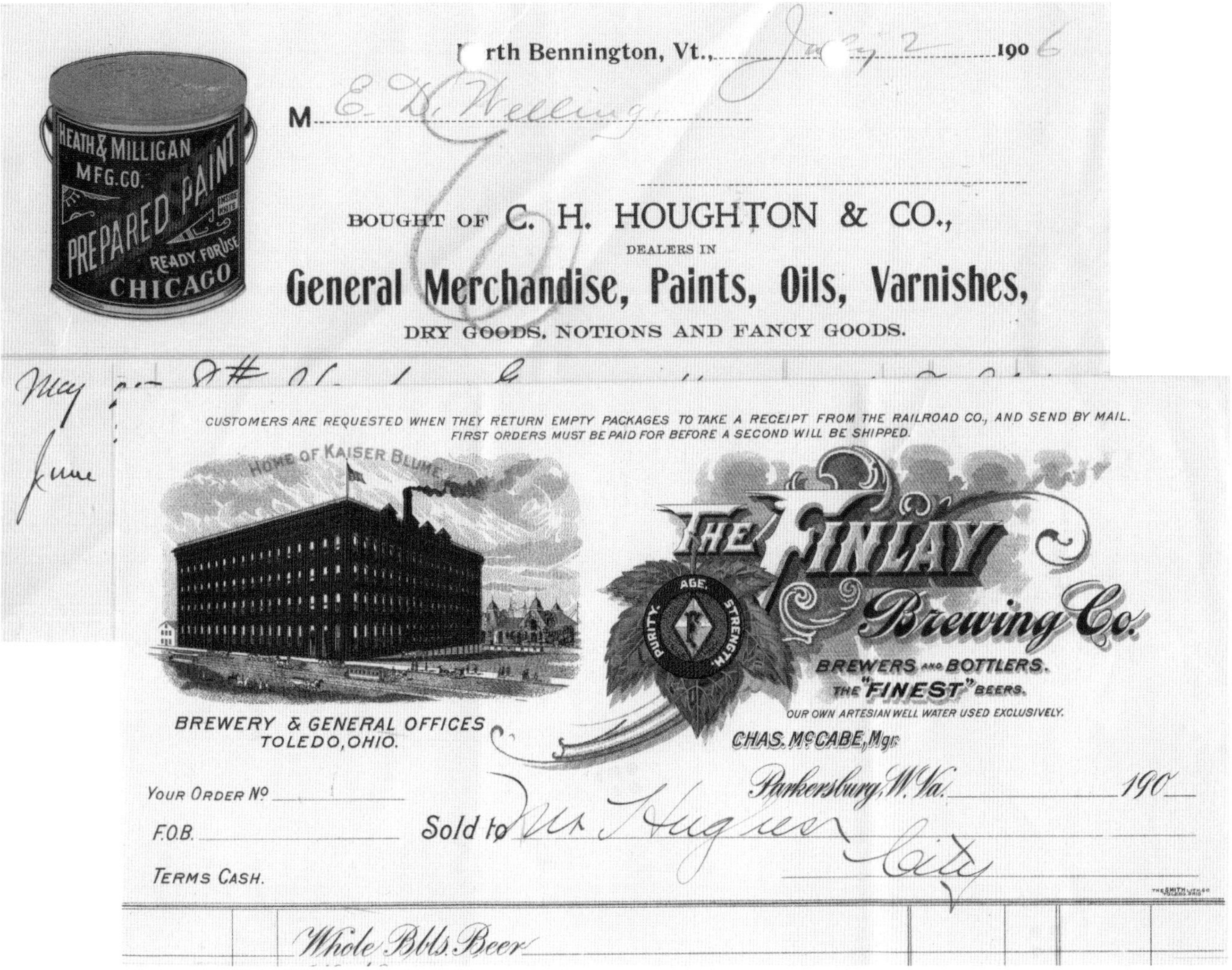

144. Colour-printed billheads. *(Top)* Advertising billhead in use 1906, promoting Heath & Millington of Chicago, printed letterpress in four colours with overprinted details for a Vermont general store. *(Below)* In red, green and black by Smith Lithographic Co., Toledo, Ohio, in use in the 1900s. Vignette and lettering are presented as separate, unrelated entities, the design thus lacking the unity of the Diem Wing heading shown in illustration 150. (74%)

145. In his *Fine Printing*, 1895, the typographer George Joyner observed that 'many compositors fail to realise the importance of the comparative relation of prominent and subordinate display', illustrating his point with this comparison pair. In the card on the left the message is confused owing to the minor lines being set in types that are unnecessarily large. The version on the right has better 'perspective' through the corresponding lines being set in smaller sizes, making the ordering of the information clearer. (78%)

and instead providing small-scale sample settings of run-of-the-mill billheads, circulars, posters and title-pages. (146). Gould's manual was probably to prove as useful to American jobbers as to British, for the Pittsburgh *Quadrat* trusted that 'none of our readers will scold [us] for advising them to send a postal order for 75 cents [to] secure a copy', while the *Michigan Tribune* said that it should be 'in the hands of every printer in the land'.[23]

Letterpress poster design continued much as described by Karl Burg in the 1860s and would do so well into the twentieth century. Gould advised that when arranging a multi-sheet poster the wood type be laid on the floor to determine which words – and for the main display lines, which letters – would go on which sheet (40); while in his *Modern Printing*, 1892, Southward recommended that the sheets be nailed on the composing room wall and the display lines either sketched in with charcoal or printed on long slips of paper, to be pinned up and moved around until the best arrangement was found.[24] Thomas Hailing won the ten-guinea prize (equivalent to $50.93)[25] for 'the best displayed and most effective four-sheet double-crown Posting Bill, in two, three, or four colours, on white or coloured paper' at the third Allied Trades Exhibition held in London in 1883.[26]

Writing in 1893, J. Anderson advised the young compositor to study the posters he saw around him, 'from the humble dog-lost bill to the more pretentious Snookum's Soap advertisement [for] knowing the means by which others obtain their effective bits, or the pitfalls into which they may have stumbled … he will find that the lessons thus learned in theory will in practice stand by him as truly faithful allies'. Anderson reiterated the adage that the chief requirement in poster design was that he who runs may read, but added that when intended chiefly for shop-window display a slightly more ornate type might be used, 'as here it is probably the loitering passer-by whose attention is desired'.[27]

During the 1880s there were advances in the design of lithographically-printed stationery comparable to those affecting letterpress. Up to this time lithographed billheads and cards had retained the look of copper or steel engravings but now, prompted by the richness of artistic printing, lithographic artists began to take their own line. Increasingly, one element in the design would now overlap another, creating a sense of space and volume, further enhanced by tone and shadow; while lettering became free and inventive, and either integrated with the pictorial element or presented on flowing or angled ribbons (149, 150). The style is thought to have been suggested by the night-time play of light and shadow on the three-dimensional lettering of shop fascias, hence the name by which it came to be known – the gaslight style.[28] It was not limited to printed stationery (143), but it was there that it was most characteristically employed.

In 1887 the *American Lithographer & Printer* inaugurated a form of specimen exchange which it described as the Travelling Portfolio. The journal had accrued a lot of spare material through its specimens column and the idea was to circulate the best of this to subscribing firms via the US postal service. (The scheme was intended to be international, but when a Mr V. G. Goshi of Poona subsequently enquired it was felt unlikely that other subscribers would willingly incur the postal charges for onward forwarding to India.) In all, some ten portfolios went on circuit, the first to firms in Philadelphia, Buffalo, NY, and Louisville, Kentucky. But ill luck dogged the scheme. Subscribers added unauthorised specimens of their own, word filtered in of specimens torn and soiled, portfolios went to the wrong recipients or were lost track of entirely. The scheme was abandoned in November 1888, the

The same job composed as a Circular and as a Poster.

F 2

POSTER.

NEW SUMMER GOODS!

J. NEWMAN,

CLOTHIER & OUTFITTER,

25, LONDON ROAD,

Begs to announce that he has just received

A LARGE CONSIGNMENT OF

GENTS' & YOUTHS'

CLOTHING

OF EVERY DESCRIPTION.

Full Suits Black Cloth, Gent's - £3 15 0

Do. Finest Grey Tweed do. - 2 12 6

Boys' & Youths' Suits from 15/- to 2 5 0

A Varied Assortment, all New Styles, to Choose from.

OBSERVE THE ADDRESS:

25, LONDON ROAD

SYDENHAM.

CIRCULAR.

NEW SUMMER GOODS.

J. NEWMAN,

CLOTHIER AND OUTFITTER,

25, LONDON ROAD, SYDENHAM,

Begs to announce that he has just received

a large consignment of

Gents' and Youths' Clothing

Of every description.

—::—

Full Suits Black Cloth, Gent's - - £3 15 0

Do. Finest Grey Tweed do. - - 2 12 6

Boys' and Youths' Suits from 15s. to - 2 5 0

—::—

A VARIED ASSORTMENT, ALL NEW STYLES, TO CHOOSE FROM.

—::—

OBSERVE THE ADDRESS:

25, LONDON ROAD,

SYDENHAM.

JOB-WORK—DISPLAY.

83

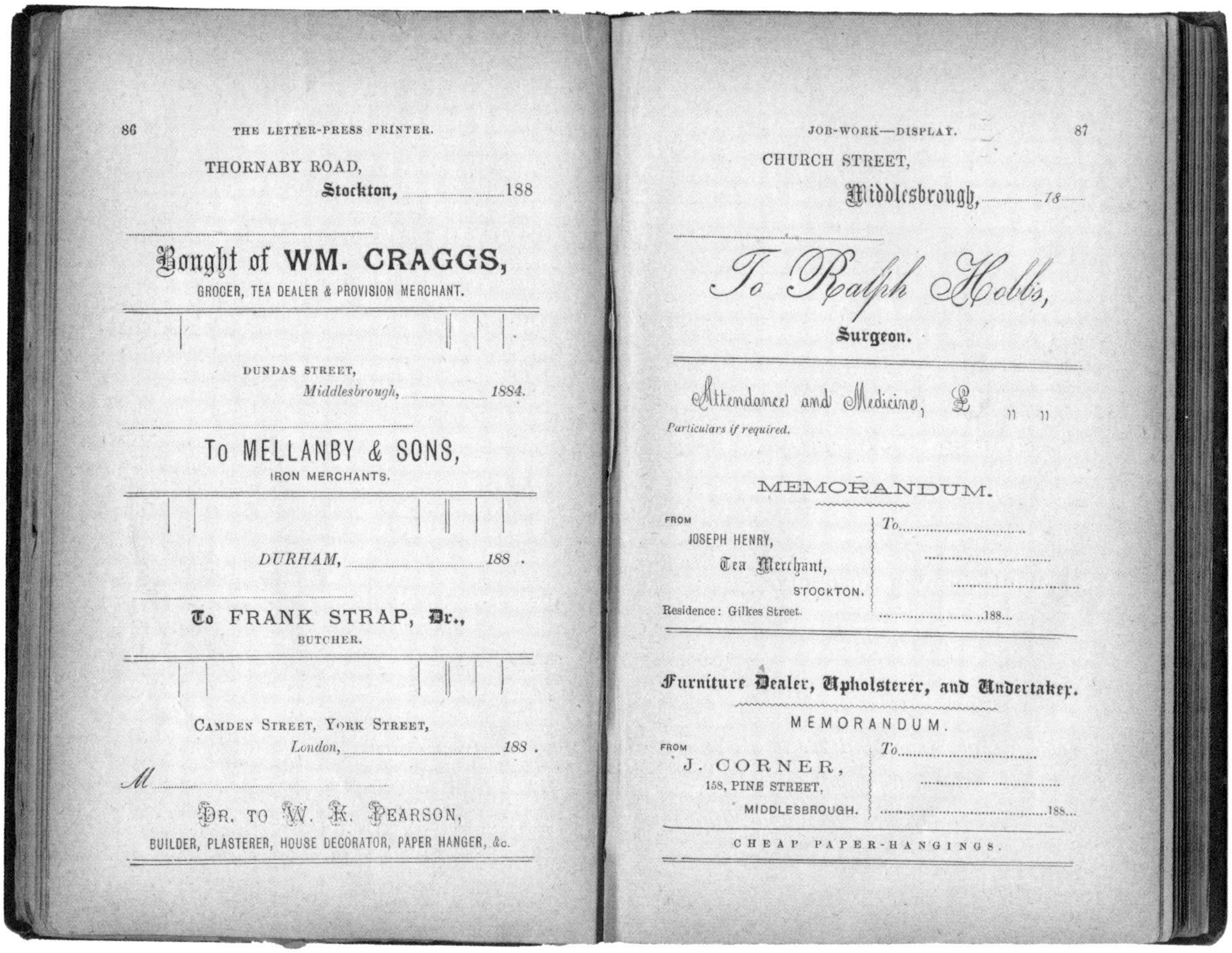

86 THE LETTER-PRESS PRINTER.

THORNABY ROAD,

Stockton, ... 188

Bought of WM. CRAGGS,

GROCER, TEA DEALER & PROVISION MERCHANT.

DUNDAS STREET,

Middlesbrough, ... *1884.*

To MELLANBY & SONS,

IRON MERCHANTS.

DURHAM, ... *188* .

To FRANK STRAP, Dr.,

BUTCHER.

CAMDEN STREET, YORK STREET,

London, ... *188* .

M ....

DR. TO W. K. PEARSON,

BUILDER, PLASTERER, HOUSE DECORATOR, PAPER HANGER, &c.

JOB-WORK—DISPLAY. 87

CHURCH STREET,

Middlesbrough, ... *18*

To Ralph Hobbs,

Surgeon.

Attendance and Medicine, £ " "

Particulars if required.

MEMORANDUM.

FROM JOSEPH HENRY,

Tea Merchant,

STOCKTON.

Residence: Gilkes Street.

To............

............188...

Furniture Dealer, Upholsterer, and Undertaker.

MEMORANDUM.

FROM J. CORNER,

158, PINE STREET,

MIDDLESBROUGH.

To............

............188...

CHEAP PAPER-HANGINGS.

146. Rule-of-thumb jobbing. Demonstration settings shown in Joseph Gould's *The Letter-Press Printer* (6th edition, 1893), showing how differently the same copy should be displayed when set as a poster and as a circular, and a two-page spread offering the printer a variety of suggestions for stationery headings. (78%)

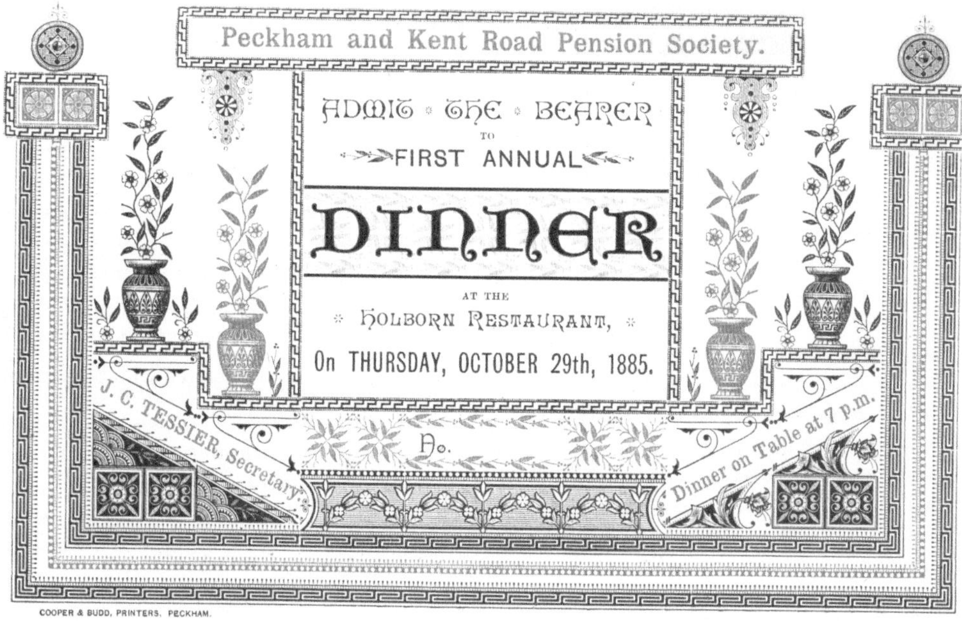

Peckham and Kent Road Pension Society.

ADMIT THE BEARER TO FIRST ANNUAL

DINNER

AT THE HOLBORN RESTAURANT,

On THURSDAY, OCTOBER 29th, 1885.

J. C. TESSIER, Secretary.

No.

Dinner on Table at 7 p.m.

COOPER & BUDD, PRINTERS, PECKHAM.

2 TO 14 CROWN COURT,
AND 72 FLEET STREET, LONDON, E.C.,

1890.

DEAR SIR,

We take the liberty of enclosing a Sample of our celebrated "CROWN COURT" NOTE PAPER & ENVELOPES, and will be glad to be favoured with your orders for same through your nearest Stationer, as we supply the Wholesale Trade only. Should you not succeed in obtaining the Paper in this way, kindly communicate with us, and oblige,

Yours truly,

Edward Lloyd, Limited.

147. *(Top)* dinner invitation by Cooper & Budd, London, 1885; and *(below)* circular letter by Robert Grayson, Leicester, 1890. Printed in gold and dark blue, with a pale-green tint of tiny leaf ornaments backing the main display line, the elaborately ornamented Cooper & Budd card seeks to rival the visual richness of chromolithography. In contrast, Grayson, working in the Leicester free style, has created an elegant arrangement that is essentially typographic. The muted colours are also characteristic of the style. Published in *Printers' International Specimen Exchange* 7 (1886) and 11 (1890), both jobs appear to represent work done for actual customers rather than ones specially designed for the *Exchange*. (85%)

148. Trade card designed by George W. Jones and set by a compositor working under his direction at the Darien Press, Edinburgh, 1888. The design exhibits the characteristics of what was later to be termed the Leicester free style: asymmetrical arrangement, vignettes chosen for their aesthetic qualities rather than relevance to subject, and the design space structured with brass printing rule. The portrait motif is another unit from the Holbein series. (72%) George Joyner, *Artistic Printing*, 1895.

journal instead inviting readers to send in their own specimens the best of which they would keep on file at the journal's office, open to the inspection of any who cared to call.[29]

Letterpress printing itself evolved through the 1880s, American work becoming quieter in colour and the standard of British typography gradually improving. Rather than seeking to imitate lithography, the trend now shifted towards developing a style of fine printing that was essentially typographic. George W. Jones moved to the Darien Press from Raithby & Lawrence early in 1888 and published the firm's first specimen book, *Something New in Letterpress Printing*, later that same year. Set to Jones's designs, the work was wholly in accord with the *British Printer*'s philosophy of combining the artistic with the practical (148), and drew the following appreciation from the journal:

> There is no very elaborate composition in any of these specimens; ornament is used sparingly, but every bit tells, and as a rule the whole of any job is almost entirely in one tint, with just an initial, a rule, a small emblem or arms in another and more decided colour. Some of the tints are difficult to describe, thus fulfilling Ruskin's definition of a true art colour. The new pictorial vignettes are used in a novel style that will find many imitators. … Another feature is that in the majority of these specimens only two or three faces of type – sometimes only one – are used, yet in every case the effect is good.[30]

What was innovative in the new vignettes was that although, being pictorial, they had subject matter, this was incidental, for their purpose was not to illustrate but simply to decorate (130, 151). Thus did typography manifest the 'art-for-art's-sake' principle of the Aesthetic movement. George Joyner described the first of these vignettes as a series introduced by Zeese & Co. of Chicago as recently as 1887, followed by a set of German sea, river and pastoral vignettes in 1888.[31]

Jones's ideas were further developed by Raithby & Lawrence's new works manager, Robert Grayson, of whom the *British Printer* was to observe 'in ever striving to obtain the maximum of effect with a minimum of labour, he has developed a style which is becoming increasingly popular with British printers, as evidenced by the free use which not only printers, but even lithographers have made of the designs'.[32]

This new typography was a far more open mode of setting than that which characterised the earlier period of Art-printing, and it had been developing for some time. In May-June 1888 the *British Printer* presented an open and well-balanced specimen by Cutherbertson & Black of Manchester, preceding Jones's *Something New* by several months, and earlier than this the *American Art Printer* had published in 1887 a very open design in brass rule as stimulus for its readers' ideas.[33] But this was a peculiarly British mode of typography, and was to be fully developed by Grayson at Leicester. To some it was the 'grouped' style; but it was widely noticed in Germany also, and it was German printers who would coin the name by which it was to be most widely known, *der ungezwungen Leicester stil* – the Leicester free style.[34]

Oscar Harpel had taken it as given that all lines would be centred, with pleasing design achieved through varying the line lengths and the weights and sizes of type. But it was not always easy to do this while at the same time respecting the natural line breaks and maintaining the appropriate emphases in the copy. With the Leicester style this problem was avoided, the compositor having the option of displaying a phrase as two, sometimes three, short lines staggered asymmetrically one below the other.

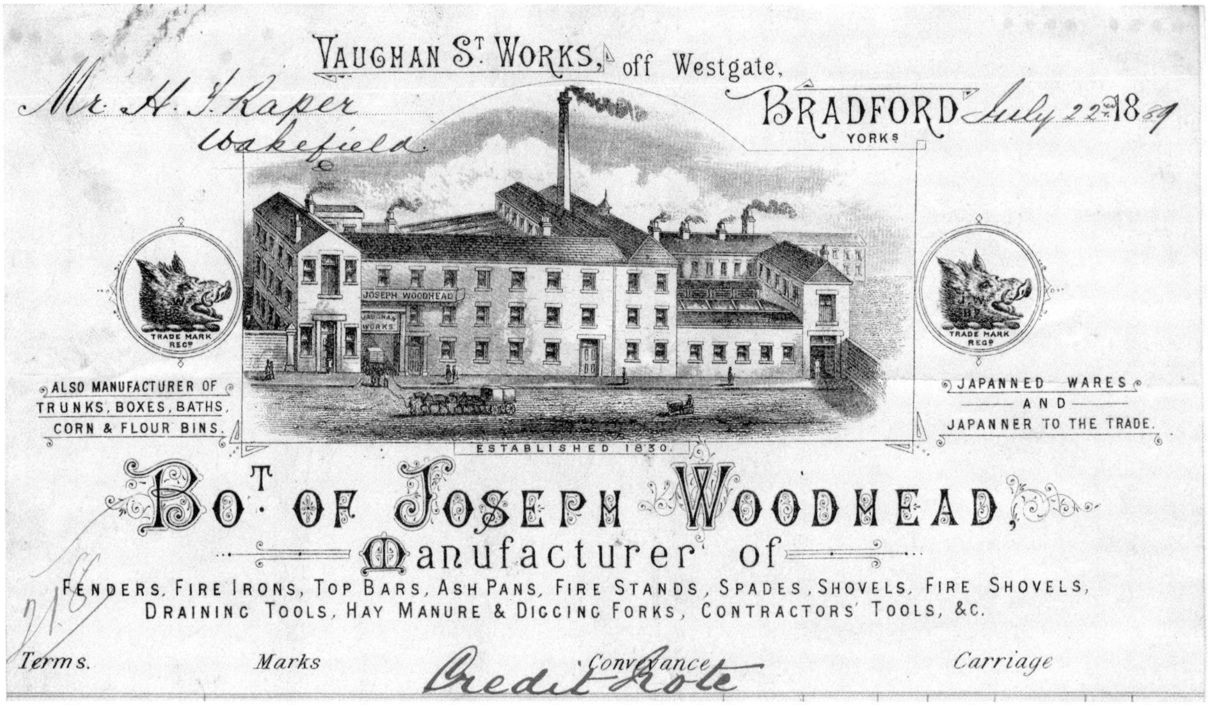

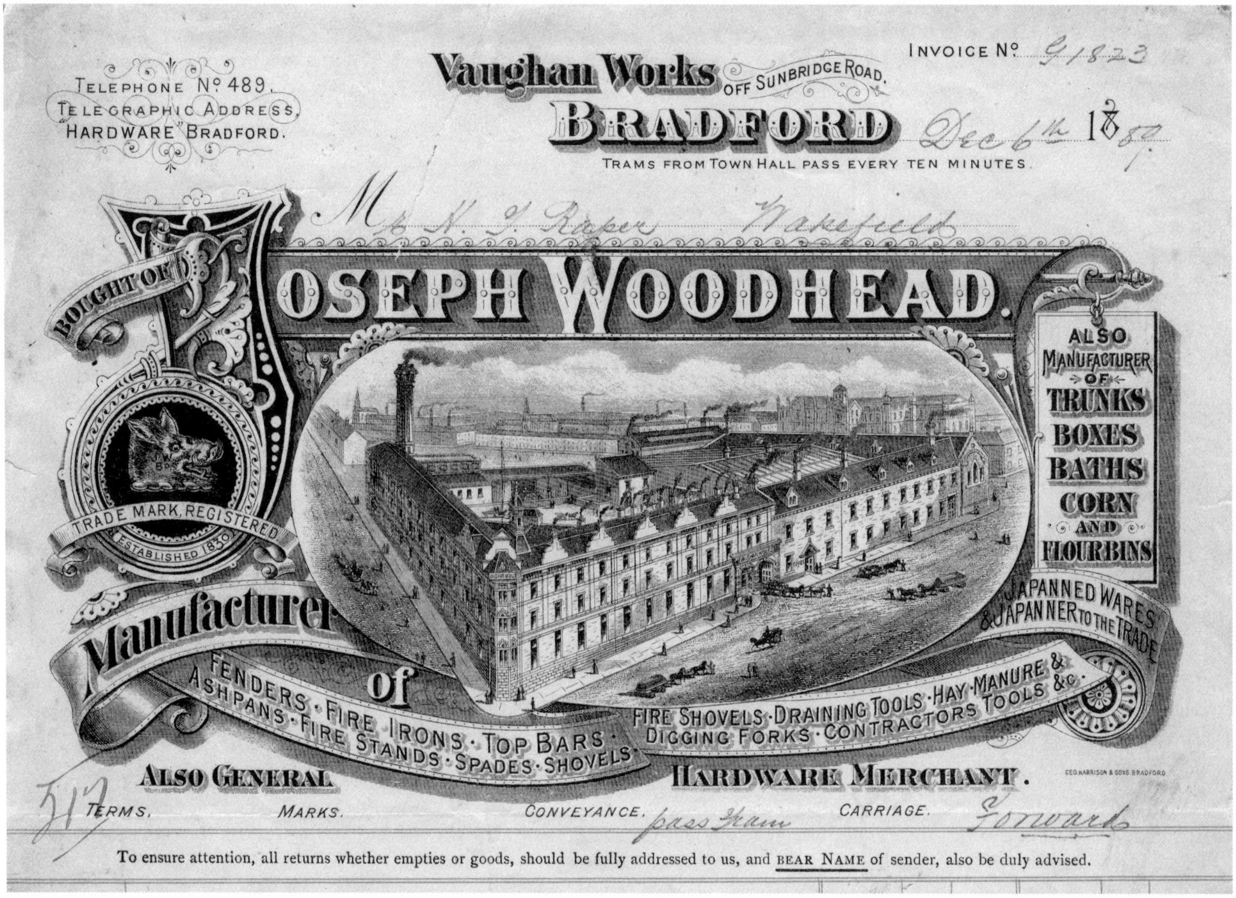

149. Lithographic design in transition. *(Top)* Billhead engraved on stone in the traditional steel-engraved manner, in use 1889; and *(below)* the 'gaslight' design that replaced it in the same year, engraved on stone by George Harrison & Sons, Bradford. The new design appears to have been prompted by a move to new premises. In both cases the figures and the horses and carts in the streets have been considerably reduced in scale to exaggerate the heights and lengths of the buildings. (78%)

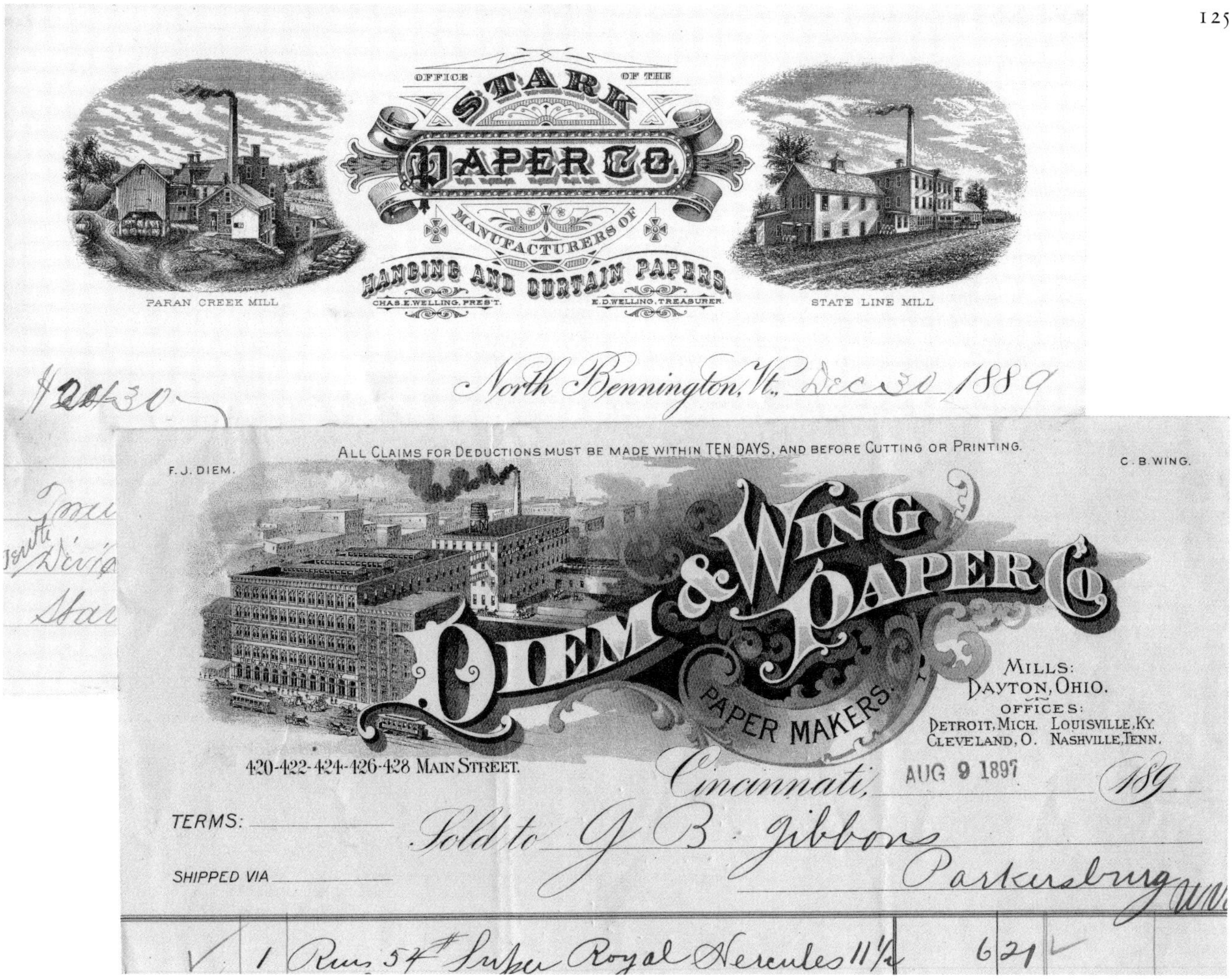

150. Engraving on stone on American billheads. *(Top)* In use 1889: the lettering carries a hint of the gaslight style, but the symmetry of the composition and the presentation of lettering and vignettes as separate items adheres to an earlier tradition. *(Below)* In use 1897: a particularly well considered expression of the gaslight style, the vignette convincingly integrated with the dynamic curving lettering. Note how the back flourish of the D neatly curves around the streetcar. On both headings, the engravings are so fine that it is likely they were reduced on a Buehring reducing machine or similar apparatus. (74%)

It was not a wholly new idea but it was in the 1890s that it became most common. The essence of the free style was space and the frequent use of asymmetry. Layout was structured on arrangements of 1½-point brass rule, or ornamental bands of border units set between fine rules, the words grouped according to sense, and space of white or tinted background paper replacing the elaborately contrived ornamentation of the 1880s (134, 147, 151). A vignette or single large unit of combination border could be employed to create a point of focus. Within the wider context of the Aesthetic movement itself, the asymmetrical balance and elegant rule work of the Leicester style had affinity with Japanese design, both in the original and as interpreted in the furniture of E. W. Godwin and others. How important printer's rule was in the 1890s is shown by the publication of a manual of exemplars on this subject alone, *Straight Rule Designs for Job Comps*, published by L. A. Macdonald of Portland, Oregon, in 1892. *Printing World* strongly advised its readers to buy a copy.[35]

Variant modes of layout which developed within the Leicester style were the *panel* style, where rectangles defined by rules were variously tinted to create the effect of overlapping panels, and the *geometrical* mode in which the panels were set at angles.

In December 1892 Robert Grayson read a paper to Leicester trade students on 'Design and Display in Job Work', which gives us a clear picture of typography as it was practised in the period. Echoing Harpel's advice of two decades earlier, Grayson observed that occasionally it would be appropriate to modify the customer's wording 'to "turn it inside out" so to speak' in order to display it effectively, 'the great majority of customers [being] only too glad to let the printer lick their copy into shape'. The key to achieving a good design was that it should have as a

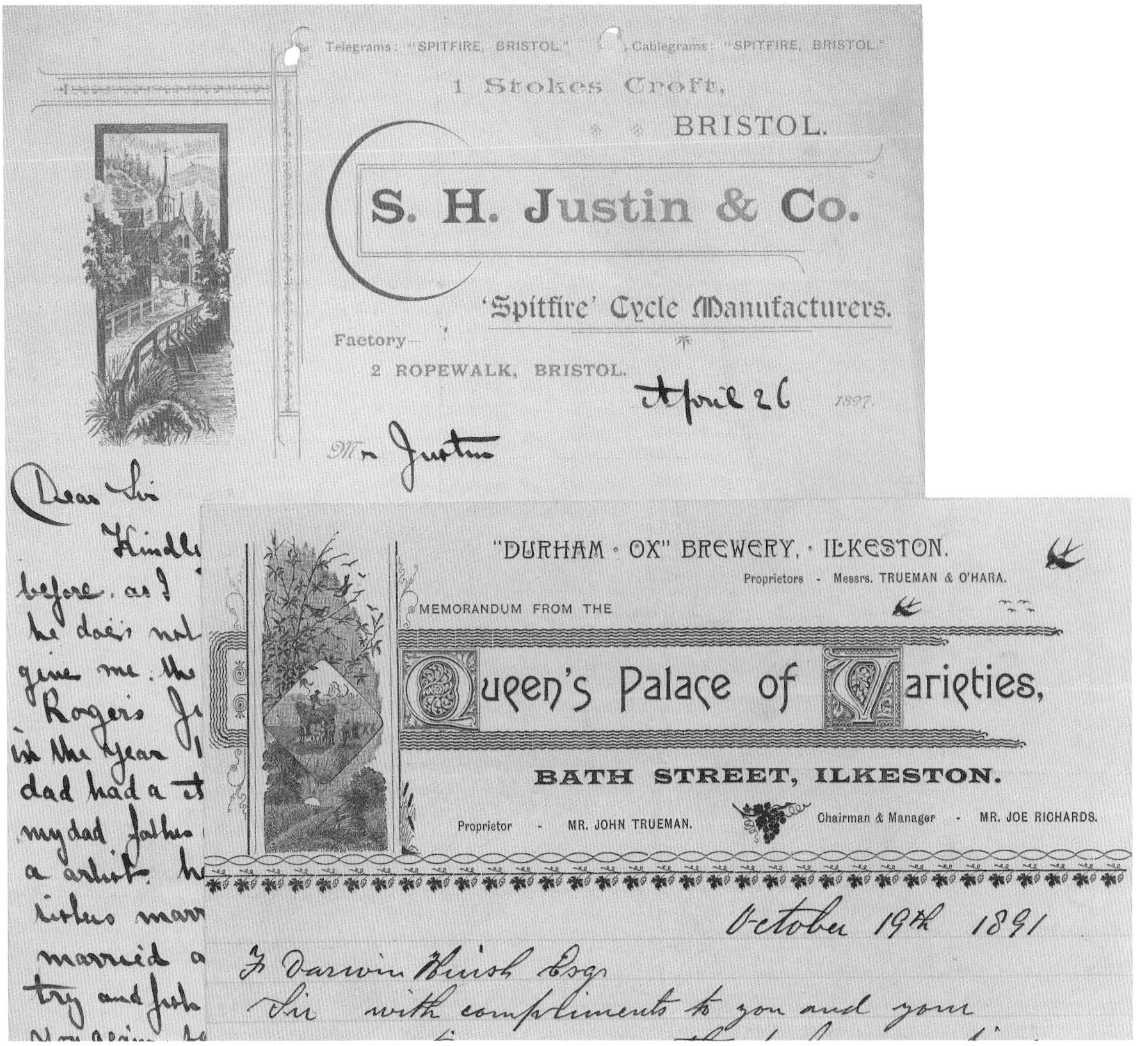

151. *(Top)* Letterhead in the Leicester free style, 1897. Printed in red and green on cream paper, the colours are unusually bright for work of this period. Pine forest, mountains and the architecture of the church confirm that the vignette is of German origin. *(Below)* Letterhead in the Leicester style in use 1891, utilising another of the new pictorial vignettes introduced but a few years earlier. In both cases the imagery is essentially part of the Aesthetic scheme of the design with no relevance to the natures of the firms represented. (57%)

main element some distinctive 'feature', by which he meant for example type overprinted on a panel of ornament, or a noticeable band of border units placed across the page or forming a frieze at the head.

Grayson instructed that main display lines should be set in a single series of type, with a contrasting series employed for the secondary lines. If the main were 'somewhat fancy' then the secondary should be plain, each thus bringing out the character of the other. Artistic setting was not to be achieved simply by putting in decorative material, but through 'the judicious arrangement or grouping of ornament, type and space'. The latter was all-important, Grayson having seen scores of jobs 'otherwise good in every respect' spoilt through insensitivity to its correct use. The eye had to be trained, which would take long practice, but once achieved the compositor might judge his spacing to the precision of a one-point lead.

When designing a job the compositor should set and proof the main lines and any vignette or large ornament he intended to use, then cut them out and try them in different groupings on a sheet of paper to find a satisfactory arrangement. That done, the finer details would follow: 'you will find the choice of main lines to influence every other part of the design; it will decide for you the general character of the other lines and of the style of ornament to be used'. Those points decided, the layout would then be completed in pencil (such a layout, it was noted elsewhere, could even be used as a customer's first proof.[36]) With the wealth of typographic material now available he added, it was possible to create a design equally effective as a similar job drawn by a lithographic artist but taking about a quarter of the time.

In conclusion, Grayson observed that of all the departments of letterpress, none were 'so exhausting as that of

152. Letterpress colour printing by John F. Earhart. Produced as a tour-de-force for *Printers' International Specimen Exchange* 4, 1883, the job is printed in gold and twelve colours. The butterfly is a wood-engraving by Earhart and the marble-like frame an example of 'chaostype' which he invented. A sense of the third dimension is created with the overlapping, piercing and curling of various parts of the imagery – all achieved with brass printing rule. The intention to match the visual richness of chromolithography is clear. (80%)

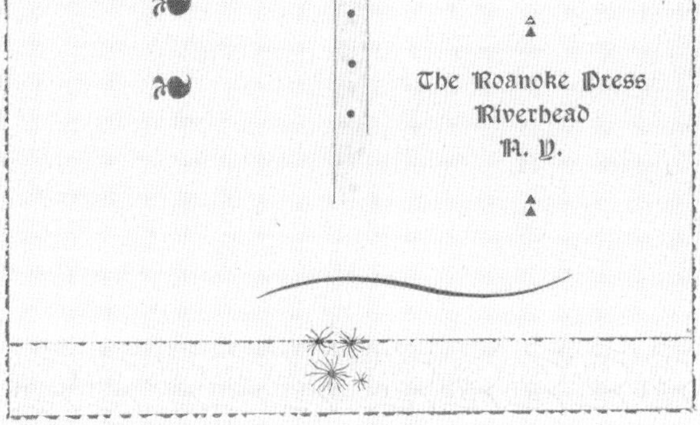

153. *(Right)* Specimen-book cover by Harry Taft of the Roanoke Press, Riverhead, NY. The asymmetry, division of space with rules and general openness of the design show the influence of the British Leicester free style, though here the layout has a distinctly individual touch, presaging the trend towards simplicity in American printing. *Printers' International Specimen Exchange* 13, 1892. (70%)

fancy or artistic jobbing'; but it had its compensations, giving 'pleasure to the designer, to the compositor, to the pressman, to the customer, and to the reading public, and the finished product is a thing of beauty, though it may not always prove a joy for ever'.[37] Job printing was, as Grayson realised, ultimately ephemeral.

With the development of the Leicester free style the initiative in typographic thinking passed to Britain. Hilton received enquiries from the United States for good men who could design and compose in 'the free Leicester style'[38], and in St Louis the *Artist Printer* described specimens from George Lewis & Son as 'work which for originality and thorough departure from our hackneyed styles surprises us'.[39]

Addressing the question of printing inks, John Southward

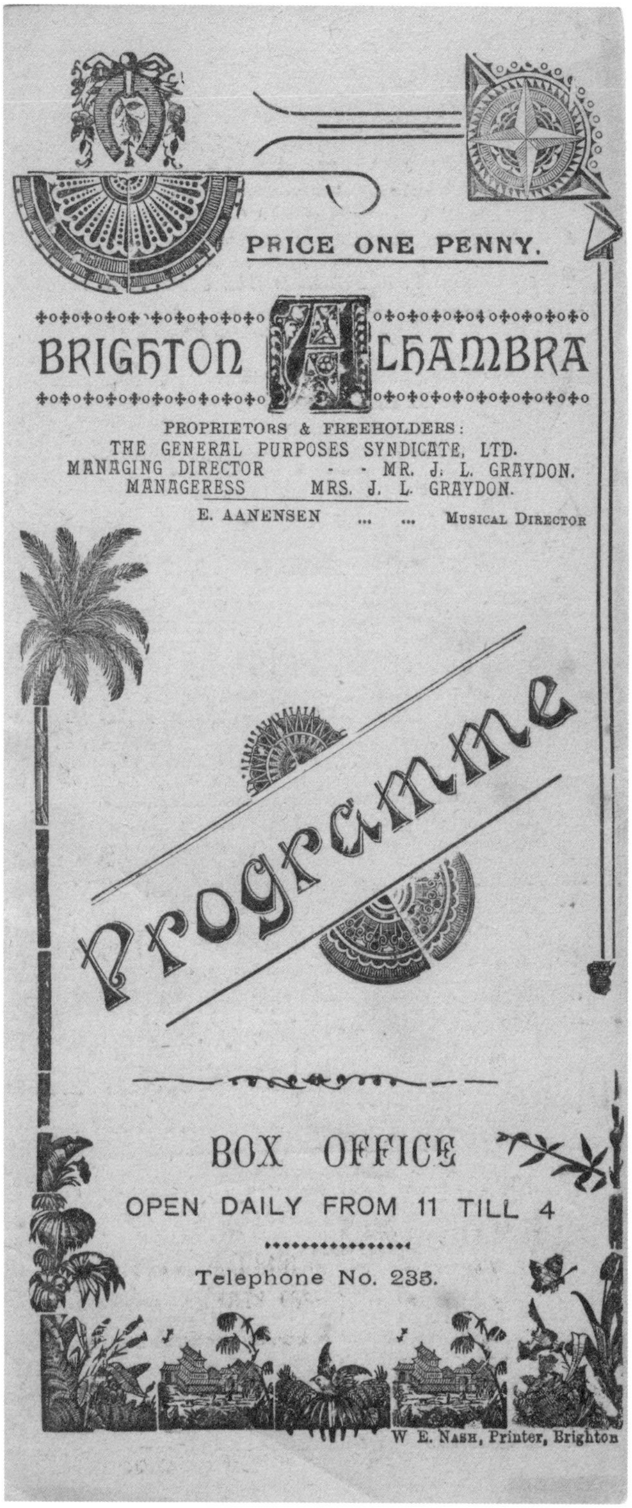

PRICE ONE PENNY.
BRIGHTON ALHAMBRA
PROPRIETORS & FREEHOLDERS:
THE GENERAL PURPOSES SYNDICATE, LTD.
MANAGING DIRECTOR - - MR. J. L. GRAYDON.
MANAGERESS MRS. J. L. GRAYDON.
E. AANENSEN ... ... MUSICAL DIRECTOR
Programme
BOX OFFICE
OPEN DAILY FROM 11 TILL 4
Telephone No. 235.
W E. NASH, Printer, Brighton

154. 'Blacksmith' work, 1896. The term was applied by the printing trade to those who took no pride in their work. On this music-hall programme, W. E. Nash of Brighton has stuck in his artistic ornaments just any old how and the presswork is execrable. (92%)

noted in 1892 that the printer's preference was for 'Art colours', similar to those used in dress and furnishing fabrics.[40] The compositor of the 1890s could now call on ready-mixed hues more subtle than those of earlier years, and in those parts of a setting where once he would instinctively have used black a dark *colour* was now more usual. Art colours were beautiful in themselves, yet a long-standing question remained: what rules were to be followed to achieve harmonious colour combinations? Advice in the trade journals was limited to descriptions in words – e.g. 'umber, combines with light violet-black, blue-black [or] claret [and] should be displayed with bright blue or green [or] geranium lake'[41], but the value of this was clearly limited. Aesthetically charged trade journalism such as the following was not much help either: 'Art cannot blend colours as does Nature; but we may learn many a colour lesson from the painted petals of Flora's children, or from the gay-winged insect that sips nectar from the glowing heart of the flower.'[42] How such lessons were to be applied in the composing room was left undetermined.

The Art-printer most skilled in his use of colour was John Earhart, whose specimens had Andrew Tuer 'lost in admiration and amazement'[43] (152). In 1884 Earhart embarked on a project aimed at demonstrating the use of colour by practical example, but it was not until 1892 that *The Color Printer* was finally completed. Earhart took as his basis twelve easily procurable base inks plus zinc white, and with them created over a thousand discernibly different colours from two- and three-ink mixes, the best of which he showed as printed samples together with the formulae for mixing them. Earhart also listed a series of two- and three-colour harmonies utilising these colours, classifying them as 'good', 'very good' or 'excellent'. Also demonstrated were the further colours achievable by over-printing, Earhart observing 'good use of these effects can be made, not only in fine label work, but also in elegant card work, or ornamental printing of any description'.[44] Receiving a copy of the *Color Printer*, Hilton described it as the richest typographic feast he had ever had.[45] A companion volume, *The Harmonizer*, illustrating the effects of printing in colours on tinted papers, was published in 1897.

Art-printing, particularly that of the 1880s, was characterised by elaboration in setting and colour, and the question arises as to how commercially viable it actually was. One who had no place for it was De Vinne, who instructed his compositors in 1883 'the business of the house is done for profit [...] the office cannot allow one-quarter of a day for the composition of a card for which it receives but fifty cents', and 'avoid fantastic arrangements of type and ornaments. Do not try to show yourself or your skill by eccentric fancies in composition.'[46] Discussing the cost question, the Philadelphia *Printer's Circular* was doubtful, but concluded that an office equipped with the right material 'may make it profitable, providing that customers come along who will give the printer unconditional terms for the sake of obtaining something

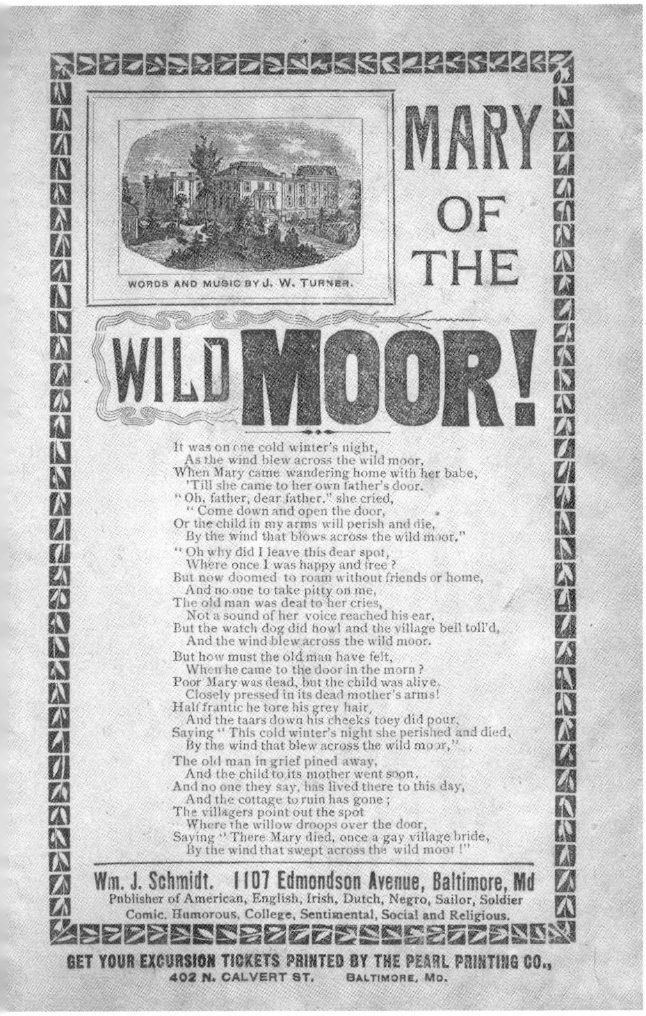

WORDS AND MUSIC BY J. W. TURNER.

MARY OF THE WILD MOOR!

It was on one cold winter's night,
As the wind blew across the wild moor,
When Mary came wandering home with her babe,
'Till she came to her own father's door.
"Oh, father, dear father." she cried,
"Come down and open the door,
Or the child in my arms will perish and die,
By the wind that blows across the wild moor."
"Oh why did I leave this dear spot,
Where once I was happy and free?
But now doomed to roam without friends or home,
And no one to take pitty on me,
The old man was deaf to her cries,
Not a sound of her voice reached his ear,
But the watch dog did howl and the village bell toll'd,
And the wind blew across the wild moor.
But how must the old man have felt,
When he came to the door in the morn?
Poor Mary was dead, but the child was alive,
Closely pressed in its dead mother's arms!
Half frantic he tore his grey hair,
And the taars down his cheeks toey did pour,
Saying "This cold winter's night she perished and died,
By the wind that blew across the wild moor,"
The old man in grief pined away,
And the child to its mother went soon.
And no one they say, has lived there to this day,
And the cottage to ruin has gone;
The villagers point out the spot
Where the willow droops over the door,
Saying "There Mary died, once a gay village bride,
By the wind that swept across the wild moor!"

Wm. J. Schmidt. 1107 Edmondson Avenue, Baltimore, Md
Publisher of American, English, Irish, Dutch, Negro, Sailor, Soldier
Comic, Humorous, College, Sentimental, Social and Religious.

GET YOUR EXCURSION TICKETS PRINTED BY THE PEARL PRINTING CO.,
402 N. CALVERT ST. BALTIMORE, MD.

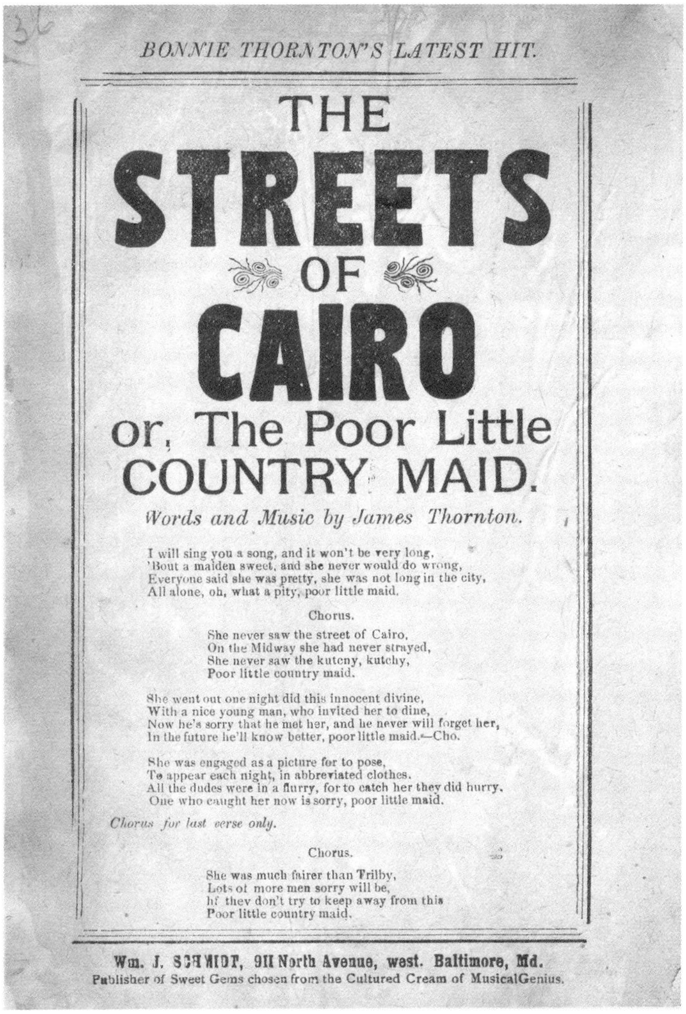

BONNIE THORNTON'S LATEST HIT.

THE STREETS OF CAIRO

or, The Poor Little COUNTRY MAID.

Words and Music by James Thornton.

I will sing you a song, and it won't be very long,
'Bout a maiden sweet, and she never would do wrong,
Everyone said she was pretty, she was not long in the city,
All alone, oh, what a pity, poor little maid.

Chorus.

She never saw the street of Cairo,
On the Midway she had never strayed,
She never saw the kutcny, kutchy,
Poor little country maid.

She went out one night did this innocent divine,
With a nice young man, who invited her to dine,
Now he's sorry that he met her, and he never will forget her,
In the future he'll know better, poor little maid.—Cho.

She was engaged as a picture for to pose,
To appear each night, in abbreviated clothes.
All the dudes were in a flurry, for to catch her they did hurry.
One who caught her now is sorry, poor little maid.

Chorus for last verse only.

Chorus.

She was much fairer than Trilby,
Lots of more men sorry will be,
If they don't try to keep away from this
Poor little country maid.

Wm. J. SCHMIDT, 911 North Avenue, west. Baltimore, Md.
Publisher of Sweet Gems chosen from the Cultured Cream of MusicalGenius.

155. 'Blacksmith' work by William Schmidt, Baltimore. Published in the 1890s, Schmidt's ballad sheets have the typographic crudity of a bygone age, but that they are of the period indicated is shown by a reference to 'Trilby' in one line of 'Streets of Cairo', George Du Maurier's novel *Trilby* being serialised in *Harper's* magazine in 1894. (58%)

specially attractive'.[47] Andreas Haight made a similar point in the New Orleans *Southern Printers' Journal* in 1886, but added perspicaciously 'a judicious arrangement of few colours can often be made more attractive, with the introduction of a new idea, though very simple, than the elaborate and difficult work that can only be appreciated by the printer'.[48]

For practical purposes the complex and multi-formed Art printing of the 1880s clearly was uneconomic; and in the early 1890s Earhart's observation found fulfilment in the typographic elegance of the Leicester free style, the practicality of which is supported both by surviving ephemera and a number of specimens in the exchanges which, although artistic in effect and thoughtfully designed, would demand no extensive time in setting. When in 1895 the *British Printer* observed 'artistic composition brings trade to a house – that is something which cannot be gain said', it was the Leicester style it had in mind.[49]

Spring and Summer, 1905.

38. Church Street.
ILFRACOMBE.

Dear Madam.
I have much pleasure in intimating that my purchases of Spring and Summer Novelties are now complete, and embrace Elegant and Dainty Designs in

French & English Millinery.
Blouses, Sunshades, &c.

Should you favour me with a visit of inspection. I can assure you no pains will be spared to meet your wishes. and any design not in my Showroom, I shall be pleased to get or copy.

Obediently yours.

A. K. MACKENZIE.

The
Dressmaking
Department
is under efficient management.

The
Children's
Department
is replete with all the latest styles.

C 227

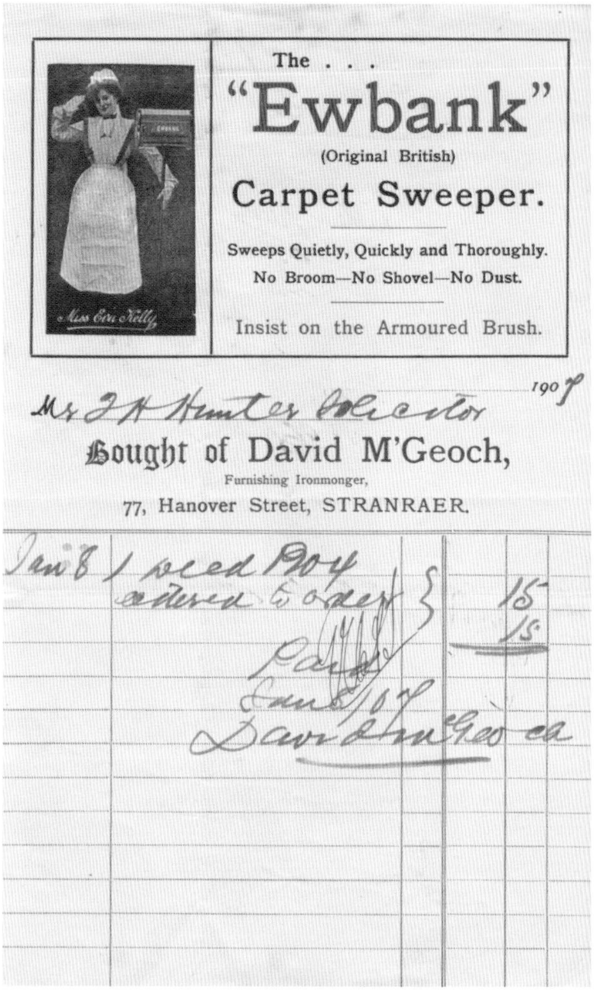

The . . .
"Ewbank"
(Original British)
Carpet Sweeper.
Sweeps Quietly, Quickly and Thoroughly.
No Broom—No Shovel—No Dust.
Insist on the Armoured Brush.

Miss Eva Kelly

190

Bought of David M'Geoch,
Furnishing Ironmonger,
77, Hanover Street, STRANRAER.

156. Letterpress halftones. *(Top left)* Circular letter with vignetted stock cut reproduced from a watercolour original. The sheet folds for posting, the bottom panel having a slit for insertion of the tab at the top. *(Top right)* Advertising billhead in use 1907, with halftone of the music hall artiste Eva Kelly promoting a carpet-sweeper. Printed in large editions, such stationery was supplied to shopkeepers at modest cost for overprinting with their individual business details. *(Bottom)* Tomato-can label, early twentieth century, combining a halftone image of the jardiniere with a line image of tomatoes. Printed in black and four additional colours. (60%)

An Eccentricity of Comicality.
MEMO. from
Harry Speller,
HUMOROUS ENTERTAINER
- - AND - -
LIVING MARIONETTE.
Every Description of Entertainment attended and Catered for at Moderate Terms.
AVIS & DELAFOND, 116, BOROUGH ROAD
Address, for Terms and Vacant Dates
London, 190
MEMOS.
AS THIS SAMPLE.
ANY ONE COLOUR,
100, 2/6. 250, 3/9.
ANY TWO COLOURS,
100, 3/0. 250, 4/6.
Photo. Block, 4/-
Prompt Delivery. Latest Styles.
AVIS & DELAFOND,
PROMPT PRINTERS,
116, Borough Road, S.E.
A Roar of Laughter from Start to Finish!
SAM WALSH,
(THE CARD SHARP)
Comedy Conjurer,
Card Manipulator, etc.
Introducing SMART AND ORIGINAL MYSTERIES.
The Only Act of its kind. Funny & Clever.
P.S.—My Act is Not a Cod Conjuring Act, . . .
. . . but all REAL CLEVER TRICKS.
Address
With Herni Gros and Adney Payne, 1904-5-6 & 7.
Encore, Feb. 28th, 1907.
MR. SAM WALSH, comedy conjuror, is going well at the Chelsea Palace this week. He has a variation of the hat and omelette trick, which is not only clever, but intensely funny. He should make headway.
Camberwell & Peckham Times
MR. SAM WALSH provided a most finished exhibition of conjuring, interspersed with witty 'patter.' His skill was decidedly above the ordinary.
8/6
100 5/6
200 6/6

157. Printer's samples, 1900s, by Avis & Delafond of London, who made a specialty of entertainers' stationery. Letterheads like Harry Speller's cost 2*s.* 6*d.* (61c) per hundred and 4*s.* (at this time equivalent to 97c) for the halftone. Two-colour headings like that of Sam Walsh would be 5*s.* 6*d.* ($1.34) per hundred plus 8*s.* 6*d.* ($2.07c) for the larger halftone. (61%)

8

Process engraving and commercial art

In 1892 Theodore L. De Vinne contributed a paper to the United Typothetaea of America on 'Masculine Printing', his mode of typography, where visual quality was achieved through using only 'easily read types of good cut, and of the plainest form';[1] and on another occasion (probably in 1893), addressing the National Editorial Association, De Vinne foresaw the day when all ornamentals would be either forgotten or 'remembered only to be hooted at'.

De Vinne was greatly admired by the British printer George W. Jones, but Jones was impelled to respond that, with all his love for a beautifully cut roman letter, he could not imagine a day 'when we shall come to the sole use of plain roman types [and] nothing of an ornamental nature proceeds from the press'.[2] It was a basic tenet, however, of Jones and other intelligent Art-printers, that Artistic types and ornaments were ultimately of secondary importance. What really mattered was the structure they enriched, and thus plain work composed with sensitivity to space, tone and scale would be more truly artistic than ornamented work executed without understanding. In this their thinking was close to that of De Vinne, and indeed Harpel, who had advocated the value of well-considered plain work rather more than twenty years before.

In June 1889 Jones had left the Darien Press, setting up his own business in London later that year.[3] Visiting the press in 1895, the editor of the *British Printer* observed that the office had now 'somewhat departed from its former enterprise in fine jobbing'. This was a good six years after Jones had left Edinburgh, but it may be that the enthusiasm there for Art printing had simply declined without his inspiration. There was similar decline elsewhere in Scotland, for the editor also noted that at Nimmo & Co., Leith, 'stern business necessities seem to have narrowed the class of production to an ordinary plain style, and very little of the higher branches of jobbing is now cultivated'; while at George Lewis & Co. 'a quieter and perhaps less elaborate style is now the order of the day, Mr. [John] Lewis, jun., who was chiefly responsible for the newer ventures of the jobbing class, having left for fields afresh'.[4] The crowded display of 1880s Art-printing had been superseded by the refinement of the Leicester free style, and now in the 1890s the trend was towards something simpler still.

The first book from William Morris's Kelmscott Press, *The Glittering Plain*, was published in May 1891, followed by *Poems by the Way* in October. Lovers of fine printing imported these and other Kelmscott books into America, Morris's thoroughly masculine typefaces thereby giving

158. Employee of a process-engraving firm using wood-engraving tools to enhance a half-tone plate. In the case of this half-tone illustration, the original was a pencil drawing by commercial artist F. G. Kitton, and here the engraver (perhaps the very man depicted) has brought freshness to the image by cutting away all half-tone dots from the areas representing white paper. *British Printer*, 7.40 (1894). (94%)

A DISHONEST playgrounds

B September Excursions

C SURPRISE NEIGHBOR
Modern American Designs

D STRONG REMINDERS

E FORMER Explorations

159. Plain printing types. (A) Caslon, from George W. Jones's specimen of 1925; (B) Satanick, imitating William Morris's Troy type; (C) Jenson Oldstyle, based on Morris's Golden type; (D) Cheltenham Oldstyle; (E) Post Oldstyle No. 1, one of a variety of faces exaggerating the effect of printing on the hand-made paper of colonial days. (100%)

further encouragement to those who saw potential in types of plainer cut. Morris's Golden, Troy and Chaucer types were unprotected in America, and legend has it that when Joseph Phinney of the Dickinson foundry requested permission to manufacture the Troy in America, he was curtly told to go to hell: consequently when American Type Founders brought out their unauthorised version in 1896 they aptly named it Satanick (159B). If the story is true, Morris had probably still been fuming over Jenson Old Style (159C), a weak imitation of the Golden type brought out by ATF three years earlier.[5] Other plain-cut types of the 1890s were original in design, among them the highly popular Cheltenham designed by Bertram Goodhue in 1896 (159D). This was the first type cut as an extensive series, some eighteen variations being produced in the period 1904–11.

In England in 1844 the printer Charles Whittingham initiated a revival of Caslon's classic roman at the Chiswick Press. In America Caslon was available again from 1859, but its use really caught on from 1896 when the young Will Bradley began using Caslon at his newly founded Wayside Press, Bradley describing it as 'the most direct, honest, vigorous and imaginative [type] America has ever known'.[6] Inspired by the qualities of Caslon type and ornaments, Bradley developed what he termed the 'Colonial' style, a mode of typography akin to Tuer's Antique but based on seventeenth- and eighteenth-century models rather than the medieval (162).

In 1887, in volume 2 of Ed McClure's *American Printers' Specimen Exchange,* the Danco Printing & Publishing Co. of Philadelphia had recommended that less showy, more everyday work be invited for volume 3. Taking the hint, McClure advertised that future specimens might be of all classes – not necessarily 'fine', but this may have diminished the subscribers' ardour for with volume 3 the number of contributors fell, and a despondent McClure announced in volume 4 (1890) that there would be no more.[7]

In England the original *Specimen Exchange* continued but contributions began to fall off in 1894, the specimens received for that and the following year being published as a single volume 15 in 1895. The decline continued, and when volume 16 finally appeared in 1898 it was the last. Hilton had sold his interest in the *Specimen Exchange* to Raithby, Lawrence & Co. four years earlier, and difficulties that had subsequently arisen between him and the firm may have led to doubts among contributors as to the future of the scheme;[8] but this is unlikely to have been a

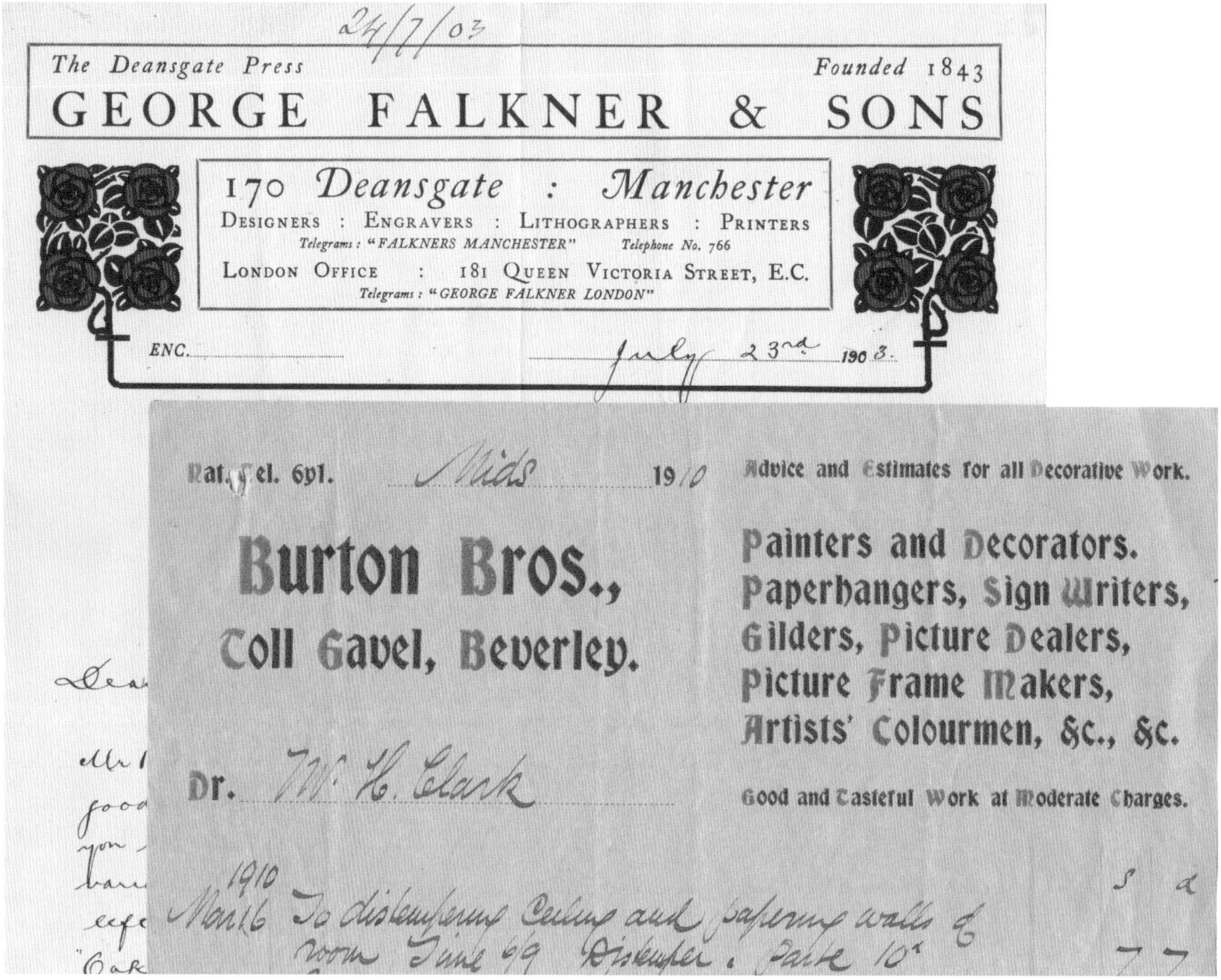

160. *(Above, top)* Letterhead in use 1903 set throughout in Caslon type, and *(below)* billhead in use 1910 set in Venetian Text – stylistically a descendant of William Morris's Troy type of 1892. The two-colours are employed to good effect on the letterhead but the use of a differently coloured initial for each word on the billhead is noticeably distracting. (76%)

major reason for the decline. It may simply be that the *Exchange* had been *too* successful, engendering similar schemes elsewhere and thus diverting potential specimens to other outlets, and perhaps also diluting the kudos of having one's work selected. The printer now had other sources of inspiration as well, in specimen books purchasable from individual printing firms and exemplars of job design published in the trade journals.

In their different ways, De Vinne, Bradley and other designers initiated a style of typography in which the type itself – strong in form, well set and carefully spaced – was the aesthetic focus. The 'severe American style' was how one writer referred to this new mode of typography.[9] Taken to the extreme it could be severe to the point of bleakness, but in both countries some use of ornament was to continue, albeit now as masculine in form as the type it complemented (160, 161, 164).

With the coming of the twentieth century typographers saw that a wide range of approaches to layout was now open to them. Edmund Gress observed that 'with De Vinne beckoning to us from the point of conservatism and Bradley from the point of radicalism, the typographer anxious to do work properly must decide for himself how to treat it'. But, then as now, even the best of typographers could lose sight of the nature of a job and simply turn out a design in the style that he personally favoured. Gress said, 'I have seen a jeweller's booklet cover so filled with ornamentation by Bradley that it was almost impossible to read the wording, and I have also seen a children's Bible typographically treated by the De Vinne company in a style as severe as if it were a book of legislative acts'.[10]

Though styles were changing, art was still seen as the essential underpinning of good typography, George French observing in the *Inland Printer* in 1903: 'the printer

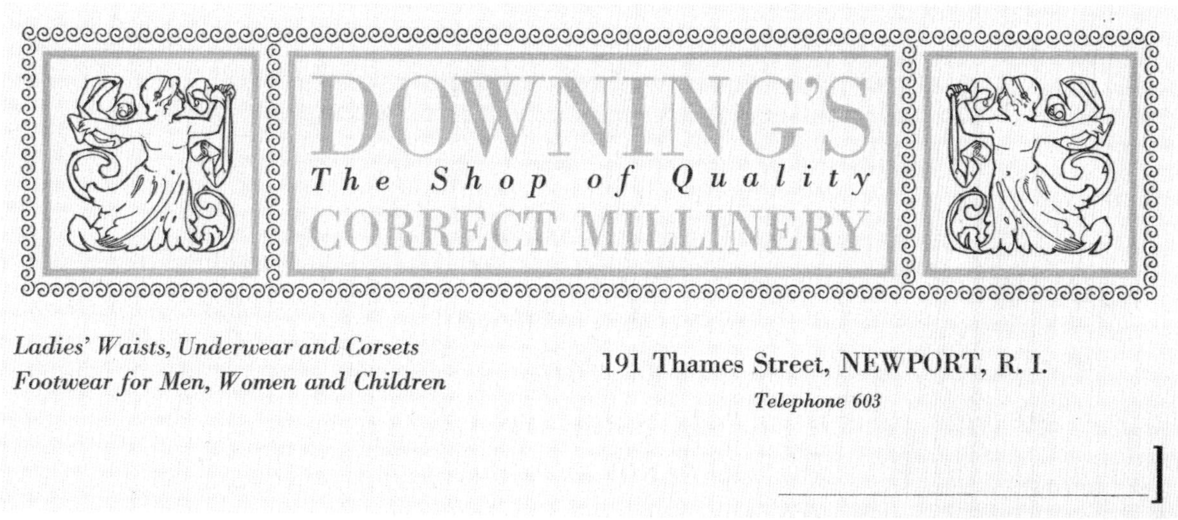
DOWNING'S
The Shop of Quality
CORRECT MILLINERY
Ladies' Waists, Underwear and Corsets
Footwear for Men, Women and Children
191 Thames Street, NEWPORT, R. I.
Telephone 603

JOHN T. KEANE & COMPANY
Upholsterers and Interior Decorators
NORTHEAST HARBOR · MAINE
AWNINGS, SHADES, DRAPERIES, CARPETS
MATTRESSES. FINE FURNITURE TO ORDER.
CUSHIONS. YACHT CUSHIONS & CANOPIES
Sold to
Date

161. *(Top)* Letterhead and *(below)* billhead, *c.*1911–12, from *Type Designs in Color*, specimen book of the Oswald Publishing Co., New York. The letterhead is set in American Type Founders' Bodoni, a modern-face type based on the designs of the eighteenth-century Italian printer Giambattista Bodoni. Here a line of lower-case has been skilfully letter-spaced to precisely match the lengths of the main display lines above and below. On the billhead, the designer has limited his typographic variation to three sizes of letter-spaced Caslon capitals and one line of italic. On both items the decoration is highly formalised. (93%)

of the future must … know a great deal about art, especially those fundamental laws of art that relate to proportion, drawing, colour, tone values, perspective, etc'.[11]

The aspiring typographer of the period was not always well served by those who proffered advice. In 1894, Wesley Washington Pasko vouchsafed 'it is a usual rule in job work to contrast the lines in length, weight, size and face. The important lines take the largest type, and frequently the heaviest, and so on down to the most unimportant.' This was banal, but Pasko's instruction that empty spaces 'should not usually be allowed to exist at the corners [of a design] when they can be filled up by words or ornament' was unforgiveable.[12] An article in the *Inland Printer* in 1907 contained some useful advice but suggested that in the preliminary sketch 'any indication of letters whatever is entirely unnecessary … whether they are to be capitals or lower-case need not be indicated on the sketch, which is not to be a piece of lettering, but simply a pleasing arrangement of the spots or forces of attraction on the page'.[13] The writer's specimen designs comprised no more than rectangles (representing the pages) enclosing more rectangles (the lines of type), and all today who have taught typography to intelligent students will know how bereft an approach this would be.

Edmund Gress's large-format *Art & Practice of Typography*, its intelligent and copiously illustrated chapters covering all aspects of the profession, was published in 1917. Fully alert to the importance of business as well as aesthetic values, Gress wrote 'art is essential to printing; so are Uncle Sam's specimens of steel engraving. The more art the printer absorbs the larger should grow his collection of these engravings.'[14]

Reflecting on typographic originality, in 1907 the *Inland Printer* observed that 'what has been accomplished has been the work of artists – men outside the printing office [and now] the tendency is for the larger offices to have an artist to lay out the work, and the printer follows orders'. The journal urged compositors to restore their status by studying the principles of design themselves.[15] But the days were passing when a man could expect to be both skilled compositor and accomplished typographer. Gress cited the case of the New Yorker Benjamin Sherbow, the freshness and individuality of whose typography Gress ascribed largely to the fact that Sherbow never had been a printer, and thus worked 'unrestrained by the traditions of the craft as handed down from compositor to apprentice'.[16] That D. B. Updike similarly entered typography from outside the industry has already been noted.

In 1905 Will Bradley was commissioned to design a series of promotional booklets for American Type Founders, and Frank B. Berry later described how Bradley laid out ATF's *Green Book of Spring*:

> Starting in on this about half-past ten one morning Bradley made up a dummy, prepared the copy and laid out the work – specifying the size and style of type to be used, the form of display and designating the exact position of each ornament with the required spacing. This was in effect practically furnishing reprint copy for the compositors. Then, to 'give good measure', as he expressed it, copy was prepared for the cover, and the work was ready for the printers before half-past one.[17]

The contrast between this practice and the *Inland Printer*'s bleak rectangles needs no comment.

The most onerous job for any printer was incurred by 'pi' – type that had become completely jumbled and had tediously to be sorted. When Sherman's army passed through Waynesboro, Georgia, on their sweep through the South in 1864, they pied one printing shop's entire stock of type, and as late as 1887 it was reported that 'though the work of sorting the mixed types has since gone steadily on there are still about two bushels of that "pie" undigested'.[18] In 1885 Otto Merganthaler patented the *Linotype*, which cast lines of 'hot metal' type from its own matrices, and though the machine's primary purpose was mechanical typesetting it also obviated pi, the type 'slugs' simply being melted down again when the job was done. The *Monotype*, invented by Talbot Lanston in 1887, had separate setting and casting units and similarly recycled its type metal. Such machines, however, designed primarily for newspaper and book production, were only slowly adopted by job printers.

In 1872 the Photo-Engraving Co. was established in New York to exploit *process line-engraving*, invented by the Frenchman Charles Gillot. This entailed making a photographic negative from an artist's line drawing, printing this on to light-sensitive zinc, then etching away the background to leave the image in relief (168). But to publishers

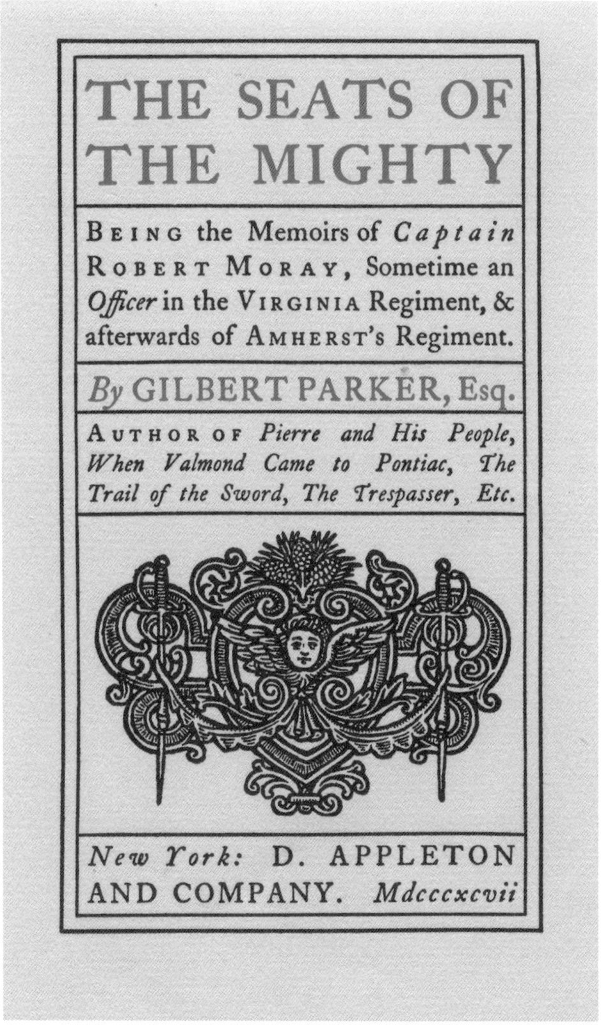

THE SEATS OF THE MIGHTY

BEING the Memoirs of *Captain* ROBERT MORAY, Sometime an *Officer* in the VIRGINIA Regiment, & afterwards of AMHERST'S Regiment.

By GILBERT PARKER, Esq.

AUTHOR OF *Pierre and His People, When Valmond Came to Pontiac, The Trail of the Sword, The Trespasser, Etc.*

New York: D. APPLETON AND COMPANY. *Mdcccxcvii*

162. Specimen title page in the colonial style by Will Bradley demonstrating the use of Caslon type on handmade paper, shown in *Bradley, His Book* (1897) and subsequently reproduced in Gress's *Art and Practice of Typography*. The ornament has been reproduced by line process engraving from a drawing by Bradley. (75%)

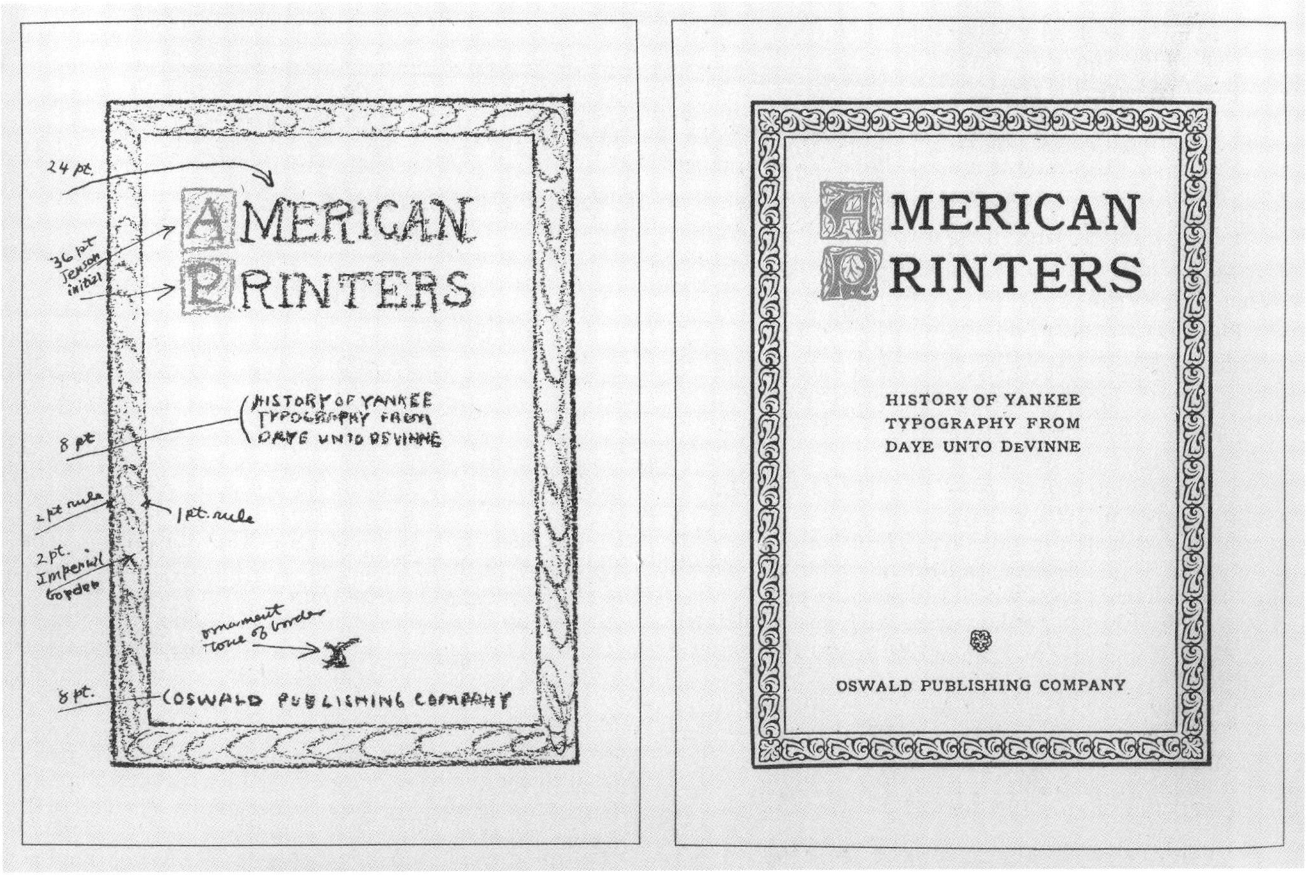

163. Illustration from Gress's *Art & Practice of Typography*, 1917, showing typographer's layout (presumably by Gress himself) and subsequent setting of a two-colour booklet cover. The decorative types are American Type Founders' Jenson initials, their design based on the wood-engraved initials used at William Morris's Kelmscott Press. (93%)

the results offered no obvious advantages over wood-engraving other than cost, and it was to be well into the 1880s before the line 'zinco' was generally adopted. Wood-engraving itself reached new heights of sophistication in America in the 1870s and 1880s when, impelled by the increasing prevalence of photography, engravers developed the ability to translate even the tonal qualities of real photographs into wood-cut textures.[19] A similar concern for photographic fidelity was evidenced in the work of steel engravers and engravers on stone (166–7).

The reproduction of actual photographs and other tonal originals by *halftone* process engraving became possible in 1881 when both George Meisenbach of Munich and Frederick Ives of Philadelphia patented varieties of halftone screen. The Ives screen proved the more successful. Essentially this was two sheets of glass each engraved with parallel fine black lines and fixed together at right-angles to form a grid, through which the original was rephotographed. This broke the image into a pattern of dots, the sizes of which when printed on to the zinc for etching varied according to the darks and lights of the original (156–7). Later all but the coarsest halftones were made on copper.

The best halftone reproduction was done in America, one British journal remarking 'there is a delicacy and at the same time a vigour and brilliancy about some [American work] which seems confined to themselves. If progress goes on uninterruptedly, wood engraving will before long be in the same moribund condition as [hand] engraving unfortunately now finds itself.'[20] To get the best out of a halftone block required a strongly built press with a precisely level bed, 'dead level' halftone blocks (the copper being mounted on wood to bring it type-high) and, equally essential, paper made specifically for halftone work. Screens were made in 'grains' of so many lines to the inch, the coarsest used by the Meisenbach Co. (who in spite of their name were using the Ives screen) in 1894 being 70 to the inch (28 per cm).[21] Even at this grain the depth of etch between the printing dots was very shallow, but the firm's finest screen was 170 to the inch (the dots all but invisible when printed) and the etch was virtually undetectable.[22] Small wonder that so much importance was attached to having the right paper for the job.

Lithographic line imagery was printed to stone photographically by Alfred Lemercier as early as 1852. Means

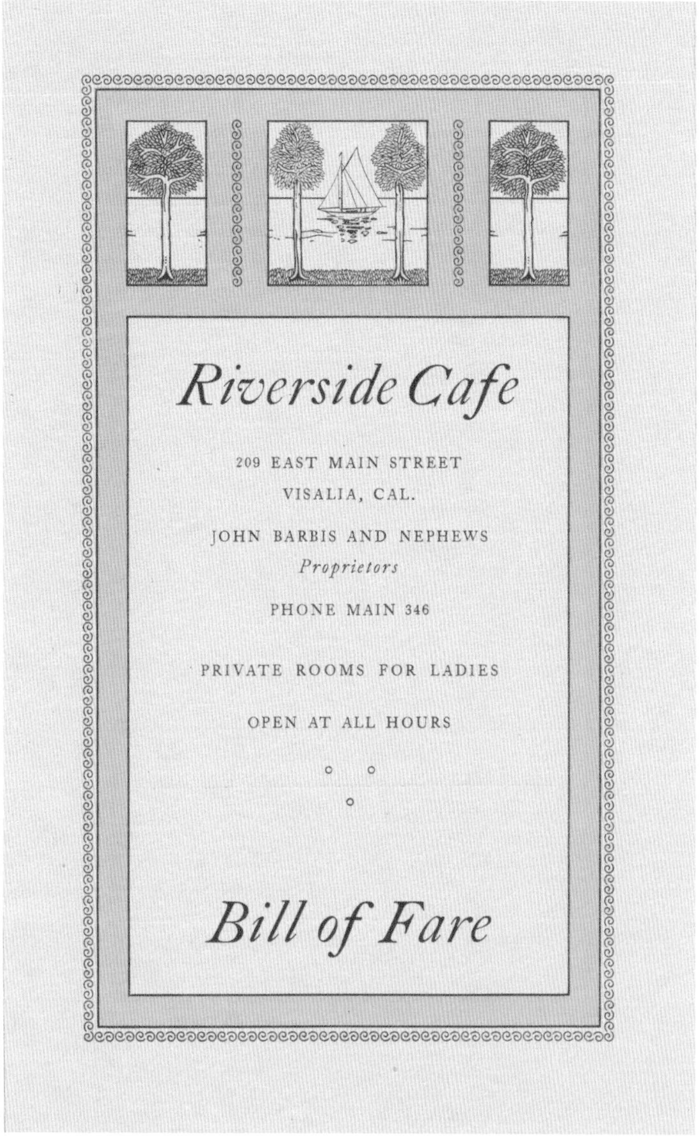

164. Menu cover in two colours by Arthur Nelson, 1912, set in Caslon type and with formalised decoration supplied by American Typefounders. Both letter- and interlinear spacing have been carefully considered. From *Type Designs in Color*, Oswald Printing Co., New York. (81%)

of creating lithographic halftones were developed in the 1880s, but it was not until the turn of the century that *photolithography* was well established, further encouraged around 1904 by Ira Rubel's invention of the rotary offset press. Here the printing image was carried on a flexible aluminium plate locked on to a revolving cylinder, the image printing first on to a second, rubber-faced cylinder, and from there on to the paper. The marked advantage for lithographers was that finer halftones could be printed on cheaper papers than was possible with letterpress.

Collotype, invented in the 1850s, utilised a glass plate coated with a layer of light-sensitive gelatine. Exposing the plate under a tonal negative rendered the gelatine in varying degrees sensitive to moisture so that when subsequently damped and inked the ink adhered according to the amount of moisture taken up. No screen was involved and the resulting image faithfully reproduced the tones of the original. Another non-screen reproduction process, *photogravure*, was invented by the Austrian Karl Klíc in 1879. This was a hand-printing process similar in principle to aquatint, with the depth of the etch varying according to the tones of the original. Developed in 1910, *rotogravure* was based on the same principle, but utilising a form of screen and working on an industrial scale. Collotype and rotogravure were employed (among several other processes) in printing picture postcards, but only to a limited extent for other ephemera.

Earhart's *Color Printer* and *Harmonizer* had given the letterpress printer a rationale for his use of colour, but even at the time of their publication they were being sidelined. The reproduction of full-colour originals by the *three-colour* process was developed following experiments by Ives in the 1880s. Here three halftones were made from a coloured original, each via a different colour filter, the result being a set of halftones which when subsequently overprinted in yellow, red and blue produced an image closely resembling the original. It took some years to develop but by 1900 the *British Printer* could say 'the process is a powerful aid to the [letterpress printer] and a corresponding loss to the chromo-lithographer'.[23] Later it became the practice to add a fourth printing in black to achieve better dark tones. Three- and four-colour reproduction was a specialist field, thus not easily adopted by all; but even where printers were restricted to more limited use of colour, it would now be black plus one or at the most two other colours (156–7), reflecting the plainer style of jobbing now in vogue. Process colour was subsequently adapted to lithography (165, 174–5), though owing to its own intrinsic qualities chromolithography was to hold a share of the market for many years (113), some firms continuing into the 1950s.

At the first annual dinner of the International Society of Wood Engravers in 1893, the proprietor of the *Graphic* recalled the days of Palmer's glyphography, at which time all had thought that wood-engraving was finished; but 'that was forty years ago', he said, and here they were now 'eating their dinners and enjoying themselves as though there was no such thing as "process"'.[24] He was too sanguine, for in the previous year the editor of *Printing World* had already observed that although process reproduction was unlikely ever to supplant wood-engraving, there was 'no getting away from the fact that it has brought [some] wood engravers very near to a state of destitution'.[25] The leading London wood-engravers Dalziel Bros failed

165. Blotter/trade card, 1920s. American stock card printed by four-colour offset lithography, overprinted in letterpress with the business details of a Southport, England, monumental masons. Bearing in mind the nature of Keeley & Sons' business, the choice of image is surprising. (100%)

shortly after the society's dinner.[26] Other wood-engraving firms added process to their existing businesses, Hare & Co. doing so as early as 1885. In 1895 this firm reported the development of half-tone plates elaborately finished with hand engraving, which 'the general public may easily take ... for wood engraving pure and simple'.[27] But halftones with 'woodcut finish' were to prove but a passing fad.

Engravers who could draw and design had the chance of continuing in employment with the process firms, and for those who could not, those early halftones often needed skilled work with a graver to freshen up the highlights or soften the edges of a vignette (158). But for men accustomed only to 'common engraving', or too old to adapt, life must have been difficult indeed. Except for some limited use in catalogue work, by the end of the century the making of printed illustrations was no longer the province of the wood engraver – it was now that of the process engraver and the commercial artist.

Discussing the new opportunities afforded by process, the *British Printer* in 1893 drew a distinction between 'artists and illustrators, Art and art', observing that for the 'smaller fry' among artists there was a new opening for employment in commercial art, 'its disappointments [being] less keen, the comparative remuneration higher, and the scope broader than in the painting of unsold canvasses'.[28] The editor of the *Process Year Book* wrote in 1901: 'process has been often declared antagonistic to artistic ideas, yet it has set up a race of artists and draughtsmen who have made it their business to draw for process, and have certainly found it more lucrative than the pursuit of art for art's sake'.[29] An addition to the artist's media in this period was the *airbrush*, a hand-held spray-gun introduced in America in 1893 with which an even or finely graded film of colour could be laid down on artwork (174–5).[30]

Judging by the trade advertising of the time, most process-engraving firms had their own art studios. There were also independent studios, and commercial artists working as freelances. Writing in 1917, Gress described the most successful artists as those who specialised in particular fields: 'classic Roman lettering and decoration; seventeenth-century French decoration; Old English or American Colonial effects; modern German coloring and decoration; art-nouveau creations, the serious and the humorous; illustrations of child life, or of the Civil War period', and concluding 'while there are versatile artists like Will Bradley who can do work in many styles, they are not numerous'.[31]

Bradley was versatile. Trained as a wood engraver, he found no difficulty in adapting to process and is credited with Edward Penfield with inspiring much of the art-poster craze of the 1890s. For some months in 1896–7 Bradley printed and published his own magazine, *Bradley: His Book*. The typography was strongly influenced by that of the Kelmscott Press, though it is unlikely that Morris would have taken kindly to its Christmas number, printed throughout in Satanick.

Gress held that in a print shop too small to employ its own layout man the head compositor or foreman might be entrusted with the work, even the firm's traveller, were they 'artistically fitted'. It was sensibility to art values that mattered. But as Gress acknowledged, few skilled compositors would actually have the necessary artistic temperament, for so often in his experience their 'calm, precise, methodical disposition' was accompanied by lack

166. The influence of photography. *(Top)* Letterhead: engraving on stone with portrait of Lydia E. Pinkham – 'Lillie the Pink' – in use 1919; *(below)* billhead with wood engraving depicting the premises of printer J. Batcheller in use 1887. In both cases the images are closely based on photographs, though on Batcheller's vignette the engraver has still managed to introduce the conventional tiny figures intended to render a building more imposing. (56%)

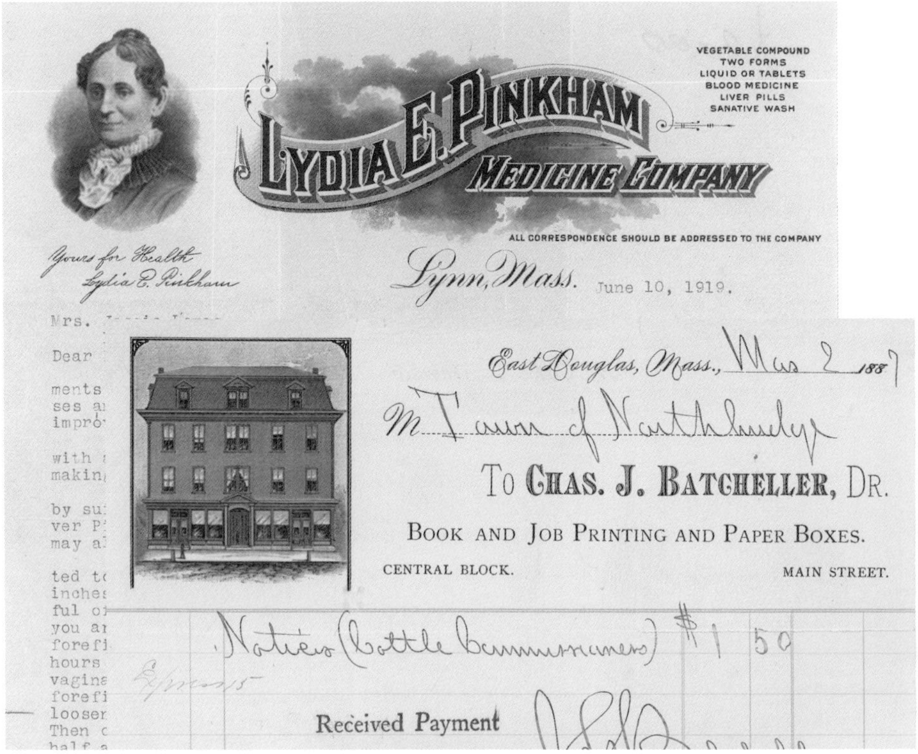

167. Steel engravings based on photographs. *(Left)* Trade card by John A. Lowell & Co., Boston (lithographed on the back with notice of a spring 1882 sale by Amy, Bigelow & Weber of Salem, MA); and *(right)* magazine inset by Waterlow & Sons, London, 1890s, with portrait of the singer Lillie Langtry after a photograph by Van der Weyde. Some elements of the lettering are American in style, and it is possible that a version of this insert circulated in America as well as Britain. (53%)

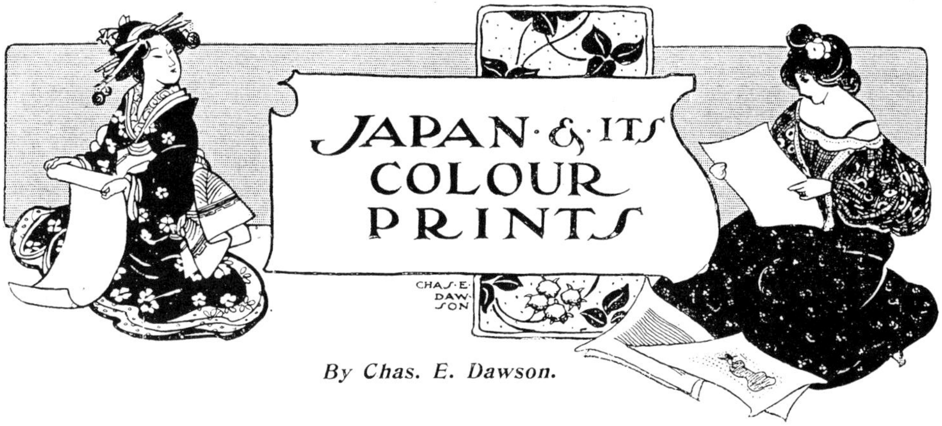

Fig. 404.

Fig. 405.

Fig. 406.

Fig. 407.

Fig. 408.

Fig. 409.

168. Process line engraving. *(Top)* Article heading from *Penrose's Pictorial Annual* 1901 by Charles E. Dawson; *(below)* various methods of treating portraits shown in Hackleman's *Commercial Engraving and Printing*, 1921. The images are not individually referred to by Hackleman, but the figure numbers would be useful to an advertising manager in discussion with a commercial artist; 408 and 409 are chiefly executed in Ben Day tint (100%)

of imagination. Thus Gress's conclusion was that: 'Each workman should have opportunity to do that which he can do best. He of the artistic temperament should lay out the jobs, and he of the mechanical turn of mind should construct them.'[32]

In 1911 George W. Jones opened a new printing works 'At the Sign of the Dolphin' in Gough Square, London. This was within a half mile of the site of the printing shop near Lincoln's Inn Fields where Benjamin Franklin had once worked as a journeyman. In 1924 Jones was to publish a magnificent specimen of Caslon Old Face, the type that had for so long featured in both British and American printing (159A). When Franklin had worked in London the printer had been his own designer, making his own decisions as to the choice and disposition of type, space and imagery. Now, in Jones's day, when text was more often set on a machine than by hand, and the layout of the printed sheet was the province of the typographer and the commercial artist, the printer was but one of a team.

169. Music cover designed, drawn and printed in three-colour chromolithography by H. G. Banks, 1894. The dancing 'Pa et Granpa' are the future kings George V and Edward VII (then Prince of Wales) while the baby is the future Duke of Windsor, destined to reign briefly (January–December 1936) as Edward VIII. (60%)

170. A lighter moment for the American GI during World War I: music cover signed de Tukace, printed letterpress in two colours. Overprinting the orange and blue has achieved a range of intermediate browns and a convincing black. Both this and the music cover on the opposite page are reminders of how closely the design of ephemera can reflect the events of the passing day. (71%)

171. Halftone stock cuts by process engravers Garratt & Atkinson, London, intended for the advertising of hair oil, face powder and other feminine goods. With the girl in the centre, for an additional charge 'the actual package or other article could be drawn in hand' by a staff artist. *British Printer*, 18.107, advertisements, p. 66 (1905) (100%)

172. Artwork for a monochrome cigar-box label by commercial artists Hudson & Son, Birmingham, England, early twentieth century. Clipped from an earlier label, the portrait has been printed in neutral colours by chromolithography, yet the artwork is intended for reproduction by letterpress process half-tone, perhaps indicating that the manufacturers were switching to the newer method. Lettering and background are executed by hand and airbrush in poster colours. (78%)

TELEPHONE 538.

SAVILE STREET, (off Bradford Road),

DEWSBURY, 31 Jany 1922

Messrs M Smith

Dr. to John Bragg & Son,

Motor Haulage & Carting Contractors.

PARTNERS { JOHN W. BRAGG. EDGAR BRAGG. Chars-a-bancs Proprietors.

173. *(Top)* Billhead of a Dewsbury, Yorkshire, motor hauliers in use 1922, with half-tone showing one of the firm's vehicles. *(Below)* Front and back of a 1906 two-colour brochure advertising sightseeing tours of New York illustrated with half-tones of two of the firm's magnificent Observation Automobiles. In both cases photography would convey a more convincing image of the firms' services than would have been possible with hand-drawn imagery. (83%, 69%)

174. Music cover illustrated by commercial artists Rolt Armstrong, printed in four-colour offset lithography by the Knapp Co., New York, 1917. The original painting was executed in watercolour, an airbrush being employed to achieve the subtle gradations on the girl's face. (70%)

175. Music cover by commercial artist Gustav Michelson employing the same media as on the Armstrong design opposite, printed in four-colour offset litho by the Knapp Co., New York, 1919. (70%)

Notes and references

Introduction

1 Arnold Bennett, *Clayhanger* (Harmondsworth: Penguin Books, 1954), p. 103.
2 W. D. Howells, 'The Country Printer', *Scribner's Magazine*, 13 (1893), p. 539.

1 The wooden press

1 '200 to 400 copies' are quoted in respect of an iron press in 'Trades and How to Learn Them', *Family Economist*, 1855, reprinted in *Bulletin* 18 (London: Printing Historical Society, 1986), p. 223. The rate for a wooden press would be only slightly less. If 400 copies per hour were achieved it would have been for a small-format job hurriedly printed, and perhaps printed two- or more up also.
2 Rob Roy Kelly, *American Wood Type: 1828–1900* (New York: Van Nostrand, Reinhold, 1969), p. 162.
3 Cited in 'Trades in the Last Century', *Paper & Printing Trades Journal* 68 (London: 1889), p. 36.
4 Joseph Collyer, *The Parent's and Guardian's Directory and Youth's Guide in the Choice of a Profession or Trade* (London: 1761), extracts reprinted in *Bulletin* 19 (London: Printing Historical Society, 1986), p. 245.
5 Thomas Bewick, *My Life*, edited and with an introduction by Iain Bain (London: Folio Society, 1981), p. 29.
6 Arthur J. Pulos, *American Design Ethic: A History of Industrial Design* (Cambridge, MA: MIT, 1983), p. 19.
7 The billhead of the London undertaker John Cooke in the John Johnson Collection appears to be an example: see illustration 61 in Julie Anne Lambert, *A Nation of Shopkeepers* (Oxford: Bodleian Library, 2001).
8 Bewick, p. 63.
9 Clarence P. Hornung, *Handbook of Early Advertising Art Mainly from American Sources*, 3rd edn, 2 vols (New York: Dover Publications, 1956), pictorial vol., p. xvi.
10 [Jared Sparks (ed.)] *The Autobiography of Benjamin Franklin* (London: Blackie & Son, nd.), pp. 80–1.
11 Edmund G. Gress, *The Art and Practice of Typography* (New York: Oswald Publishing Co., 1917), frontispiece.
12 Berthold Wolpe, 'Caslon Architectural', *Alphabet* 1 (Birmingham: James Moran/Kynoch Press, 1964), p. 63 and plate 9. These types were cast as capitals only, enabling the letters to occupy the full depth of the face. Had a lower-case been provided, the bottom portion of the face would have been reserved for the descending strokes, thereby limiting the size of the capitals.
13 Robin Myers (ed.), *The Autobiography of Luke Hansard, Printer to the House, 1752–1828* (London: Printing Historical Society, 1991), pp. 7, 17.
14 Imprint on undated turnpike ticket, Wakefield City Museum, Yorkshire.
15 Clarence P. Hornung and Fridolf Johnson, *200 years of American Graphic Art* (New York: George Braziller, 1976), p. 24.
16 Karen Nipps, 'Far from Ephemeral: the Career of Lydia Bailey, Philadelphia, Job Printer', *Job printing in America: Ephemera Journal*, 8 (Schoharie, NY: Ephemera Society of America, 1993), p. 17.
17 Numerous examples are reproduced in Eric P. Newman, *The Early Paper Money of America* (Iola, WI: Krause Publications, 1997).
18 Joseph Moxon, *Mechanick Exercises on the Whole Art of Printing* (London: 1683–84; edited by Herbert Davis and Harry Carter, Oxford: Oxford University Press, 1958), pp. 212–14.
19 John Smith, *The Printer's Grammar* (London: 1755), pp. 217-18.
20 J. A. Cochrane, *Dr Johnson's Printer: the Life of William Strahan* (London: Routledge & Kegan Paul, 1964), p. 27.

2 The iron press

1 James Moran, 'How Many Columbian Presses did George Clymer and his Successors Make?', *Journal of the Printing Historical Society*, 13 (London: 1978–9), p. 78.
2 Stephen O. Saxe in *American Iron Hand Presses* (Delaware: Oak Knoll, 1991), p. viii, states that no Albions were used for commercial printing in America. However, in 'Have We Reached the End?, Chicago: *Inland Printer* 3.12 (1886), p. 748, the experienced printer is spoken of as one who 'contrasts the old "Albion" or "Washington" of his apprentice days with the lightening changes of modern times', which suggests that American printers were familiar with the press to some degree at least.
3 William Savage, *Practical Hints on Decorative Printing* (London: 1822), p. 21. It is possible that the characteristics of these bold display letters were suggested by the lettering of signwriters.
4 Ray Nash, 'Ornamented Types in America', in Nicolete Gray, *Nineteenth Century Ornamented Type Faces*, 2nd edn (London: Faber, 1976), p. 115.
5 T. C. Hansard, *Typographia* (London: 1825), p. 618.
6 *Horniman's Reading Directory* [1827], back cover.
7 S. N. Dickinson, *Boston Almanac 1846*, p. 149
8 Rob Roy Kelly, *American Wood Type: 1828–1900* (New York: Van Nostrand, Reinhold, 1969), p. 74.
9 Kelly, p. 34. The early history of wood type in England is obscure, but to judge by John Parry's well-known watercolour of a London poster site wood letter was in common use by 1835; Parry exaggerates the scale of the posters, but even allowing for this the letter-forms are too large to have been cast in metal. Parry's painting is reproduced on page 1 of the author's *The Victorian Printer* (Princes Risborough: Shire Publications, 1996) and on the jacket of Alastair Johnston's *Alphabets to*

Order: The Literature of Nineteenth-Century Typefounders' Specimens (New Castle, DE: Oak Knoll, 2000)

10 There is a difference between British and American usage however: in Britain the nominal sheet is 20 × 30 in. (505 × 763 mm); in America 30 × 40 in. (763 × 1010mm). In the present work British usage is followed.

11 Charles Dickens, 'Bill-sticking', *Household Words*, 52 (London: 1851), p. 605.

12 William Savage, *Dictionary of the Art of Printing* (London: 1841), p. 478.

13 Thomas Houghton, *The Printer's Practical Every-Day Book* (Preston: 1841), pp. 35–7.

14 Nicolete Gray, *Nineteenth Century Ornamented Type Faces*, 2nd edn (London: Faber, 1976), p. 34, describes the Italian face as 'a crude expression of the idea of perversity'.

15 Henry Sampson, *A History of Advertising from Earliest Times* (London: 1875), p. 511.

16 Iain Bain, Bewick MSS.

17 Bain.

18 Bain.

19 Bain.

20 Clarence P. Hornung, *Handbook of Early Advertising Art Mainly from American Sources*, pictorial volume, 3rd edition (New York: Dover Publications, 1956), p. xiii.

21 Iain Bain, *The Watercolours and Drawings of Thomas Bewick and His Workshop Apprentices*, 2 vols (London: Fraser, 1981), I, pp. 51–2.

22 John Johnson, *Typographia, or the Printer's Instructor* (London: 1824), p. 549. The engraving is shown in Stephen Calloway, *English Prints for the Collector* (London: Lutterworth Press, 1980), p. 118.

3 The rise of lithography

1 C. F. Partington, *The Engraver's Complete Guide* (London: *c.*1825), pp. 102–3, 106–7.

2 Peter C. Marzio, *The Democratic Art: Pictures for a 19th-Century America* (Boston: David R. Godine, 1979), p. 239.

3 British Library shelfmark L.R.271.b.8(1).

4 Marzio, pp. 69–71.

5 *British Lithographer*, 1.2 (1891–2), p. 33.

6 Respectively: Michael Twyman, *Early Lithographed Music* (London: Farrand Press, 1966), p. 59 (Britain and France); Marzio, p. 65 (Kentucky); *British Lithographer*, 1.5 (1892), p. 10 (Indiana).

7 *Horniman's Reading Directory* [1827], back cover.

8 *Horniman.*

9 Heber Mardon, *Landmarks in the History of a Bristol Firm, 1824–1904* (Bristol: Mardon, Son & Hall, 1908), p. 16.

10 Michael Twyman, *Breaking the Mould: The First Hundred Years of Lithography* (London: British Library, 2001), p. 31.

11 Lawrence H. Officer, 'Dollar-Pound Exchange Rate from 1791', MeasuringWorth.com, 2007.

12 Officer.

13 *Typographic Advertiser*, 9 (1863), p .66.

14 *American Lithographer & Printer*, 11.17 (1889), p. 264.

15 W. D. Richmond, *The Grammar of Lithography* (London: E. Menken, 11th edition, 1895), pp. 58–9.

16 Richmond, p. 67.

17 Richmond, p. 68.

18 Richmond, pp. 68–9.

19 Officer.

20 '"Plant Form" Supplements', *British Lithographer*, 1.1 (1891–2), p. 12; 2.9 (1893), p. 77; 2.10 (1893), p. 113.

21 *British Lithographer*, 2.9 (1893), p. 77.

22 Richmond, pp. 42–3.

23 Richmond, p. 52.

24 *British Printer*, 6.34 (1893), p. 304.

25 Iain Bain, 'Thomas Ross & Son, Copper- and Steel-plate Printers Since 1833', *Journal of the Printing Historical Society*, 2 (1966), p. 9.

4 Advancing technology

1 *Printers' Register*, 19 (1865), p. 10.

2 'Wood-Cutting and Type-Founding', *Penny Magazine*, 101 (1833), p. 421.

3 John Buchanan-Brown, 'British Wood-engravers c.1820–c.1860: a Checklist', *Journal of the Printing Historical Society*, 17 (1982–3), p. 39.

4 'Employment for Women: Schools of Design', *The Lady's Almanac* (Boston: John P. Jewett, 1854), p. 71.

5 *Typographic Advertiser*, 10 (1863), p. 77.

6 Jane R. Pomeroy, 'On the Changes Made in Wood Engravings in the Stereotyping Process', *Printing History*, 17.2 (1995), p. 38.

7 *Typographic Advertiser*, 20 (1863), p. 47.

8 *Printers' Register*, 56 (1868), p. 43.

9 *The Printer*, 10 (1864), unpaginated advertisement.

10 Lawrence H. Officer, 'Dollar-Pound Exchange Rate from 1791', MeasuringWorth.com, 2007.

11 *Typographic Advertiser*, 10, (1863) centre spread; 12 (1863) p. 95. The original American version of the cut is shown in Clarence P. Hornung, *Handbook of Early Advertising Art Mainly from American Sources*, 3rd edn, 2 vols (New York: Dover Publications, 1956), pictorial vol., p. 99.

12 Officer.

13 *Typographic Advertiser*, 25 (1864), p. 96; 27 (1864), p. 120.

14 Officer.

15 *Typographic Advertiser*, 9 (1863), p. 71

16 Heber Mardon, *Landmarks in the History of a Bristol Firm, 1824–1904* (Bristol: Mardon, Son & Hall, 1908), p. 26.

17 Officer.

18 Martin Andrews, 'Hare & Co., Commercial Wood-Engravers: Jabez Hare, Founder of the Firm, and His Letters 1846 to 1847', *Journal of the Printing Historical Society*, 24 (1995), p. 85.

19 Derek Forbes, *Illustrated Playbills: A Study Together with a Reprint of 'A Descriptive Catalogue of Theatrical Wood Engravings' (1865)* (London: Society for Theatre Research, 2002), reprint pp. 2, 72, 92, 95.

20 Rob Roy Kelly, *American Wood Type: 1828–1900* (New York: Van Nostrand, Reinhold, 1969), p. 184.

21 Stanley Applebaum, *Advertising Woodcuts from the Nineteenth-century Stage* (New York: Dover, 1977), pp. vii–viii, 147.
22 William Frost Mobley, *A Superlative Selection of Nineteenth-century Historical and Advertising Broadsides* [catalog] (Wilbraham, Mass: the author, 1980), item 57.
23 Robert Wood, *The Victorian Printer and the Stage* (Newcaste: Newcastle Imprint Club, 1972), pp. 19–20.
24 Letter (19 July 1831) Charles Stanton to George Robert Gitton, Bridgnorth, quoted in Diana R. Mackarill, 'George and George Robert Gitton, Printers, Bridgnorth' *Journal of the Printing Historical Society*, n.s. 4 (2002), p. 43.
25 In conventional type founding, the original for each character was cut in the end of a short steel rod: this was the *punch*. When struck into a small brass plate this made the *matrix*, which fitted into an adjustable mould for casting.
26 'Quadrat', 'Discursions of a Retired Printer', *Inland Printer* 28 (1907), p. 675.
27 W. D. Howells, 'The Country Printer', *Scribner's Magazine*, 13 (1893), p. 552.
28 Karl Burg, 'On Show Bills', *Printers' Register* 37 (1866), p. 12.
29 J. Luther Ringwalt, 'Display of Type', *American Encyclopaedia of Printing* (Philadelphia: 1871), pp. 141–5, 'condensed from a paper read a few years ago by Theo. L. DeVinne in the rooms of the New York Typographical Society'.
30 The competition may be followed in the respective issues of the *Typographic Advertiser*: 35, p. 80; 37, pp. 99–102, 104; 38, pp. 111–14, 116; 39, pp. 120–1 (1864); 40, p. 2; 41, p. 18 (1865).

5 Colour and special processes

1 Joseph Moxon, *Mechanick Exercises on the Whole Art of Printing* (London: 1683–84; edited by Herbert Davis and Harry Carter, Oxford: Oxford University Press, 1958), p. 300.
2 Michael Twyman, *Printing 1770–1970: An Illustrated History of its Development in England*, 2nd edn (London: The British Library, 1998), p. 45; Robert Banham, 'Gye and Balne: Printing Families', *Journal of the Printing Historical Society*, n.s. 5 (2003), pp. 23, 26, 32, 39–40.
3 T. C. Hansard, *Treatises on Printing and Type-Founding* (Edinburgh: 1841), p. 144.
4 J. Luther Ringwalt, *American Encyclopaedia of Printing* (Philadelphia: 1871), p. 371.
5 Karl Burg, 'On Show Bills', *Printers' Register* 37 (1866), p. 12.
6 'Some Remarks on Posters', *Printing World*, 1 (1891), p. 216.
7 Reprinted in Arthur Oldfield, *A Practical Manual of Typography* (London: E. Menken [1890]), pp. 87–8.
8 The technicalities of Victorian embossing appear to have been shrouded in secrecy. Despite intensive searching in the trade literature the only satisfactory description of how such embossing could have been achieved found by the author is that in Charles W. Hackleman's *Commercial Engraving and Printing*, 2nd edn (Indiana: Commercial Engraving Publishing, 1924), p. 594, on which the author's brief description is based.
9 Henry Fitzcook, 'The Graphotype', *Typographic Advertiser*, 47 (1886), p. 73.
10 Fitzcook.
11 'Colour Printing in Excelsis', *Printing World*, n.s. 12 (1893), pp. 579–80; 'Knöfler Reproductions of the Early Italian Masters', *British Printer*, 37 (1894), pp. 21–6.
12 Lester S. Levy, *Picturing the Songs: Lithographs from the Sheet Music of Nineteenth-Century America* (Baltimore: John Hopkins University Press, 1976), pp. 34, 60.
13 S. Leighton, 'The Art of Chromo-Lithography', *British Printer*, 18 (1905) pp. 186–7.
14 Sharon Uhler, 'My Dear Mr Prang', *Ephemera Journal*, 1 (1987), p. 30.
15 Leighton, p. 186.
16 Sir Alfred Munnings, *An Artist's Life* (London: Museum Press), pp. 51, 55.
17 *Printers' Register*, 23 (1884), p. 185.
18 Heber Mardon, *Landmarks in the History of a Bristol Firm, 1824–1904* (Bristol: Mardon, Son & Hall, 1908), p. 37.
19 Peter C. Marzio, *The Democratic Art: Pictures for a 19th-Century America* (Boston: David R. Godine, 1979), p. 131.
20 Alain Weill and Jack Rennert, *Masters of the Poster: 1896–1900* (London: Academy Editions, 1977), p. 11. In America many posters were printed from zinc plates rather than stone and their keyline images, drawn by the artists themselves, were enlarged to printing size by photomechanical means.
21 S. Manors, 'The Hoardings', *Poster*, June 1898, p. 7.
22 Russell Ash, *Toulouse Lautrec: The Complete Lithographs* (London: Pavilion, 1991), plate 1 (unpaginated).
23 Frank Millward, 'A Chat with Stewart Browne', *Poster*, April 1899, p. 146.
24 Lawrence H. Officer, 'Dollar-Pound Exchange Rate from 1791', MeasuringWorth.com, 2007 .
25 'Posters Wanted', *British Lithographer*, 11 (1893), p. 152.

6 Artistic Printing

1 Thomas Lynch, *The Printer's Manual: A Practical Guide for Compositors and Pressmen*, 5th edn (Cincinatti: Cincinnati Type Foundry, 1859; repr. Peter M. Van Wingen; New York: Garland Publishing, 1981), introduction.
2 Oscar Harpel, *The Typograph or Book of Specimens* (Cincinnati: 1871), p. 1.
3 Harpel, p. 8.
4 Harpel, p. 16.
5 Harpel, p. 23.
6 Harpel, p. 17.
7 Harpel, p. 17.

8 Thomas Hailing, 'Autobiography', *American Art Printer*, 1.2 (1887), p. 9.
9 *American Model Printer*, 1.1 (1879), p. 5.
10 'American Style', *American Model Printer*, 1.1 (1879), p. 5.
11 'Our London Letter', *American Model Printer*, 1.2 (1879), pp. 30–1.
12 *Printers' International Specimen Exchange*, 1 (London: 1880), p. 9.
13 *Printers' International Specimen Exchange*, 1 (London: 1880), p. 5.
14 *American Model Printer*, 1.4 (1880), p. 52.
15 'Printers' Specimen Exchange', *American Model Printer*, 1.5 (1880), p. 62.
16 'The Printers' International Specimen Exchange and Technical Education', *Printers' International Specimen Exchange*, 1 (1880), pp. 7–8.
17 'The Printers' International Specimen Exchange', *Paper & Printing Trades Journal*, 33 (1880), pp. 8, 9.
18 'The Printers' International Specimen Exchange', *Hailing's Circular*, 1 (1881), p. 53.
19 'World's Album of Fine Printing', *American Model Printer*, 2.4 (1884), p. 72.
20 A. V. Haight, 'About Job Composition', *Hailing's Circular*, 2 (1888), p. 118.
21 *Paper & Printing Trades Journal*, no. 26 (1879), p. 21. Tuer's comments were prompted by Harner's cartoon (131).
22 'Printer's Types', *Hailing's Circular*, 7 (1880), p. 48.
23 'To Aspiring Printers', *Hailing's Circular*, 10 (1882), p. 85.
24 'Spacing and Display', reprinted in *Hailing's Circular*, 10 (1882), p. 86.
25 Norman Kelvin (ed.), *William Morris on Art and Socialism* (Mineola, NY: Dover, 1999), p. 2.
26 Peter Stansky, *Redesigning the World: William Morris, the 1880s, and the Arts and Crafts* (Princeton, NJ: Princeton University Press, 1985), p. 217.
27 'Ornament', *Hailing's Circular*, 1 (1882), p. 98, quoting from the *Printers' Friend*.
28 'Craft Jubilee Dinner', *Caxton Magazine*, 24 July 1924, p. 406.
29 'Andreas V. Haight', *American Art Printer*, 1.5 (1887), p. 12.
30 George W. Jones, 'Messrs George Lewis & Son', *Printing World*, 1 (1891), p. 343.
31 George Joyner, *Fine Printing: Its Inception, Development and Practice* (London: Cooper & Budd, 1895), p. 31.
32 Herbert L. Baker, 'The Suggester', *Inland Printer*, 11.4 (1893), pp. 311–12.
33 Joyner, p. 4.
34 'Specimens', *Paper & Printing Trades Journal*, no. 67 (1889), p. 11.
35 'Specimens', *Paper & Printing Trades Journal*, no. 68 (1889), p. 10.

7 The Leicester free style

1 'Printing as an Art', *Hailing's Circular*, 2 (1884), p. 43.
2 'The Advance of Typography', *Inland Printer*, 5.11 (1888), p. 823.
3 Kelvin, p. 15.
4 Wider Halén, *Christopher Dresser: A Pioneer of Modern Design* (London: Phaidon, 1993), p. 31.
5 'Specimens', *Paper & Printing Trades Journal*, no. 65 (1888), p. 14.
6 'Drawing as Part of a Printer's Education', *Typographical Circular* (Manchester), no. 333 (1880), p. 11, repr. from *British & Colonial Printer & Stationer*.
7 'Original Design', *Printers' Register* (London), 24 (1884) p. 254.
8 'On Display', *Modern Printer*, 1.1 (1884), p. 8.
9 Robin Myers (ed.), *The Autobiography of Luke Hansard, Printer to the House, 1752–1828* (London: Printing Historical Society, 1991), pp. 49, 79.
10 Oscar Harpel, *The Typograph or Book of Specimens* (Cincinnati: 1871), p. 17.
11 'Dissecting a Job', *American Art Printer*, 1.2 (1887), p. 6; and 1.4 (1887), p. 7.
12 *Printers' International Specimen Exchange*, 4 (London: 1883), p. 5.
13 Alfred Pye, 'Job Compositors', *Inland Printer*, 1.2 (1883), p. 13.
14 'Helpful Hints', *British Printer*, 2 (1889), p. 6.
15 'Specimens', *British Printer*, 1.4 (1888), p. 17. The name of the enterprise was changed from Co-operative Printing Co. to Darien Press about the time of Jones's arrival: Lawrence Wallis, *George W. Jones, Printer Laureate* (Nottingham: Plough Press, 2004), p. 22.
16 'Specimens', *British Printer*, 37 (1894), p. 56.
17 Alexander Lawson, *The Compositor as Artist, Craftsman and Tradesman* (Athens, GA: Press of the Nightowl, 1990), p. 3.
18 E. W. Hill, 'Place aux Dames', *British Printer*, 5.30 (1892), p. 6.
19 In America the 5½pt size was more commonly known as Agate.
20 *British Printer*, 1.1 (1888), p. 1.
21 John Southward, *Artistic Printing* (London: Printer's Register, 1892), pp. 364–5.
22 Joseph Gould, *The Letter-Press Printer* (Middlesborough: 1876), pp. 85-6.
23 Joseph Gould, *The Compositor's Guide* (London: 1878), unpaginated advertisement.
24 John Southward, *Modern Printing*, 1 (London: 1898), pp. 364–5.
25 Lawrence H. Officer, 'Dollar-Pound Exchange Rate from 1791', MeasuringWorth.com, 2007.
26 'The Exhibition', *Hailing's Circular*, 2 (1883), p. 28.
27 J. Anderson, 'The Composition of Posters', *Printing World*, n.s. 1 (1893), p. 395.
28 Maurice Rickards, *Collecting Printed Ephemera* (Oxford: Phaidon, Christie's, 1988), p. 116.
29 The story of the Travelling Portfolio can be followed in successive issues of the weekly *American Lithographer & Printer* from 8.6 (1887) to 11.2 (1888).
30 George Joyner, *Fine Printing: Its Inception, Development and Practice* (London: Cooper & Budd, 1895), p. 36.
31 Joyner, p. 36.
32 'Robert Grayson', *British Printer*, 18 (1890), p. 6

33 'The Specimens', *American Art Printer*, 1.3 (1887), p. 3 and unpaginated specimen.
34 *Printers' International Specimen Exchange*, 13 (London: 1892), un–paginated introduction.
35 'Straight Rule Design', *Printing World*, 2 (1892), p. 342.
36 'Nosredna', '"Artistic" Jobbing', *Printing World*, 2 (1892), p. 26.
37 Robert Grayson, 'Design and Display in Job Work', *British Printer*, 6.31 (1893), pp. 13–20.
38 *Printers' International Specimen Exchange*, 13 (London: 1892), unpaginated introduction.
39 *Printers' International Specimen Exchange*, 13 (London: 1892), John Lewis specimen.
40 Southward, *Artistic Printing*, pp. 48–9.
41 'Some Useful Colour Combinations', *British Printer*, 5.29 (1892), p. 28
42 '"Artistic" Printing', *British Printer*, 4.22 (1891), p. 7, reprinted from *Modern Engraver*.
43 'Specimens', *Paper & Printing Trades Journal*, no. 63 (1888), p. 13.
44 John F. Earhart, *The Color Printer: A Treatise on the Use of Colors in Typographic Printing* (Cincinnati: 1892), p. 33.
45 *British Printer*, 5.29 (1892), p. 41.
46 Douglas C. McMurtrie, ed., *Manual of Printing Office Practice by Theodore L. De Vinne* [1883] (New York: Press of Ars Typographia, 1926), p. 51.
47 'Fancy Printing', *Hailing's Circular*, 2.16 (1884), p. 42, reprinted from the Philadelphia *Printers' Circular*.
48 *Printers' International Specimen Exchange*, 7 (1886), p. 4.
49 'The Artistic Job Compositor', *British Printer*, 8 (1895), p. 88.

8 Process engraving and commercial art

1 Theodore L. DeVinne, 'Masculine Printing', *United Typothetaea of America*, Sixth Annual Convention (1892), p. 164.
2 'Artistic Printing at the Borough Road Polytechnic', *Printing World*, n.s. 3 (1893), pp. 127–8.
3 Lawrence Wallis, *George W. Jones: Printer Laureate* (Nottingham: Plough Press, 2004), pp. 25, 29.
4 [Harry Whetton], 'On Tour in the Land o' Cakes', *British Printer* (47), pp. 297–9.
5 William S. Peterson, 'William Morris and His Types', Serif Magazine (www.serifmagazine.com/wp-morris.php4), p. 10.
6 Wendy Kaplan, *'The Art that is Life': The Arts & Crafts Movement in America, 1875–1920* (Boston: Museum of Fine Arts, 1987), p. 160.
7 Ed McClure, 'Final Words', *American Printers' Specimen Exchange*, 4 (Buffalo, NY: 1890), unpaginated.
8 Graham Hudson, 'Artistic Printing: A Re-evaluation', *Journal of the Printing Historical Society*, n.s. 9 (2006), p. 62.
9 Lewis C. Gandy, 'A Plea for Simplicity', *British Printer*, 18.106 (1905), p. 201.
10 Edmund G. Gress, *The Art and Practice of Typography* (New York: Oswald Publishing Co., 1917), p. 33.
11 George French, 'The Education of a Printer', *Inland Printer*, 30.5 (1903), p. 865.
12 Wesley Washington Pasko, *American Dictionary of Printing and Bookmaking* (New York: 1894), p. 309.
13 'Job Composition: Design in Job Printing', *Inland Printer*, 38.4 (1907), pp. 555–9.
14 Gress, p. 53.
15 'Editorial notes', *Inland Printer*, 38.4 (1907), p. 531.
16 Gress, p.78.
17 Gress, p. 32.
18 'American Notes', *Paper & Printing Trades Journal*, 57 (1887), p. 8.
19 David Woodward, 'The Decline of Commercial Wood-Engraving in Nineteenth-century America', *Journal of the Printing Historical* Society, 10 (1974–5), p. 60.
20 'Notes on Periodicals', *Paper & Printing Trades Journal*, 65 (1888), p. 23.
21 'Photographic Engraving, and the Work of Mr. Frederick Ives', *British Printer*, 37 (1894), p. 67.
22 'The Meisenbach Company, Ltd', *British Printer*, 39 (1894), pp. 165–77. (Screen rulings determined by the author with a screen gauge.)
23 'Hints and Wrinkles: Three-Colour', *British Printer*, 73 (1900), p. 16.
24 Boreham Wood, 'Trade News & Notes', *Printing World*, n.s. 4 (1893), p. 186.
25 'Type-Righter', 'Trade News & Notes, *Printing World*, 2.9 (1892), p. 387.
26 Boreham Wood, 'Trade News & Notes', *Printing World*, n.s. 5 (1893), p. 246.
27 'Hare & Co. Ltd: Half a Century of Engraving', *British Printer*, 47 (1895), pp. 270, 272.
28 Noax, 'Black and White Art for the Press', *British Printer*, 35 (1893), p. 369.
29 William Gamble, 'A Wonderful Process', *The Process Year Book* (London: 1901), p. 11.
30 *British Lithographer*, 3.16 (1894), pp. 124–5.
31 Gress, p. 77.
32 Gress p. 37.

Further reading

Ash, Russell, *Toulouse Lautrec: The Complete Lithographs* (London: Pavilion, 1991)
Aslin, Elizabeth, *The Aesthetic Movement, Prelude to Art Nouveau* (New York: Frederick A. Praeger, 1969)
Bain, Iain, *The Watercolours and Drawings of Thomas Bewick and His Workshop Apprentices*, 2 vols (London: Gordon Fraser, 1981)
— *The Workshop of Thomas Bewick, a Pictorial Survey* (Stocksfield: Thomas Bewick Birthplace Trust, 1989)
Banham, Robert, 'Gye and Balne: Printing Families', *Journal of the Printing Historical Society*, n.s. 5 (2003)
— 'Nineteenth-Century Jobbing: The Printing Methods of Gye and Balne', *Journal of the Printing Historical Society*, forthcoming.
Berry, W. T., and H. E. Poole, *Annals of Printing: a Chronological Encyclopaedia from the Earliest Times to 1950* (London: Blandford, 1966)
Bewick, Thomas, *My Life*, edited by Iain Bain (London: Folio Society, 1981)
Boyd, Julia, *Bewick Gleanings* (Newcastle: Andrew Reid, 1886)
Caparga, Leslie, *Letterheads: One Hundred Years of Great Design, 1850–1950* (San Francisco: Chronicle, 1992)
Chatto, W. A., and J. Jackson, *A Treatise on Wood Engraving, Historical and Practical* (London: 2nd edn, 1861)
Cochrane, J. A., *Dr Johnson's Printer: The Life of William Strachan* (London: Routledge & Kegan Paul, 1964)
Courtney Lewis, G. T., *George Baxter (Colour Printer), His Life and Work* (London: Sampson Low, Marston, 1908)
Davis, A., *Package and Print: the Development of Container and Label Design* (London: Faber, 1967)
DeVinne, Theodore L., 'Masculine Printing', *United Typothetaea of America*, Sixth Annual Convention (1892)
Duchochois, P. C., *Photographic Reproduction Processes* (London: 1892)
Earhart, John F., *The Color Printer: A Treatise on the Use of Colors in Typographic Printing* (Cincinnati: 1892)
Fenton, William, *Railway Printed Ephemera* (Woodbridge: Antique Collectors' Club, 1992)
Fertel, Martin Dominique, *La Science pratique de l'imprimerie* (Saint Omer: 1723)
Fielding, T. H., *The Art of Engraving, with the Various Modes of Operation* (London: 1841)
Fitzcook, Henry, 'The Graphotype', *Typographic Advertiser*, 47 (1886)
Gascoigne, B., *How to Identify Prints* (London: Thames & Hudson, 1986; repr. 1995)
Gould, Joseph, *The Letter-Press Printer* (Middlesbrough: 1876, and later editions)
Gray, N., *Nineteenth Century Ornamented Type Faces*, 2nd edn (London: Faber, 1976)
Gress, Edmund, *The Art and Practice of Typography* (New York: Oswald Publishing, 1917)
Gretton, G., *Murders and Moralities: English Catchpenny Prints, 1800–1860* (London: British Museum, 1980)
Hackleman, C., *Commercial Engraving and Printing*, 2nd edn (Indiana: Commercial Engraving Publishing, 1924)
Haill, Catherine, *Fun Without Vulgarity: Victorian and Edwardian Popular Entertainment Posters* (London: HM Stationery Office, 1996)
Hansard, Thomas C., *Typographia* (London: 1825)
Harpel, Oscar, *The Typograph or Book of Specimens* (Cincinnati: 1871)
Heal, A. *London Tradesmen's Cards of the XVIII Century: an Account of Their Origin and Use* (London: Batsford, 1925; repr. New York: Dover, 1968)
Hillier, B., *Posters* (Hamlyn: London, 1974)
Holme, Bryan, *Advertising: Reflections of a Century* (London: Heinemann, 1982)

Hornung, Clarence P., *Handbook of Early Advertising Art Mainly from American Sources*, 2 vols (New York: Dover, 1956)
— and Fridolf Johnson, *200 Years of American Graphic Art: a Retrospective Survey of the Printed Arts and Advertising since the Colonial Period* (New York: George Braziller, 1976)
Houghton, Thomas, *The Printer's Practical Every-Day Book* (Preston: 1841, and later editions)
Howells, W. D., 'The Country Printer', *Scribner's Magazine*, 13 (1893).
Hudson, G., 'Artistic Printing: A Re-evaluation', *Journal of the Printing Historical Society*, n.s. 9, 2006
James, Louis, *Print and the People, 1819–1851* (Harmondsworth: Penguin, 1976)
Jenny, Adele, *Early American Trade Cards from the Collection of Bella C. Landauer* (New York: William Edwin Rudge, 1927)
Johnston, Alastair, *Alphabets to Order: The Literature of Nineteenth-Century Typefounders' Specimens* (New Castle, DE: Oak Knoll Press, 2000)
Johnson, John, *Typographia, or the Printer's Instructor* (London: 1824)
Joyner, George, *Fine Printing: Its Inception, Development and Practice* (London: Cooper & Budd, 1895)
Kelly, Rob Roy, *American Wood Type 1828–1900: Notes on the Evolution of Decorated and Large Types* (New York: Da Capo, 1969)
Kiehl, David W., *American Art Posters of the 1890s in the Metropolitan Museum of Art, including the Leonard A. Lauder Collection* [catalogue] (New York: Metropolitan Museum of Art, 1987)
Lambert, Julie Anne, *A Nation of Shopkeepers: Trade Ephemera from 1654 to the 1860s in the John Johnson Collection* (Oxford: Bodleian Library, 2001)
Last, Jay T., *The Color Explosion: Nineteenth-Century American Lithography* (Santa Ana, CA: Hillcrest, 2005)
Leighton, S., 'The Art of Chromo-Lithography', *British Printer*, 18 (1905)
Levy, Lester S., *Picturing the Songs: Lithographs from the Sheet Music of Nineteenth-Century America* (Baltimore: John Hopkins University Press, 1976)
Lewis, J. *Printed Ephemera* (Ipswich: W. S. Cowell, 1962)
Linton, W. J., *The History of Wood-Engraving in America* (Boston: 1882)
— *The Masters of Wood Engraving* (London: 1889)
Lynch, Thomas, *The Printer's Manual: A Practical Guide for Compositors and Pressmen*, 5th edn (Cincinatti: Cincinnati Type Foundry, 1859; repr. Peter M. Van Wingen; New York: Garland Publishing, 1981)
Mardon, Heber, *Landmarks in the History of a Bristol Firm, 1824–1904* (Bristol: Mardon, Son & Hall, 1908)
Margolin, Victor, *American Poster Renaissance* (New York: Castle, 1975)
Marzio, P. *The Democratic Art: Pictures for a 19th-Century America: Chromolithography 1840–1900* (Boston: David R. Godine, 1979)
McLean, R., *Victorian Book Design and Colour Printing* (London: Faber, 2nd edn, 1972)
McMurtrie, Douglas C., ed., *Manual of Printing Office Practice by Theodore L. De Vinne* [1883] (New York: Press of Ars Typographia, 1926)
Meggs, P., *A History of Graphic Design* (London: Allen Lane, 1983)
Moran, J., *Printing Presses: History and Development from the Fifteenth Century to Modern Times* (London: Faber, 1973)
Moxon, Joseph, *Mechanick Exercises on the Whole Art of Printing* (London: 1683–4; edited by Herbert Davis and Harry Carter, Oxford: OUP, 1958)
Munnings, Sir Alfred, *An Artist's Life* (London: Museum Press, 1950)
Myers, Robin (ed.), *The Autobiography of Luke Hansard, Printer to the House, 1752–1828* (London: Printing Historical Society, 1991)

Oldfield, Arthur, *A Practical Manual of Typography* (London: E. Menken [1890])
Officer, Lawrence H., 'Dollar-Pound Exchange Rate from 1791', MeasuringWorth.com, 2007.
Partington, C. F., *The Engraver's Complete Guide* (London: *c.*1825)
Pearsall, R., *Victorian Sheet Music Covers* (Newton Abbot: David & Charles, 1972)
Peterson, William S., 'William Morris and His Types', *Serif Magazine* (www.serif-magazine.com/wp-morris.php4)
Pulos, A. J., *American Design Ethic: a History of Industrial Design to 1940* (Cambridge, MA: MIT, 1983)
Richmond, W. D., *The Grammar of Lithography* (London: 1878, and later editions).
Rickards, M., *Collecting Printed Ephemera* (Oxford: Phaidon, Christie's, 1988)
— *The Encyclopedia of Ephemera: a Guide to the Fragmentary Documents of Everyday Life for the Collector, Curator, and Historian*, edited and completed by Michael Twyman with the assistance of Sarah du Boscq de Beaumont and Amoret Tanner (London: The British Library, 2000)
Ringwalt, J. L., *American Encyclopaedia of Printing* (Philadelphia: 1871)
Sampson, Henry, *A History of Advertising from Earliest Times* (London: 1875)
Savage, William, *Practical Hints on Decorative Printing* (London: 1822)
— *Dictionary of the Art of Printing* (London: 1841)
Saxe, Stephen O., *American Iron Hand Presses* (Delaware: Oak Knoll, 1992)
Southward, John, *Artistic Printing* (London: 1892)
— *Modern Printing*, 4 vols (London: 1898, and later editions).
[Sparks, Jared, ed.], *The Autobiography of Benjamin Franklin* (London: Blackie & Son, n.d.)
Staff, F., *The Valentine and its Origins* (London: Lutterworth Press, 1969)
Stansky, Peter, *Redesigning the World: William Morris, the 1880s, and the Arts and Crafts* (Princeton, NJ: Princeton University Press, 1985)
Sutton, J. and A. Bartram, *An Atlas of Type Forms* (London: Lund Humphries, 1968)
Turner, M. L., *The John Johnson Collection: Catalogue of an Exhibition* (Oxford: Bodleian Library, 1971)
Twyman, M., *John Soulby, Printer, Ulverston* (Reading: University of Reading, 1966)
— *Early Lithographed Books, A Study of the Design and Production of Improper Books in the Age of the Hand Press* (London: Farrand Press, 1990)
— *Printing 1770–1970: An Illustrated History of its Development and Uses in England*, 2nd edn (London: The British Library, 1998)
— *The British Library Guide to Printing: History and Techniques* (London: The British Library, 1998)
— *Breaking the Mould: The First Hundred Years of Lithography* (London: The British Library, 2001)
Uhler, Sharon, 'My Dear Mr Prang', *Ephemera Journal*, 1 (1987)
Wallis, Lawrence, *George W. Jones, Printer Laureate* (Nottingham: Plough Press , 2004)
Weill, Alain, and Jack Rennert, *Masters of the Poster: 1896–1900* (London: Academy Editions, 1977)
Wolpe, Berthold, 'Caslon Architectural', *Alphabet* 1 (Birmingham: James Moran/Kynoch Press, 1964)
Wood, Lawrence, *The Victorian Printer and the Stage* (Newcastle: Newcastle Imprint Club, 1972)
'Wood-Cutting and Type-Founding', *Penny Magazine*, 101 (1833)

Index

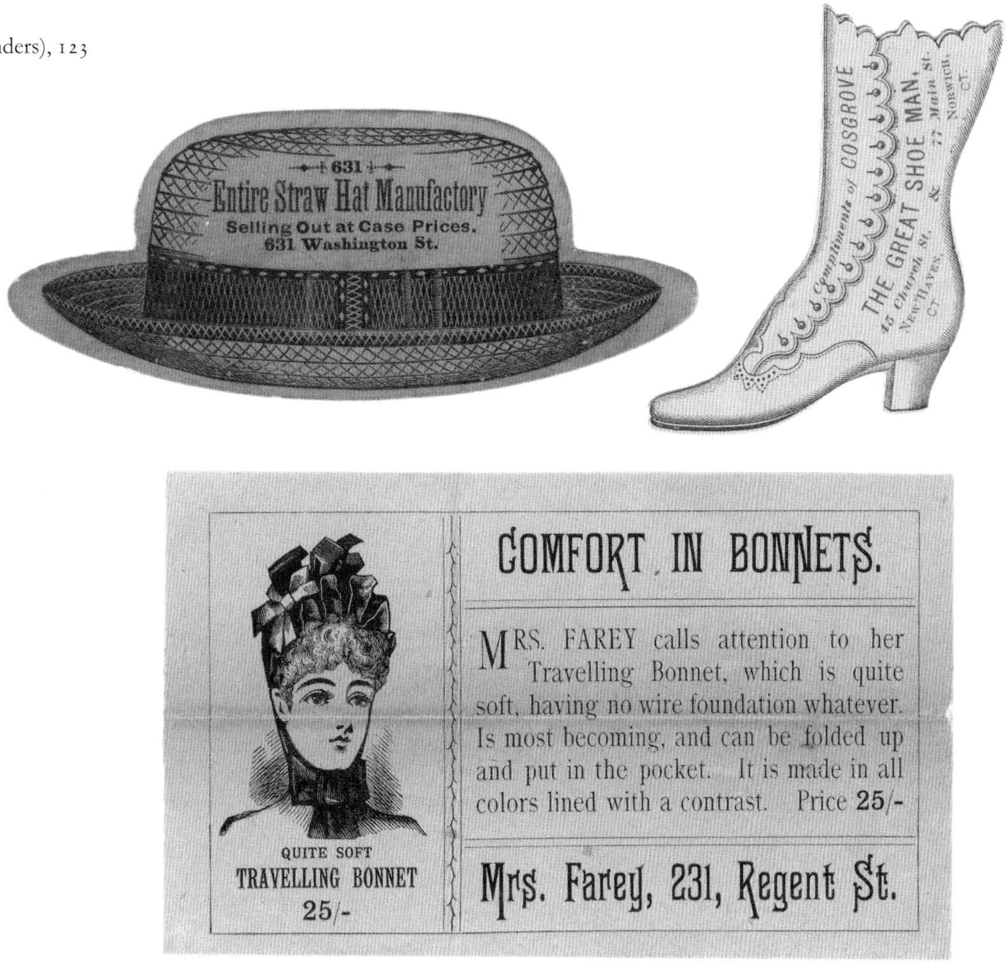

176. *(Top)* Two late-nineteenth-century American advertising trade cards and a British advertising slip c.1890. (80%)

The image over the page is an Art Ornament from the American Type Founders' *American Speciment Book of Type Styles,* 1912.

No. 120001 40c